The IMF and Ghana
The Confidential Record

The IMF and Ghana
The Confidential Record

Eboe Hutchful

Institute for African Alternatives
Zed Books Ltd.
London and New Jersey

The IMF and Ghana was first published in 1987 by
Zed Books Ltd., 57 Caledonian Road, London N1 9BU and
The Institute for African Alternatives, 23 Bevenden Street,
London N1 6BH

Copyright © Eboe Hutchful 1987

Cover design by Andrew Corbett
Printed and bound by Biddles of Guildford

All rights reserved

British Library Cataloguing in Publication Data

The IMF and Ghana : the confidential record.
  1. International Monetary Fund 2. Ghana—
  Economic conditions—1979-
  I. Hutchful, Eboe
  330.9667'05   HC1060

ISBN 0-86232-614-1
ISBN 0-86232-615-X Pbk

Contents

Preface	1
Introduction	3
'Socialism' and Planning in Ghana	4
What type of Consolidation?	8
The IMF and the World Bank Intervene	9
Socialism or Welfarism?	16
'New Deal' for Ghana's Economy	18
Effects of IMF Stabilization Policies	20
The Agreements with Foreign Private Enterprise	29
Performance of the Manufacturing Sector	36
Conclusion	38
PART I: THE IMF, THE WORLD BANK AND THE WEST	41
Introductory Note	43
Documents:	
1. IMF Report on the Ghana Economy	45
2. World Bank Mission Preliminary Report	47
3. Ghana Government's Response on Bilateral Payments Agreements	50
4. Finance Minister's Statement on IMF/World Bank Recommendations	50
5. National Economic Committee Meetings	53
6. Ghana Government's Request for IMF Consultations	57
7. Adomakoh to Schweitzer	57
8. Schweitzer to Adomakoh	58
9. Ghana Embassy, Washington, to N.A. Quao	58
10. Adomakoh to Schweitzer	58
11. Request for World Bank Assistance	59
12. World Bank Position on Aid to Ghana	60
13. Proposed Letter of Intent, IMF Standby Agreement	61
14. Report of Ghanaian Delegation to the West	66
15. World Bank Assessment of the Military Regime	74

PART II: FROM 'SOCIALISM' TO THE 'WELFARE STATE' — 83
Introductory Note — 85

Documents:
16. Military Government's Economic Policy — 86
17. Further Aspects of Military Government's Economic Policy — 92
18. World Bank Recommendations on Private Foreign Investment — 97
19. Recommendations on Promotion of Indigenous Business — 100
20. Agricultural Policy — 102
21. World Bank Recommendations on Stabilization Policy — 111

PART III: ECONOMIC RELATIONS WITH THE EAST — 117
Introductory Note — 119

Documents:
22. Fate of Soviet and Eastern Projects — 120
23. Recruitment of Crew for Russian Boats — 123
24. Bilateral Trade and Payments Agreements Recommendations — 124
25. Bilateral Trade and Payments Agreements Recommendations — 125
26. Bilateral Trade and Payments Agreements Recommendations — 129
27. Report of Ghanaian Delegation to USSR and Yugoslavia — 132

PART IV: STATE ENTERPRISES FOR SALE — 141
Introductory Note — 143

Documents:
28. Performance of State Enterprises — 145
29. Recommendation of World Bank Mission on 1966/67 Development Budget — 160
30. Terms of Lease of State Hotels — 165
31. Private Participation in State Rubber Project — 171
32. Private Participation in State Cement Factories — 179
33. Private Participation in State Pharmaceutical Corporation — 185
34. Acquisition of Ashanti Goldfields by Lonrho — 190
35. Acquisition of Ashanti Goldfields by Lonrho — 192
36. Lonrho: Proposals for Participation in Sugar Industry — 193
37. Lonrho: Proposal to Establish Beer Industry — 195
38. Proposals for Privatization of National Investment Bank — 197
39. Liberalization of Bank Financing of Cocoa Sector — 199
40. Government Response to Criticisms of Participation Agreements — 200
41. Objections to Management Agreement with Inter-Continental Hotels — 208
42. Economic Committee Response — 212
43. Political Committee Response — 213

PART V: LABOUR AND THE MILITARY   217
Introductory Note   219
Documents:
44. The Condition of the Ghanaian Working Class   220
45. TUC Comments on Proposed Changes to Labour Laws   223
46. Threat of General Strike to Protest Shootings of Workers   225
47. Tax Exemptions for Members of the Armed Forces   229

PART VI: 'A LOAD OF INDEBTEDNESS'   233
Introductory Note   235
Documents:
48. Ghana's Debt Service Burden
49. Abuses in Pre-Finance Contracts   241
50. Contractor-Finance Projects   243
51. Rearrangement of Ghana's Medium-term Debt   244
52. Ghana's Medium-term Debt: Agreed Minute, 1968   249
53. Impact of Rescheduling on Ghana's Debt Service Burden   254
54. The Case for Possible Debt Repudiation or Default 254
55. Proceedings of the Ghana Debt Conference, London   257
56. Proceedings of Ghana Debt Conference   264
57. Proceedings of the Ghana Debt Conference   266
58. Proceedings of Ghana Debt Conference   268
59. Ghana's Medium-term Debt   271
60. Finance Minister's Report on Ghana Debt Conference 273
61. Lt. Col. Acheampong's Statement on Ghana's External Debts   281
62. Repayment of Ghana's Medium-term Debt   286

Notes   290

Preface

Although the period following the military coup and the overthrow of Nkrumah in 1966 has often been regarded as a critical point of transition in the development of Ghana's economy, there have been no detailed or systematic analyses of the economics of the period outside the extensive policy documents of the International Monetary Fund and the World Bank. There are probably several interrelated reasons for this, among them the decline in scholarly interest in Ghana following the coup, the difficulties posed for research by the decay in the planning and statistical organs of the state, and the increasingly secretive context of economic decision-making brought about by the militarization of the Ghanaian state and the intervention of the international financial agencies. This present volume is not intended to constitute the type of study referred to above, but may rather be regarded as a (sometimes polemical) contribution towards laying the foundation for such a study. In the absence of publicly available data, I regard the confidential documents published here as essential for any reconstruction of the economics and politics of the post-1966 period.

A word is necessary about the sources of the documents reproduced here. These documents were collected during intermittent periods of research in Ghana from 1970 to 1980. The main sources were: first, the records of the National Economic Committee of the National Liberation Council (NLC), the military junta that ruled Ghana from February 1966 to October 1969. This was the most important single source of documents, and includes the records of the NLC negotiations with the IMF and World Bank in Part I, the economic policy documents in Part II (including the World Bank mission reports), the material on relations with the socialist countries in Part III, and most of the material on the state enterprises in Part IV. A second source was the private documents of various former government and bank officials. The entire records of the debt negotiations presented in Part VI were obtained in this way. A third, and, for the purposes of this present collection, less important source was the minutes and memoranda of the Political Committee of the National Liberation Council, although these were used extensively in my earlier doctoral dissertation on the NLC (University of Toronto, 1973). Finally, the Trades Union Congress in Accra was the source of several documents on labour presented in Part V. Where necessary, documents from open sources, such as parliamentary records, have been used to supplement or clarify the confidential data.

Regrettably (but also inevitably in an enterprise of this sort) it has not been possible to acknowledge publicly the officials and individuals whose invaluable assistance (and confidence) made it possible for me to secure these papers. I trust that my unilateral decision to publish them will not cause undue embarrassment to any of these benefactors.

As soon as circumstances permit, the materials presented in this collection and others not included will be lodged at the Balme Library at the University of Ghana, Legon.

E.H.
Port Harcourt

Introduction

> In 1966 Ghana stood at the crossroads. With the right direction, the nation could have been saved, not for any privileged few, but for the broad masses of the people.
>
> 'Was it a revolution for the elite?' *The Spokesman*, February 27 1971

In many ways 1966 was a turning point for Ghana. This was the year in which a military coup overthrew the government of President Kwame Nkrumah. The following four years of military government were probably the most crucial in Ghana's contemporary history. It is with this period (1966 to 1969) and its immediate aftermath (the period of civil rule from 1969 to 1971), the repercussions of which are still felt today, that these confidential documents are concerned. The fact that military governments never willingly give the information necessary for the dissection of the realities they represent would alone be enough justification for publishing these documents, and for giving the ordinary citizen the opportunity to peruse memoranda and reports designed only for the eyes of the most secretive manipulators of his fate. But these papers also help to answer the most urgent question posed by this period: why did the Ghana economy, after a much publicized application of IMF austerity after that coup, enter a period of deepening stagnation and underdevelopment from which, two decades later, it has yet to recover?

As these documents suggest, one of the immediate factors precipitating the coup was the disagreement between the International Monetary Fund and the Nkrumah Government on how to resolve the crisis in Ghana's 'socialist' development. From the advantage of hindsight it is more than ever clear that this crisis had nothing to do with 'socialism', indeed presaging a crisis with which virtually every African country was subsequently to be confronted.[1] A period of export-led growth and 'prosperity', the development of a semi-industrial structure and socio-economic infrastructure on the basis of state spending and extensive foreign credits, followed by a sudden fall in primary commodity prices and the onset of balance of payments complications, in turn accentuated by the failures of import-substitution industry and domestic agricultural stagnation – these are familiar elements in the structural crisis facing virtually every African country today. And, indeed, many if not all the measures adopted by Nkrumah to respond to this crisis – state intervention and regulationalism, exchange and import controls, primary producer cartels, bilateral arrangements – have similarly been adopted, even by the most conservative African countries. Most regimes have gone further: nationalization of multinational company property, specifically rejected by Nkrumah as a dangerous 'expediency', has become commonplace. Even Nkrumah's political ideas, such as the advocacy of continental unity, the establishment of a military defence force, and assistance to liberation movements, have been accepted and even (in some respects) surpassed. Compared to contemporary radical manifestos, the *Programme for Work and Happiness* of the Convention Peoples' Party (CPP), and the *Seven-Year Development Plan*, the 'socialist blue-print' of Nkrumah's government, are almost restrained in their moderation. Yet with the possible exception of Nasser, no African leader (and this includes contemporary leaders much more radical than Nkrumah) has attracted more vitriolic or cerebral dislike from imperialism, and to date no African coup has proved more controversial than Ghana in 1966.

Why was this? Many of the ideas and actions of Nkrumah, if commonplace in the 1980s, were by no means so in the 1960s, particularly in the African context. At the time both his political and economic ideas were regarded (often incorrectly) as a threat to imperialism. Now, however, imperialism tolerates, and even *defends*, positions to which it was previously hostile.[2] On the one hand the collective struggle of Third World peoples has wrested concessions from imperialism, forcing it to retreat from dogmatic positions; on the other, imperialism now has a much better understanding of the objective character and limitations of 'radical' petty-bourgeois regimes, and is thus able to exercise much more 'flexibility' in order to continue its extraction of surplus-value. To both aspects of this development Nkrumah contributed disproportionately. His political heritage was thus profoundly ambivalent.

'Socialism' and Planning in Ghana

It is then within the context of the more primitive imperialism of the 1960s, rather than that of the 1980s, that the events depicted in these documents, as well as Nkrumah himself, must be understood. 'Nkrumahism' had envisaged the economic transformation of Ghana on the basis of collaboration between the state and finance capital in a 'big push' towards industrialization. In this 'dual mandate' finance capital would be permitted to reap higher than average profits, but in return would be expected to help in laying the technological foundations for transition to an independent socialist Ghana. Private foreign capital would not be nationalized or abolished, but would be outstripped and eventually squeezed out in 'fair competition' by state capital. Industrialization would commence with light consumer industry on the basis of data furnished by existing foreign trade data, and would take the form of (a) export valorization on the one hand, and (b) local substitution of imported commodities on the other. Light industry operations were expected to lead cumulatively to the establishment of a basis for heavy (producer-goods) industry. Industrial structure was to be capital-intensive, partly because of (what was assumed to be) limited capital/labour substitutability in modern industrial processes, and partly because only through adoption of the latest technology were Ghana's products expected to be export-competitive.[3] The leading role of the state-socialist sector was seen variously as an objective necessity imposed by the limitations of the neocolonial economy (the absence of a native bourgeoisie, the requirements of large-scale planning, etc.) and as the product of conscious ideological choice (the desire to prevent exploitation).[4]

What was to be the class basis of this 'socialism'? On this question there was particular ambivalence. Nkrumahism simultaneously asserted and denied the existence of classes in Ghanaian society. To the extent that classes did exist, they were seen as the product not of the objective logic of capitalism but as 'evils' imposed by 'money economy' on pre-colonial society (which was itself communalist and classless). In the final analysis the class question was 'laid to rest' with the argument that in a peripheral social formation with a multiform economy like Ghana, the capital/labour contradiction was only one source of contradiction in the social formation; Ghana's history could thus not be seen exclusively in terms of class struggle.[5] This 'theory' was advanced not to clarify problems of revolutionary transformation in societies with multiform structures, but to justify the amorphous social base of the Convention Peoples' Party. Logically it followed, then, that the primary objective of 'consciencism' could be neither class struggle nor the abolition of classes, but rather that of aborting their development. This was to be done by forestalling the development of Ghanaian private capitalism and concentrating the ownership of the social means of production in the hands of the state. Neither could socialism be the mode of activity of a particular class; rather the leading role was attributed to the party leadership, which would monopolize political power. In the same way as the party was not seen as the agency of specific classes, so the state was seen not as the expression of class antagonisms, but rather as an instrument by which the party leadership (elevated above any and all social classes) arbitrated contending social interests. Thus reorganizing the state, the party and the parastatals to reflect the mobilized will of the working classes was never seen by Nkrumahism as a serious problem.

Some of these contradictions in Nkrumahist socialism were undoubtedly the result of necessary compromises imposed by the fragmented and multiform nature of the Ghanaian social formation, the relatively low level of development of productive forces, the reality of Ghana's relationship both with imperialism and with the majority of neocolonial African states, as well as by the specific circumstances under which the CPP had been formed. But, as shall be seen, they were the result also of objective weaknesses in the class basis of the ruling stratum represented by the party. In spite of these weaknesses, the achievements of Nkrumahism in the economic sphere were impressive. Substantial nationalization and state control of crucial sectors (banking, insurance, import/export, the internal distributive trade and gold-mining) occurred. There was also an exceptionally high rate of capital investment in industry, agriculture, and social infrastructures, financed primarily through state appropriation of cocoa surplus but also through expansion of the tax revenue base of the state; a major expansion of cocoa exports (over 200% between 1959 and 1965) and significant re-orientation of external trade; and finally, in spite of continued dependence on imports, a major shift in the composition of imports from consumer to capital goods and raw materials. In these areas Ghana's achievements were unparalleled in Black Africa.

Nevertheless, by 1965 this 'socialist' experiment had run into serious difficulties. The economy was plagued by shortages and inflation, exhaustion of foreign exchange reserves and a rising external debt-service burden, poor performance of state industrial enterprises, stagnating food agriculture, and unemployment. Although factors outside Ghana's control, particularly the precipitous fall in cocoa prices, had some responsibility for the crisis, these merely served to demonstrate the extent to which massive state investment had failed to move the economy in the direction of meaningful transformation. A central element in this was the kind of 'industrialization' attempted in Ghana, emphasizing imports of plant, machinery, semi-finished materials, management and technical services, and high-cost credits. First, given its high import content, this kind of industrialization may actually accentuate rather than relieve pressure on the balance of payments; at best it results not so much in a decline in absolute import levels as in a shift in the composition of imports. Second, export valorization, combined with import substitution, merely preserved the inherently disarticulated character of the economy, with the export on the one hand of semi-processed raw materials and the import on the other of raw or semi-finished industrial inputs. Little integration of national industry and domestic agriculture, a necessary condition for transforming other areas of the local economy, actually took place. Third, to the extent that most 'industrial activity' was in fact simple terminal stage processing (assembly activities, etc.) the bulk of value was already embodied in the imported semi-finished materials. 'Manufacturing' was thus unable to generate the value necessary for accelerated accumulation and transformation. Fourth, the high organic composition of capital in the foreign technology adopted, which was designed specifically to eliminate manual labour processes to the greatest extent possible, led to marginal or even negative growth in employment. So complete was the faith in foreign technology that no programme was foreseen for the development of local forms of technology that would respond to the availability of vast reserves of surplus labour. This kind of local 'manufacture' thus posed little threat to the interests of foreign capital, and in fact led to new levels of profit and penetration by multinational companies.

The problem of the stagnation first of domestic, and later of export agricultures, which was sometimes seen as a separate problem, was in fact linked to this form of industrialization. To the extent that exploitation of the peasantry was necessary to finance industrial take-off, the peasantry was unable to reproduce itself, and responded with migration, withdrawal from the market, etc. But with industrialization agriculture itself is transformed into an industry. However this presupposes prior links between industry and agriculture. Massive state investment was made in large-scale agriculture in Ghana but this was not successful for a variety of reasons.[6]

The problem then was not simply the 'viability' of the state or private industrial enterprises, if by this was meant (as was usually the case) 'profitability' at the micro (plant or corporation) level, but their lack of transformational potential. This was the limitation of the 'development without growth' argument, its overall strength notwithstanding. The problem could not have been solved either by shifting the pattern of investment from 'long-gestation' to 'quick-gestation' projects.[7] In this sense the investment pattern of the 1960s differed quantitatively but not qualitatively from that of the 1950s; what differed was the *scale* of investment rather than the underlying logic, which remained the reproduction of the colonially derived demand structure. Hence the 'closed economy' of the 1960s remained essentially open.

What was required was a change in the whole conception of industry, to a strategy which would have incorporated the following features:

(a) development of domestic agriculture and the local resource base
(b) linkage of national manufacture to this resource base;
(c) the progressive development of indigenous technology, including the domestication wherever possible of foreign technologies, with the long-term objective of building up (within a regional or non-African framework) basic industry and an intermediate goods sector; and
(d) production for mass needs rather than élite consumption. This includes the promotion of agricultural and industrial exports, not as a separate sector but as an extension of production for the home market.

However, the crisis of 'socialism' in Ghana cannot be seen simply in terms of these planning 'errors', but ultimately in terms of 'socialist' production relations and the class content of the Nkrumah state. As I have indicated elsewhere, the nationalizations that occurred in the domestic economy under 'socialism' were designed simultaneously to extend the material base of the party and bureaucracy and to challenge imperialism and Ghanaian merchant capital for control over trading surplus.[8] A considerable degree of private accumulation, channelled through the state organs, thus occurred. The 'passbook' system, which rested on an alliance of the party and the parastatal bureaucracy, transferred potential surplus from the state enterprises downstream into the hands of party traders and tightly regulated access to trading stocks. In the final analysis powerful sectors of both party and bureaucracy had an interest in a dependent, import-oriented but 'commandist' economy that facilitated the collection of private revenue in the form of commissions, bribes, and so on.

What Type of Consolidation?

Thus the question in 1965 was not whether or not 'consolidation' was required, but *what kind* of consolidation. One possibility was a policy of consolidation which would have laid the basis for further advance to national economic independence and genuine socialism on the basis of the economic measures suggested above, in addition to a whole series of associated reforms: popular participation in planning, restructuring of the operations of the state enterprises to realize worker participation and control, reorientation of the educational structure, etc. The guiding principles of such a consolidation policy would have been that it (a) should be conducted under national management; (b) be consistent with the objectives of further long-term socialist transformation; and (c) should shift the burden of austerity on the rich rather than on the working poor. In the final analysis, however, these economic measures would have derived their force only from corresponding political measures; measures which could have included: dismantling the privileges of the traditional bourgeoisie as well as the party *nouveau riche* and the state bureaucracy; rectification of the excesses of 'Nkrumahism' in order to set socialism on a correct theoretical basis; democratisation and strengthening of party structures and installation of the principle of popular control over party and state organs; and mobilization for raising productivity. In the short term these political measures were crucial for rekindling popular enthusiasm and ensuring the survival of the regime. And indeed some 'radicalization' was attempted in response to the crisis, such as the extension of bilateral agreements, proposed membership in the socialist CMEA, a squeeze on major Western economic enterprises (including giving consideration to nationalization), reorganization of the party and the installation of a more progressive National Assembly. But these measures were too limited and too hesitant to have a significant impact either on the economy or on the mass of working Ghanaians.

A second option was the type urged by the IMF and the World Bank, involving cutbacks in state spending and the state role in production, the restoration of the private sector to its former prominence, slowdown or termination of trade relations with the East, dismantling of exchange controls and trade restrictions, and imposition of further austerity on cocoa farmers and/or urban working classes.[9] In turn, attracting foreign capital implied abandoning the anti-imperialist line. These measures would thus not only have forestalled further radicalization but reversed most of the progressive directions in the Ghanaian economy undertaken since 1960.

The IMF and the World Bank Intervene

To understand why these measures were advocated, and the role played by the IMF and the World Bank in these records, some knowledge of the background of the two institutions is essential. The IMF and the World Bank were initially created to regulate inter-imperialist rivalries and to prevent a recurrence of the ruinous competition between the main capitalist powers that led to the collapse of the gold standard and to two 'world' wars. In the late 19th and early 20th centuries, the major trading nations of the world had all tied their currencies to the value of gold. These currencies were therefore stable in relation to each other. Under this system balance of payments deficits corrected themselves automatically because the country which suffered a deficit in its foreign trade made up the balance by shipping gold abroad; this contracted the money supply, depressed the prices of goods and labour in the country and therefore made them more competitive on the world market, thus (in theory) attracting capital and export orders.

To prevent chronic deficit or surplus, this mechanism was combined with corrective measures to restore the balance of international trade. These involved monetary contraction and increase in interest rates in the gold-losing country, and monetary expansion and reduced interest rates for short-term credit in the gold-receiving country, with the result that:

(a) prices would tend to fall in the country losing gold and rise in the country receiving gold, thus leading to an expansion of exports and contraction of imports in the gold-losing country and the reverse in the gold-receiving country;

(b) a flow of short-term funds from the surplus country to the deficit country. The deficit would then disappear and gold movements would be reversed.

As long as this mechanism of adjustment worked, gold moved between trading countries in alternating currents, with every country now losing, now receiving gold. This system had presumed, *inter alia*, freedom of international gold movement, fixing by law of the gold content of national currency, the convertibility of national currency into gold (at least for export purposes) and vice versa, the adoption of appropriate domestic financial and economic policies to rectify a deficit or surplus, and 'reasonable' freedom of international trade. The movements of international trade were thus the main determinant of domestic economic policies. However, the difficulty with this system was that exchange stability could often be maintained only at the cost of extreme instability of the national economy. The deflation of the economy to improve an unfavourable balance of payment situation induced domestic recession and unemployment, and many governments found the social and political pressures generated thereby increasingly intolerable.

The collapse of world capitalist trade during the Great Depression led to the final abandonment of the gold standard. To recover or maintain their share of export trade, the leading trading nations resorted to competitive devaluations designed to lower the prices of their exports on the world market, while the poorer countries, unable to finance their imports, raised restrictions against imports or created bilateral trading blocs in which imports from one trading partner were paid for by exports to that country, without the transfer of scarce gold. These were often combined with exchange controls and discriminatory currency practices. At the same time widespread default and repudiation of foreign debts led to the collapse of the international bond market. These developments were regarded as a fundamental threat to the investment and trading interests of the United States, which had now grown powerful enough to challenge Britain as the leading power in world trade.

It was thus to reconstruct the international monetary system and evolve new ground rules for competition between the main capitalist powers that the 1944 conference at Bretton Woods was called. It was this conference which gave rise to the International Monetary Fund (IMF) and the International Bank for Reconstruction and Development (World Bank). The agreements reached at Bretton Woods reflected a compromise between ascendant American trading interests advocating the restoration of the gold standard and a return to the days of free trade and rigid exchange rates, and Britain, which demanded more freedom from each nation to determine its own economic policies in order to reduce the likelihood of dislocations and unemployment. The IMF was thus seen as an 'alternative to the desperate tactics of the past – competitive currency depreciation, excessive trade barriers, uneconomic barter deals, multiple currency practices, and unnecessary exchange restrictions' which had characterized pre-war inter-imperialist rivalry.[10] In spite of the concessions, the two Bretton Woods institutions reflected American trading and investment aspirations[11] and their voting arrangements ensured American political and economic dominance.[12]

The objectives of the Fund were, among other things, 'to promote exchange stability, to maintain orderly exchange arrangements among members, and to avoid competitive exchange depreciation', and 'to assist in the establishment of a multilateral system of payments in respect of current transactions between members and in the elimination of foreign exchange restrictions which hamper the growth of world trade' (Article I, Sections iii and iv). Article VIII forbids members to impose restrictions on international payments and transfers on current account, or to engage in discriminatory currency practices without the approval of the Fund. Article XIV provides that any country maintaining such restriction five years after the commencement of operation of the Fund, and each year thereafter that the restrictions are in force, should hold consultations with the Fund 'as to their further retention'. The Fund may, if necessary, make representations to any member that conditions are favourable for the withdrawal of a particular or all restrictions. A member persisting in maintaining such restrictions thereafter may be declared ineligible to use the resources of the Fund. Finally, to prevent competitive devaluation as a way of rectifying a balance of payments problem, the Fund was empowered to determine the proper levels of exchange rates. Each member nation was required to establish a 'par value' for its currency, expressed in gold, in consultation with the Fund. Changes in par value of above 10% could not be made without the permission of the Fund.

However, at Bretton Woods the inadequate supply of foreign capital was also considered one of the most important reasons for chronic deficits in the balance of payments. The World Bank was established to 'promote private foreign investment by means of guarantees or participation in loans and other investments made by private investors; and when private capital is not available on reasonable terms, to supplement private investment by providing... finance for production purposes out of its own capital, funds raised by it and its other resources'. (Article I (iii)). The hope had been expressed at Bretton Woods that the World Bank would thus act as an 'enormously effective stabilizer and guarantor of loans which [private bankers] might make'[13], and in this way 'inaugurate a new period of vast movement of investment capital throughout the worlds.[14] To avoid competition with private sources of capital, the World Bank would act as a lender of last resort, and its investments would be planned in a manner likely to expand the sphere of activity of private capital. Its dependence on the capital markets of the leading capitalist countries for the bulk of its investment funds would also impose on it an obligation to carry out prudent and conservative investments with an adequate rate of profit, and bar it from carrying out policies offensive or contrary to the interests of the main capital markets.

The Articles establishing the Fund thus demonstrated fundamental hostility to the restrictive trade and payment practices and the bilateral payments arrangements imposed or entered into by countries like Ghana. The reason for this is that this shuts off finance capital from important markets or inhibits free movement of capital and profits. The advent of the 'Cold War' introduced another, explicitly political reason which was clearly demonstrated in the case of Ghana: although bilateral agreements may be entered into by both capitalist and socialist nations, their frequent utilization by socialist countries (who are not members of the IMF) had led to their identification with 'communist' penetration. Hence where a country has attempted to 'close off' its markets either in order to diversify its external trade, to protect its trading balance, or promote a nascent domestic manufacturing base, the IMF facilitates its re-absorption into the circuit of finance capital by demanding the removal of restrictive barriers, while the World Bank and its institutions act on 'safe pilots' to guarantee foreign capital. In spite of 'reforms' to Bretton Woods leading to reinterpretation and broadening of their functions and the current efforts of the Bank in particular to cultivate a liberal 'development' image, these remain the essential objectives of the two institutions. It must also be noted that while the Fund was originally evolved to regulate rivalry between the main capitalist nations, few of these nations have required recourse to the Fund, and in practice the control of the IMF over the economic policies of these nations is marginal at best. The regulatory role of the Fund has been mainly in relation to the underdeveloped countries. In this respect the Fund and the Bank constitute the most potent instruments of multilateral imperialism in general and American imperialism in particular.

The key to the 'alternative' strategy represented by the Fund is the fund of currencies held from the quotas of its members. These funds are designed to act as an extension of the foreign exchange reserves of a member country; a member suffering from a short-term disequilibrium in its international payments can call on the resources of the Fund to permit it to ride out seasonal or cyclical fluctuations in its external trade and payments, and to correct the source of the disequilibrium without resorting to restrictive measures 'destructive' to world trade, such as exchange controls, import restrictions, or competitive devaluation, or, if such measures had already been imposed, to permit them to be eliminated. However, there is a catch. IMF funds are to be utilized strictly for meeting short-term disequilibria, and are explicitly prevented from being used to finance persistent deficits. Why 'short-term'? Initially because it was believed that balance of payments problems were due to an excessive but temporary decline in exports or increase in imports of goods and services, or both. Increasingly, however, the definition of the problem as 'short-term', and extension of IMF funds on that basis, was seen to facilitate control over the economic and political direction of recipient countries. IMF funds are disbursed in such a way as to ensure maximum compliance with strict 'performance criteria'; failure to meet these criteria may lead (as Zaïre and Brazil have recently discovered) to suspension of further disbursements and a demand by the Fund for renegotiation of the terms of the standby arrangement.

Progressive drawings on Fund resources attract increasingly more severe conditions. Permission is granted almost automatically for a drawing to the extent of the gold tranche; drawings on the next, or 'first credit tranche' (25%) are conditional on the member country making 'reasonable attempts' to solve its problems, while requests for drawing beyond these limits require 'substantial justification', i.e. prior agreement with the Fund on a 'stabilization package'. The Fund system is reinforced by the fact that neither the World Bank agencies nor private international banks and state insurance agencies will usually extend further loans or credits, or reschedule existing ones until such agreement is reached.

Over the years, the IMF developed a standard prescription for a balance of payments disequilibrium which combines deflationary monetary and fiscal policies with devaluation. These measures include cutbacks in government expenditure and reduction in the size of the budgetary deficit, tax reforms (including higher taxes) and improvements in revenue collection, the abolition of subsidies on consumer items, tighter credit policies and higher interest rates, and controls on wage and salary increases. The objective of these measures is to cut consumption (and therefore the demand for imports and foreign exchange), increase public savings (to enable resumption of debt-service and current transfers) and shift the weight of economic activity from the public to the private sector. Other standard ingredients are demands for the assurance of a more favourable climate for foreign private investment (the adoption of the stabilization programme is conditional on the injection of large quantities of foreign capital and loans) and for the removal where necessary of restrictive trade and payments barriers. As a last resort the exchange rate of the national currency may be devalued to make exports more competitive and imports more expensive.[15]

'Structuralists' have argued within the context of Latin America that these IMF monetarist policies rest on a fundamental misunderstanding of the causes of inflation in peripheral capitalist economies, and are not only irrelevant to the problem but may actually exacerbate the contradictions in these economies. According to the structuralists, inflation is not a transient phenomenon resulting from 'short-term disequilibria' but is embedded in internal and external structural imbalances basic to such economies. The most important of these imbalances include the fluctuation and slow growth of primary export earnings (particularly relative to imported manufactures) the dependent 'enclave' character of import-substituting industrialization, the stagnation of domestic food agriculture, excessive dependence on capital imports, and chronic shortages of consumer imports. A basic and lasting cure to inflation can thus come about only through structural changes, including the breakdown of the highly unequal internal distribution of property, regressive tax systems and restricted educational opportunities. Sunkel has made a useful distinction here between 'inflationary pressures', which are 'structural', 'exogenous', or 'cumulative' in origin on the one hand, and 'propagation mechanisms', such as wage demands, price increases and increasing government expenditures, which reflect and propagate these inflationary impulses but do not themselves constitute causes of inflation. In Sunkel's view IMF stabilization attacks these propagation mechanisms without attacking the structural and other sources of inflationary pressures, leading in the process to a substantial regressive shift in income distribution.[16] This analysis has obvious relevance to the Ghanaian experience in the 1960s. Yet these arguments have had little effect on IMF policies, perhaps because *domestic* 'economic recovery' is not in itself the primary objective of Fund stabilization. Rather this is the liberalization of international trade and payments enjoined by the articles of the Fund, the purpose of which (as we have seen) is to facilitate repenetration by foreign capital.

In any case, according to its official ideology, the IMF is not directly concerned with questions of development as such. This is the province of the World Bank and its two affiliates, the International Development Association (IDA) and the International Finance Corporation (IFC). The bulk of World Bank/IDA lending to Third World countries have been for infrastructural projects, primarily for the development of electric power and transportation.[17] In most cases these have been large-scale projects carried out in cooperation with the public sector, but designed primarily to create economies-of-scale, or to open up new markets and areas of operation for private (usually foreign) enterprise. The Volta Project is an example of this kind of World Bank 'development' project.

On the other hand the IFC does lend directly to industry, but always as a lender of last resort and in association with foreign and/or domestic private capital. Like the Bank, the essential function of the IFC is to 'assist the economic development of its less developed member countries by promoting the growth of the private sector of their economies'.[18] Unlike the rest of the Bank group however the IFC is the 'only international agency whose function is to assist the development of private industry on an international scale.'[19] The IFC operates by bringing together foreign and domestic private capital in Third World projects and by assisting in the establishment and financing of investment banks which support the activities of private enterprise within their respective countries;[20] increasingly, also, it has acted as an 'international investment bank' in its own right. The IFC's role is essentially 'catalytic', acting (like the Bank itself) as a 'safe pilot' for foreign investment; for every $1 committed by the IFC in a project, $4–$5 are obtained from other (mainly private) sources.

The concerns of the Bank, however, go beyond specific projects. Once the World Bank/IDA have invested in a project, they go on to initiate measures designed to create 'a general environment conducive to the economic and financial success of projects and sound management'. This task provides a springboard for increasing intervention in the economy and policy making of the host country.[21] This includes sectoral policies to stimulate production or reduce costs, removal of 'price distortions' and other policies which interfere with incentives in agriculture, improvements in power and transport, rationalization of tariffs and tax structures, etc. Particular emphasis has been laid by the Bank on strengthening public finance systems and increasing public sector savings.

However, it would be a mistake to see the Fund and the Bank solely in terms of their advocacy of certain economic policies. The articles of the Fund bar it explicitly from taking the 'domestic, social or political policies' of any member into account in its operations. The Bank also claims that it has 'no political, commercial, or other non-developmental objectives to distract it from its functions of assisting the economic growth of its developing member countries.[22] Both institutions put considerable emphasis on their claim to be 'impartial international institutions'. It is precisely this pretence of the two institutions to be 'non-political' that defines their political character. Neither the Fund nor the Bank can act against the wishes of the U.S. Government, or of the Western powers collectively.[23] The denial by Fund–Bank officials that their work has any political significance is, of course, entirely an illusion. In many cases the intervention of the IMF in the economy of a member country has resulted in 'the overthrow of governments or at least the resignation of the Finance Minister'.[24] Not surprisingly, both the Fund and the Bank have had difficulty responding to charges of Western domination and political bias.[25]

This outline provides some understanding of the significance of the policy measures proposed to the Nkrumah Government by the IMF in May 1965, and supported by the World Bank mission of September.[26] Taken separately, many of the areas of criticism by the Fund and Bank could hardly be questioned: from a technical point of view their observations on the state industries, the state farms and other aspects of economic practice were often uncontestable. But to focus on this aspect of the question would be to commit a fundamental error. The basic issue was the very direction of economic policy in Ghana. In the view of the World Bank, the fundamental problem was Ghana's 'voluntary exclusion from accepted approaches to economic development'.[27] According to the Bank this had proved 'detrimental to growth'. Ghana's development programme was thus not only to be reduced but 'reoriented'. Here lies the basic incompatibility between Nkrumah and the Fund/Bank missions that set the stage for the coup. While Nkrumah emphasized the leading role of the state 'socialist' sector, the Bank espoused the primacy of foreign capital in development, and saw as its 'first priority' in Ghana the task of 'confirming a positive environment for private investment'.[28] While Nkrumah stressed equity and structural transformation, the World Bank saw the issue almost entirely in terms of 'growth'.

Nevertheless it would be too simple to cast the 1966 coup in these terms, which tend to subordinate the role of class forces within Ghana itself. The military coup became necessary only because the IMF did not appear to have succeeded in putting a brake on Nkrumah; in the words of the state bureaucracy, Nkrumah's government 'was not prepared to subject its policies to the financial discipline that was recommended by the [IMF and World Bank] missions', hence the coup.[29] And according to General Ankrah, Nkrumah had tried to turn Ghana 'into one vast public service machine'. It was 'this kind of ideology that the revolution was intended to cure.'[30] The 'cure' proposed was the 'Welfare State'. Thus while the ambivalence of the Nkrumah government towards the 'recommendations' of the Fund and Bank missions was due partly to the weak and contradictory political base of the regime and the lack of clarity of the leadership, it was also the result of a split between wings of the Ghanaian state.

Socialism or Welfarism?

The character of the contending class forces exposed in the coup may be best understood by analysing the change from 'socialism' to the 'welfare state' – or rather the restoration of 'welfare state' rhetoric – facilitated by the coup (see Part II). In opposition to 'socialism', the 'welfare state':

(a) emphasized the leading role of private capital in development, with the state playing 'pragmatic' residual and regulatory roles, and a 'partnership' between, on the one hand, the state and, on the other, foreign capital allied with a dependent domestic bourgeoisie;

(b) saw capitalistic relations of production not in terms of contradiction and exploitation and therefore of classes, but in terms of complementarity – 'sectors', 'division of labour', 'rational division of responsibilities', etc., aimed at 'growth';

(c) advocated separation between economic action and politics, e.g., 'non-political' unions, cooperatives, students organizations, etc., within bourgeois-democratic forms;

(d) conceptualized the state not as a repository of class power and attitudes, but as an abstract and undifferentiated 'public interest'; and

(e) perceived no contradiction between imperialism and national development. On the contrary foreign capital is seen as a primary and beneficial engine of growth. As a corollary, 'development' is conceptualized in terms of a complex of 'technical' problems, soluble given the application of 'rational technique' and 'management'.

Thus, while 'socialism' was anti-imperialist, non-capitalist and populist, the welfare state was pro-imperialist, capitalist in orientation and frankly anti-mass. Nevertheless both 'socialism' and 'welfare state' had their antecedents in the CPP. Officially 'welfare state' ideology had been transcended in favour of 'socialism'; in reality it was alive and well in the state planning organs and in important sectors of the CPP.[31] By and large the planners who were the architects of the 'Seven-Year Development Plan' were also the draughtsmen of the 'Economic Policy' of the military government. The immediate genesis of the *coup* would thus appear to be the policy differences within the party leadership itself – pulled in different directions by its contradictory social base – and between its 'socialist' wing and the state bureaucracy and planning organs, focusing the collective aspirations of the rising bureaucratic class, domestic capital and imperialism. This defined the limits both to the 'leftward turn' after 1960 and the 'rightward turn' after the coup.

What basic 'unity' had facilitated the coexistence of these rival concepts within the Nkrumah state? The advocates of both paths of development were in agreement that (a) 'industrialization' was the key to development, (b) that state accumulation should be an important aspect of this process, and finally (c) that this accumulation should be on the basis primarily of the expropriation of cocoa surplus. What fundamentally differentiated the two concepts (rhetoric apart) was first the definition of the objective of state accumulation, and second the question, at the political level, of how to mediate the problems of social control that accumulation entailed. Welfare Statism saw state accumulation in the service of private accumulation and the creation of a national bourgeoisie. Convinced of the naturalness of capital and of its own social superiority, the upper petty bourgeoisie (the bedrock of Welfare Statism) saw the necessity for social control less clearly, and were content to advocate bourgeois democracy tempered by social welfare.[32] (In reality of course its weak base in civil society made it no less dependent on state intervention.) On the other hand Nkrumah's 'socialism' saw the state as a substitute for private accumulation, intended to frustrate the deepening of the class structure. However, to the extent it envisaged the centralization of the means of production not under the control of the working classes but of a bureaucracy *per se,* his 'socialism' should be seen really as a form of bureaucratic collectivism. This was not a theoretical 'error'. I have suggested that this 'collectivism' was a response on one level to the objective realities of Ghana's peripheral social formation (economic underdevelopment, national fragmentation and political disunity) and on another to the weak material base of the ruling class and the exigencies of labour control posed by forced accumulation. By concentrating economic as well as political power in the hands of the party leadership, collectivism would have facilitated the simultaneous achievement of otherwise contradictory objectives.[33]

The quintessential political expression of this collectivism was the CPP. In spite of the vaunted image of the CPP as a party of the 'common man', the essence of the party lay in its 'social corporatism' – its ability to incorporate diverse social strata and to manipulate contending class, ethnic, regional and local rivalries, thus refracting and absorbing the tensions inherent in a dependent formation undergoing rapid capitalist transformation. This 'corporatism' facilitated effective labour control (through direct organization of the producers in a system of 'integral wings') and at the same time allowed the party leadership to exercise relative autonomy by detaching its power from any specific social base.

'Nkrumahism' must thus be understood with reference both to the concrete conditions of Ghanaian society and the nature of the lower petty-bourgeois class that formed the leadership cadre of the CPP. Of course this class was not in the strictest sense a 'petty bourgeoisie' but a variegated subordinate stratum of petty traders, small commodity producers and businessmen as well as clerks, primary school teachers and other petty intelligentsia, characterized by its intermediary roles in the economy and its 'negative' social characteristics (non-peasant, non-wage, non-chief). More so than the upper petty-bourgeoisie of merchants, intelligentsia, chiefs and rural landlords, this class was in close articulation with urban wage-labour and with the small and middle peasantry. Its role as carrier of 'nationalism' allowed it to assert an autonomous interest vis-à-vis all other social strata, centering on the possibilities opened up by control over state power. However, this class was inherently torn between contradictory positions: proletarian sympathies versus bourgeois aspirations, subjective anti-imperialism versus objective dependence, and (given the division between its salaried and capitalistic wings) the advocacy of 'salary' versus the craving for profit. It was this ambivalence which was manifest in the popularity of the CPP and in the contest within the party itself between 'socialism' and the 'welfare state'. By implication, therefore, the 1966 coup could not be explicated by reference to any alleged differences in the class basis of the CPP and military regimes. The real issue was how to effectuate and rationalize the exploitation of the Ghanaian peasant and working classes, and what role imperialism should be permitted to play in the process.

The differences, if less substantial than they might have appeared, were nevertheless important. If its incorporation of contradictory social tendencies made the CPP incapable of surmounting the deepening crisis, precisely that fact also endowed the party (as opposed to the military) with its dynamism and creativity. Within the party there was always a possibility – advanced by the deepening crisis – that progressive forces would seize the upper hand, transcend the 'social hotch-potch' represented by the party and transform it in a genuinely progressive direction. This, the achievement of real socialism at home and continental liberation abroad, was seen as the real danger.[34] It was this possibility that the coup was intended to foreclose. The coup thus purged Ghanaian neo-colonialism of its ambivalence: but it also, in the process, took the country backwards into structural and historical time.

It is with the economic policies of the coup that these documents are concerned. The rest of this introduction will attempt to analyse the consequences of those policies.

'New Deal' for Ghana's Economy

The IMF stabilization policy applied in Ghana in 1966–68 contained most of the classic features (see the 'Letter of Intent' in Document 13). Government budgetary expenditures and the size of the deficit were to be sharply curtailed and limited to receipts from current revenue and borrowing from non-inflationary sources. Central Bank lending to the government was limited to a ceiling of ₡159 million, and loans and advances to the private sector and commercial banks (excluding cocoa financing) to ₡15.3 million. The Central Bank lending rate was to be raised from $4\frac{1}{2}\%$ to 7% and commercial bank lending was to be limited to ₡200 million and reduced by between 25% and $33\frac{1}{4}\%$ in non-priority areas. In the area of foreign trade and payments the import licencing system and the importation of selected inputs were to be liberalized, discrimination in import and the exchange policies was to cease, and controls in these fields were eventually to be abolished. The bilateral and payments agreements were to be reviewed in order to abolish their restrictive features, barter agreements were to be terminated, and no new restrictions on external trade to be introduced without prior consultation with the Fund. No new external loans of less than 12 years maturity (other than normal trade credits of up to 360 days maturity) were to be contracted without prior consultation with the Fund. Reliance on suppliers' credits was to cease. Finally, the NLC was to reorganize state enterprises and terminate state subsidies to them, and cut expenditures on diplomatic representation, administration, and the national airline. The IMF was also granted wide powers of supervision over the Ghana economy. Ghana was obliged to 'remain in close consultation with the Fund, and to keep the Fund informed of developments in the exchange, trade, monetary, credit and fiscal situation'.

Budget-balancing, rather than the transformation of Ghana's economy, became the main objective of NLC economic polity. Total state budgetary expenditure was cut by ₵60 million in 1966–67 over 1965, all but ₵2 million of the cuts coming from the development budget. Wage increases were limited to 5% and strict limits imposed on bank credit. The bilateral agreements with China, Albania and Guinea were cancelled, while the remaining agreements with the socialist countries were suspended pending re-negotiation. The result was that trading links with socialist economies were drastically curtailed. In July 1967 the exchange rate of the *cedi* was devalued by 30% against the dollar.

The 'development package' evolved through various Bank missions and reports constituted the other aspect of the stabilization programme. The essence of this package was as follows: In agriculture the contraction of the state-sector and large-scale farms, the limitation of the state sector to extension services, research, and provision of infrastructure, and encouragement of small-scale agricultural producers through credit and other support services. In industry the state sector was to be scaled down, through the sale of assets or participation with private investors, and the private (particularly foreign) sector expanded; the curbing of local (especially public) monopolies and lowering of tariffs to generate competition; the removal of subsidies, decontrol of market prices, import and licensing controls and greater encouragement of the market mechanism; removal of special capital investment privileges and generalization of incentives; more even spread of the tax burden, and the elimination of duty concessions on imported inputs to encourage more local raw material production and linkages, the rectification of the problem of currency over-valuation (through devaluation) and encouragement of more export-oriented production. More incentives were to be granted to plant management and wages were to reflect skill differentials.

Effects of IMF Stabilization Policies

In theory this was the programme that was to ensure Ghana's 'economic recovery'. In reality stabilization was to deepen foreign control of the Ghanaian economy and intensify its structural and social contradictions, laying the foundation not for further 'development' but for accelerated decline and future political instability.

(a) The 'Socialist' Projects

From the beginning 'stabilization' was used as an excuse for large-scale destruction of socialist projects. With the expulsion of their technical personnel in March 1966 all the Eastern projects were brought to an abrupt halt. The subsequent fate of some of these projects was instructive. The reinforced concrete panel factory, which at the time of the coup had been completed at a cost of N₵2.3 million in civil works and required only working capital to commence operations, was abandoned. It was not until 1973 and two governments later that an effort was made to put the factory into operation on the basis of a partnership between the government, the National Investment Bank, and a West German construction company. The Tarkwa gold refinery, 90% completed at the time of the coup, was abandoned altogether. According to the World Bank, it was 'understood that the ore could be refined more cheaply abroad'. In fact this project, designed to make Ghana self-sufficient in the processing of gold ores, had been opposed by the Ashanti Goldfields Corporation and other foreign gold interests. Under Nkrumah it was anticipated that national control over the gold industry would be further advanced by plans to nationalize the Obuasi mines of Ashanti Goldfields after the expiration of the lease in 1986. This was also forestalled by the coup. In 1968 Lonrho took control of Ashanti in the 'most important single take-over in the company's history', with the NLC Government as a junior partner.[35] Similarly the ferromanganese project, intended to eliminate under-invoicing by African Manganese Company, the Ghanaian subsidiary of Union Carbide, and to create conditions for the forward integration of the industry, was permanently shelved. Instead the NLC entered into a joint venture with Union Carbide through the National Investment Bank for the manufacture of batteries. The NLC also entered into a joint venture with UAC and Ghana Textile Manufacturing Company (GTMC) to take over the Chinese integrated textile mill, the only one of its kind in Ghana, at Juapong. By combining management and commercial control of Juapong with its existing management and technical partnership in Ghana Textile Printing (also a joint venture), UAC was able to transform its previous domination of the trade in imported textiles into substantial control of domestic textile manufacture. As will become clear, these were only a few of the benefits accruing to individual multinationals from the 1966 coup.

Although not an 'Eastern project' the cocoa storage silos were also abandoned, thus effectively ending Nkrumah's world cocoa market strategy. This was not in itself surprising. As a UN mission that reviewed the cocoa processing industry after the coup observed:[36]

> The economic effects of creating and using cocoa storage capacity to the tune of 200,000 tons of beans could be very great. It is to be recognised that if Ghana and other producing countries had been able to make financial arrangements whereby the cocoa surpluses of recent years had remained in storage in the possession of the cocoa producers then the course of the cocoa market during this period would have been very different from what it turned out to be. And it is to be expected that all kinds of pressures from the side of established market interests will be exerted to prevent the emergence of this situation which could give great power on the cocoa market to a producing country like Ghana.

Instead the World Bank, which had consistently opposed the project, recommended that the silos be converted into general storage for the Tema Harbour, and conveyor belts built to connect them to the docks some two miles away. Since none of Ghana's subsequent rulers found this advice palatable, the massive shells of the semi-completed silos have continued to stand to this day, stark and decaying against the Tema skyline. But the decision to discontinue the silos was of academic significance. Consumer countries had already assumed that Ghana's new rulers, utterly dependent on Western charity, 'would be very reluctant to adopt any such aggressive tactics [as withholding cocoa].'[37]

Even more flagrant waste attended the disposal of the agricultural projects of the state farms corporation. An Agricultural Committee established by the NLC to advise on agricultural policy had recommended the abolition of the corporation and the disposal of its 125 farms (see Document 20). Between 1966 and the end of 1968 state farms and agricultural projects transferred or abandoned amounted to ₡6.6 million in net book value. In spite of the substantial value of the assets there were no controls or proper documentation of the transfers.[38]

Much of the farm machinery was simply abandoned where it lay, and by late 1966 various parts of the Ghanaian countryside were littered with rusting Soviet and Eastern machinery, some still uncrated.

One may finally consider the case of the fishing industry. Twenty-eight fishing vessels belonging to the State Fishing Corporation (SFC) and private Ghanaian fishing companies were laid up at Tema Harbour when their 350 Soviet crew and technicians were expelled in March 1966. The timing of the expulsion coincided with the withdrawal from service of the remaining (Japanese and Norwegian) vessels of the Fishing Corporation, either for maintenance or to await the arrival of fresh crews from abroad. The result was that 'within a few months after the coup, almost the whole of the deep-sea fishing operations of the SFC had come to a halt.'[39] Efforts were initially made to get UAC to arrange the recruitment of a replacement crew but nothing came of this. The resulting fish shortages had to be met by imports of frozen fish and landings from foreign vessels in foreign exchange. The ten Soviet vessels of the SFC continued to lie idle until 1968, when the Negotiating Committee of the Economic Committee decided to offer them for sale. The main justification advanced for this was that the Soviet fleet was uneconomical to operate, although Mankoadze, a private Ghanaian fishing company, had been able to operate their fleet profitably. This same company insisted that the vessels could be operated profitably given 'proper management and facilities'. For another year the vessels remained unsold; deterioration was so advanced that one of them sank in the harbour and had to be refloated. The problem was transferred to Busia's Government; an attempt to sell the ten boats to a foreign buyer (for $120,000; a loss of some $3.6 million on the original purchase price of $3.72 million) in 1970 fell through when irregularities in the transaction were suspected and the sale was halted by order of the High Court. By the time of the 1972 coup eight of the vessels continued to be tied up at the harbour, their rusting hulks tying up valuable docking space and threatening shipping. Of the remaining SFC fleet, five transfer vessels and two carriers were handed over to the two largest private Ghanaian fishing companies, Mankoadze and Ocean Fisheries. Neither transfer was governed even by a formal contract.[40]

(b) Employment and Incomes

Such then was the 'rationality' with which the military government approached Ghana's economic problems. The monetarist policies of the IMF proved no less disastrous for Ghana, and especially for her working classes. Between the coup and August 1968, over 66,000 workers, constituting almost 10% of the total wage-labour force, were dismissed from their jobs, 36% of these in the Accra capital district alone. Unskilled and semi-skilled labour in the construction industry took the brunt, with 26,000 jobs. Employment in the private commercial sector also fell by almost 50%. Only 7,400 of the workers dismissed were officially said to have been relocated. Since these figures referred only to redundancies in the medium and large-scale industrial and commercial establishments (ten or more workers), which were less affected by stabilization, they can be considered as a definite understatement. In addition, although by decree all retrenchments involving more than ten workers were supposed to be reported to the Special Commission for Redeployment of Labour, in practice this provision could be evaded by progressively laying off less than ten workers at a time. Figures issued by the National Employment Service (NES) for the period from 1966 to 1969 demonstrated clearly the growing ranks of unemployed. While the NES received 285,349 applications for employment in 1966, 391,148 in 1967, 423,115 in 1968, and 366,130 in 1969, vacancies notified to the NES never exceeded 70,000 per annum in the four-year period, and these were mainly in unskilled and semi-skilled categories.

But the growth in the reserve army of labour was only one aspect of the continuing deterioration in the living standards of working people. In theory labour benefited directly or indirectly from falling rates of inflation. Wages and earnings were said to have risen 7.6% in 1966, 8% in 1967, 8.7%

in 1968, and 5% in 1969, mainly as a result of rises in productivity and the sloughing-off of the excess labour force. However, this improvement occurred in the medium and large-scale sectors and was realized at the expense of unskilled and semi-skilled labour. In reality the real income of the working class as a whole improved only marginally in absolute terms (see table below) and declined relative to capital and management.

Table 1   Income Distribution

Year	Minimum Daily Wage (Cedi)	Index of Minimum Wage	Cost of Living Index	Index of Real Minimum Wage
1960	0.65	100	100	100
1964	0.65	100	135	74
1965	0.65	100	170	59
1966	0.65	100	178	56
1967	0.70	108	168	64
1968	0.75	115	185	65

Source: Kodwo Ewusi: *The Distribution of Monetary Incomes in Ghana,* University of Ghana: ISSER, 1974, p. 34.

The share of labour in total value-added in the large-scale manufacturing sector (where most of the gains were said to have been realized) fell from 30.4% in 1962 to 20.6% in 1970, meaning that capital had increased its profits at the expense of labour. In a study of the manufacturing sector the World Bank admitted that 'the industrial workers did not benefit from the growth of productivity which took place during this period... Recipients of non-wage incomes [i.e. capital] have gained most from the industrial expansion that has occurred'.[41] This was not unexpected, given the extensive concessions to big business and foreign investors by the NLC. Stabilization policies thus had the effect of intensifying existing income differentials in Ghanaian society, both between labour and capital and within the various strata of the working classes. For the masses of the working poor 'stabilization' meant further immisceration: 'How the workers [have] existed and continue to do so now is a miracle', the Secretary-General of the Trades Union Congress wrote in 1968.[42] Mass unemployment and economic hardship bred crime and social unrest: 'Towns and villages [in the Central Region and Ashanti]... are being subjected to a wave of terrorism and dacoity unparalleled in the history of this country', complained the *Ghanaian Times* in February 1967. To deal with this situation the NLC turned increasingly to legal repression and military force.

It was not only private capital that raised its profits at the expense of labour. A similar process of differentiation was at work in the public sector.

IMF salary and wage guidelines, vigorously enforced for the working class, were simply ignored in the case of the higher state and parastatal bureaucracy. In 1967 a committee was appointed to review salaries and wages in the public sector. The trade unions presented proposals arguing that increases in the cost of living necessitated a daily expenditure of ₡3.67 by an average Ghanaian family of four (exclusive of education and medical care) and urging a rise in the minimum wage from ₡0.70 to between ₡1.00 and ₡2.00. The unions also demanded a redistribution of national income, reduction of salary differentials in the public service from 1.22 to 1.10, as well as a ceiling on profits plus incentives for higher productivity. While conceding that there had been a 'serious decline in the general standards of living throughout the country' which had been 'most severely felt among the lower wage-earners', the committee nevertheless rejected arguments for a general improvement in wages, arguing that higher wages would cause inflation, upset the relationship between 'the real income of the cultivator and the labourer in wage employment' and 'reduce the attraction of work on the land'.[43] On the other hand redistribution must 'await the development of a more technologically-based economy and a better trained and educated labour force'. The committee advised that the minimum wage be raised by 5 *pesewas* (to ₡0.75), and that negotiated wage increases be restricted to 5%. Nevertheless the committee recommended salary increases for top civil servants that would have raised the differential between the highest and lowest paid public servants upwards to 1.39. Even before the salary committee sat substantial salary increases had been granted to state lawyers, doctors and university lecturers. Salary increases of up to 106% were also granted to the managing directors of state banks and corporations.[44]

More scandalous still was the treatment of the military and police force by this regime of 'austerity'. According to directives issued by General Kotoka, the leader of the coup, to the National Economic Committee in March 1966 all military officers and ranks were to be granted total exemption from income tax, payment of quartering charges, electricity, water and conservancy, in addition to the restoration of pension rights and special maintenance and transfer grants abolished by Nkrumah's Government. Faced with this proposed plunder of the state treasury, the Ministry of Finance quaked and vacillated, finally concluding that 'a loss of ₡4.8 million is undoubtedly not too high a price to pay for the true freedom that has been brought to the Nation by the Armed Forces and Police'.[45] The defence budget increased by over 100%, from ₡25.4 million in 1965 to ₡54.2 million in 1969, the total budget for military salaries alone increasing by 230% in the same period. This may be contrasted with an overall increase of only 10% in total government expenditure in 1966–69, and a decline of 35% in the budget for agriculture over the period. Thus while IMF stabilization imposed severe austerity on the working classes, it was in practice much less successful in extending this to the ruling classes; indeed (subsequent Fund and Bank criticisms notwithstanding) rising income and privileges to these classes may be regarded as the 'bribe' required to facilitate the intensified exploitation of the country and its working classes by imperialism. These deepening class contradictions under military dictatorship were not lost on the popular consciousness. In 1968 it was reported that 'As you walk through the market, in the public places, and in fact in every public gathering, you hear "Ebi te yie, ebi nte yie, ebi so nte yie Koraa" '[46]

(c) Currency Devaluation

The irrelevance of monetarist 'solutions' to Ghana's problems was again indicated by the 1967 devaluation of the *cedi* (by 30% against the dollar) in order to stimulate exports and further reduce import levels.

In 1969 the *Economic Survey* complained that 'in spite of the devaluation, the *quantum* of exports, instead of increasing, rather decreased... for all commodities except timber and diamonds, while the *quantum* of imports increased, contrary to expectations'. What happened? The fact is that as an export promotion device devaluation, one of the policy instruments favoured by the IMF in its dealings with underdeveloped economies, was (as we have seen) originally developed in the context of the advanced capitalist economies. The main differences between these and the peripheral capitalist economies were firstly that export trade constituted an extension of production for the home market rather than a separate sector, and secondly that pricing inputs and final prices are mainly locally determined, either because of the high degree of integration of domestic production or high local value-added. In addition local substitutes exist for most imported manufacturers. But even in these self-centred industrial economies, as Livingstone has rightly argued in his study of the British experience, devaluation is 'at best a gamble' as far as improving a balance of payments situation is concerned.[47]

Applied to an externally oriented primary-commodity exporting economy like Ghana's with a dependent semi-industrial base, devaluation raises serious problems, even granted the existence of spare large industrial capacity and the ability to hold down wage demands and domestic inflation. In these situations devaluation is often an expedient designed to avoid more fundamental questions of the restructuring of the domestic economy and external commodity markets. The prime immediate benefits of devaluation can be expected to be confined to higher prices to primary commodity producers/exporters and alleviation of the liquidity problems of government, but both will be achieved at high cost. In the first place it can be assumed that given the basic dependence of the system on imports and the absence of short-term local substitutes (particularly for manufactures), import volumes will tend to be relatively unresponsive to any but the largest price increases induced by devaluation, so that the probable benefits of devaluation will have to be expected from the export side. Even in this area the evidence is not optimistic. In the first place, among Ghana's leading exports, cocoa, gold, diamonds, and coffee, which constituted about 70% of total exports by value, were sold in well-organized international markets with prices posted in foreign exchange (rather than *cedis*).[48] Devaluation could thus not be expected to lead to increased foreign exchange earnings, although higher prices to local primary commodity producers may have the effect of locking the country even more securely into primary export production. But this did not happen. On the contrary cocoa exports plunged steeply from the high of 557,000 long tons in the peak 1964–65 harvest to 334,000 tonnes in 1968–69. This was because increased cocoa production also depended on control of inflation in non-cocoa sectors and on effective solutions to the structural and other problems facing the industry (aging farm population, labour shortages, limits on cultivable land, poor extension, shortages of imported inputs), and as in the past little was done to remove these bottlenecks. But even given effective solutions to these problems, the increasing exactions of the state on cocoa surplus in this period would have constituted a final brake on the return of cocoa wealth to the producers.[49]

A second category of exports (timber, manganese, bauxite) constituting about 20% of total exports, also had prices set in foreign exchange but could benefit from devaluation owing to the imperfect organization of their markets. The problem was that production in these extractive industries (as of gold and diamonds) could not be extended without large infusions of foreign exchange to replace worn-out machinery and equipment. Only a third category comprising industrial exports, textiles, shoes, plastic goods, vegetable oils, etc., constituting 5% of total exports, stood to benefit most directly from devaluation, owing to the existence of large spare industrial capacity and the fact that (at least in theory) their market prices were determined in Ghana rather than on international markets. Again these gains could not be realized owing to the scarcity of complementary factors of production (such as skilled labour, competent management, etc.) which could not be rectified in the short term, and the almost total dependence of the industrial structure on imports of machinery, spare parts and raw materials. Given this dependence, devaluation could only drive up import prices and production costs, adversely affecting the more marginal and smaller manufacturers and making Ghanaian industrial exports even less competitive.[50]

Devaluation was even less successful in restraining imports. At the time of devaluation imports of industrial spare parts and chemicals (almost 15% of total imports) were liberalized and placed on Open General Licence, but the initial rush for licences was so great that their issuance had to be temporarily suspended. Requests for import licences in 1967 were more than triple the amount actually issued. By the end of 1967, the net reserve position of the Bank of Ghana was down to about $10 million or less than two weeks' imports, leading the World Bank to advocate the suspension of further trade and payments liberalization and the retention for the time being of direct controls.[51]

(d) Agriculture

The approach of the NLC to the substantive problems of agriculture and industry remains to be seen. The most serious shortcoming of the stabilization policy was the absence of a domestic agricultural programme.[52] This was a fundamental weakness. Apart from its leading role in stimulating inflation, domestic agriculture should have played a crucial role in linking Ghanaian industry to the local resource base and relieving pressure on the balance of payments. To the extent that an 'agricultural policy' did exist it was meant to lock Ghana even more firmly into export agriculture. In the domestic sector policy consisted almost solely in retrenching the state agricultural sector rather than stimulating private or cooperative agriculture. As late as 1968 the World Bank observed that 'program priorities and operational plans [in agriculture] are generally not yet established much less implemented'. The relevant portion of the Bank report is worth quoting in greater detail:[53]

> Effective management for the two sugar refineries and plantations has yet to be obtained and it will take considerable time and additional investment to grow sufficient input for the factories. Processing plants for pineapple, tomato and mango are still idle for lack of raw materials and no concrete proposals to grow the necessary inputs are yet in sight...Other programs such as the encouragement of production and marketing co-operatives, the improvement of extension services, the distribution of farm supplies and programs to improve water management, to mention only a few, are equally important and programs in these areas have been most uneven. Program priorities and operational plans are generally not yet established much less implemented. Instead of this type of work, it appears that too much time and resources are devoted to unproductive [sic] on-going programs like farm mechanisation and land settlement or the discussion of policy in very general terms without due regard to requirements for their implementation.

Both state investment in agriculture and commercial bank credit to the sector fell substantially throughout the stabilization period (Table 2) Shortfalls in local food production were met by increasing resort to commodity imports from the Western countries, thus further eroding the capacity of the agricultural sector for self-sufficiency. Although an unusually favourable harvest briefly brought down food prices in 1967, the local food price index continued to climb, from 167 in 1967 to 200 in 1969 and a record 236 in 1971.

The State Enterprises

Unlike agriculture however industry was the subject of a systematic policy. The central target of this policy was the state industrial enterprises. Before the coup the position of the state enterprises stood roughly as follows. Total estimated investment in the enterprises (considered understated) amounted to £39.8 million. Accumulated profits to end 1965 for 32 of the 35 enterprises stood at £1.2 million, while accumulated losses stood at £15.1

Table 2 Commercial Bank Loans and Advances to Agriculture[1] 1965 to 1969 (₡ million)

Year End	Total[2]	Public Institutions	Cooperatives	Private Sector	(Total Loans and Advances to Commerce)[3]
1965	10.0	8.9	0.013	1.1	40.3
1966	13.8	11.6	0.015	2.2	31.0
1967	3.2	0.27	0.005	2.8	42.2
1968	3.8	0.61	0.004	3.1	37.8
1969	10.0	2.3	2.2	5.5	43.8

Source: *Economic Survey*, various issues: Commercial Bank reports.

[1] Includes credit for Forestry and Logging (both negligible).
[2] Figures may not add up due to rounding.
[3] For comparison only.

million. However, of the total losses £13.6 million were accounted for by only three enterprises: Ghana Airways, the State Mining Corporation, and the State Farms Corporation. The losses of the airline were attributed mainly to flying uneconomic routes. These were routes intended to reduce travelling time and improve communications between African countries at a time when most African flights were routed through Europe. Those of the State Mining Corporation were due to high costs of production relative to the fixed world price of gold, investment in mine development, and provision for heavy depreciation. Finally the losses of the State Farms Corporation were partly inherited from the defunct Agricultural Development Corporation, and partly due to development expenditure on new plantations (which should have been capitalized in the accounts rather than charged directly to income and expenditure).[54] The remaining 29 enterprises had recorded total losses of £1.5 million. The poor performance of these enterprises was attributed to a variety of factors; high wage and salary bills relative to turnover, heavy overheads, poor and inefficient management, poor costing systems and production controls, improper pricing and sales policies, and under-utilization of plant capacity, due mainly to shortages of imported raw materials. Of 24 manufacturing enterprises studied by a World Bank mission in November 1965, 6 were said to be currently profitable and 18 were unprofitable. Of the 18, 5 could become profitable in a year or two without further investment, 2 had profit potential but had been constrained by unfavourable policies and bad planning, 4 were to be wound up, 2 required market studies, and the profitability of 3 could not be determined.[55] According to the Bank, apart from the four enterprises to be wound up, 'the remainder, provided that the management and technical efficiency are improved, can probably be run with a measure of financial success.'[56]

The condition of most of the state enterprises, though by no means buoyant, was thus not necessarily hopeless. A number of reforms had been contemplated to streamline the operations of the enterprises and to improve their profitability, including a new form of instrument of incorporation for all state enterprises. By the time of the coup the problem of management had been partly resolved, owing to courses and seminars organized for management and supervisory staff by the Ghana Association for Advancement of Management (GAAM) and the National Productivity Centre. Thus seven months after the coup a review of state enterprises had concluded that progress in management during the preceding two years had been 'quite encouraging'. Managements had begun to show awareness of their responsibilities, and even those enterprises which had hitherto shown heavy losses had either reduced their loss levels considerably, begun to break even, or were already showing profits.[57] However, at the time that it came to power the NLC was already predisposed to sell or invite private participation in at least some of the enterprises, and in any case Fund ceilings on government expenditure gave few other options. Nevertheless there were specific pressures from the World Bank, the US Embassy and American Government agencies, and the Chamber of Commerce and foreign companies in Accra to transfer interest in some of the enterprises to private concerns.[58] In addition a basic conditionality attached to much Western 'aid' to the NLC was willingness to curtail the state sector and expand the sphere of operations of private capital.[59]

The Agreements with Foreign Private Enterprise

During 1966 and early 1967 a sub-committee of the National Economic Committee, the economic advisory organ of the NLC, negotiated with a number of foreign companies for participation (in reality, virtual takeover) in selected state enterprises. During the negotiations[60] the companies demanded and obtained wider-ranging management and policy control over the enterprises as well as extensive tax and other concessions. In the agreement governing the establishment of the Ghana Cement Works, Norway Cement Export S.A. ('Norcem') with only 25% of the shareholding in the joint venture, obtained parity with the Ghana Government on the Board of Directors. One of Norcem's representatives on the Board was to be both Chairman of the Board (with a casting vote) and Managing Director of the company. Norcem's Managing Director was to have exclusive power to manage the company, including, but not limited to, the hiring and firing of local and expatriate employees, placing of all orders for the company's requirements, the determination of the prices for cement and of company sales policy. The Board was to exercise only those powers not already conferred on the Managing Director, but even these were to be exercised at the behest of Norcem. These included the appointment and dismissal of the Managing Director, the declaration of dividends, the sale or acquisition of company property, and the raising of loans and the mortgaging of company property – but only on the recommendation of Norcem. Similarly in the pharmaceutical joint venture, Abbott Laboratories of Illinois, with 45% of the shares, acquired complete control of the management, including appointment and dismissal of personnel, determination of product lines and quality standards, marketing organization and controls, product pricing and packaging standards, decisions over sources of raw materials, and the award of contracts for legal, accounting, and auditing services. Abbott was also to furnish the technical, consulting, and management services in respect of all aspects of the company's operations, for which services it was to be reimbursed by Abbott–Ghana. Finally Abbott was to have a majority on the Board of Directors and voting control of the company including the appointment of the Chairman of the Board, the Managing Director and the Company Secretary.

Why then were these agreements signed? In the first place Ghana entered into the negotiations from a subjectively inferior bargaining position. According to the NLC's chief negotiator, Ghana really had no alternative to capitulation to foreign capital; the state enterprises 'would otherwise have been dying'.[61] In fact, in all cases the original agreements governing the projects included training programmes designed to completely Ghanaianize management (in addition to complete ownership) in a few years. Deeper reasons may be found in the views of the military regime on the beneficial effects of multinational penetration. Multinational companies would assure a net inflow of capital into Ghana; they would develop local productive forces by importing into Ghana a 'stream of modern industrial technology' and by introducing 'those practices of labour and management which make for a high level of productivity in advanced countries.'[62] The NLC had therefore been advised at an early stage that in joint ventures technical and commercial management should be left in the hands of the foreign private partner. Consequently the state negotiators were much less concerned with management or policy control over the joint-venture enterprises than with maximizing state revenues and sources of budgetary support. The insistence on state majority shareholding during the negotiations was primarily for this reason. As Ghana's chief negotiator once again explained: 'Ghana insisted on and obtained a majority holding in the shareholding so as to earn a large share of the distributable profits which will now surely be forthcoming because of the efficient management which will be brought to bear on the factory operations [of Abbott–Ghana].' What was good for the multinational was good for Ghana: 'The investor is in the business of making money; and given average honesty, he will only make money when he makes money for us as well.'

Naturally the investor abroad also expects, and was expected, to reap super-profits: 'All private enterprise, whether domestic or foreign, in a developing country like Ghana expects to make substantial profits. The reason is that the risk of investing in such countries is greater than that of placing an investment in the developed economies where the determinants of profitability are better known and more easily controlled.' Thus: 'to attract foreign capital from elsewhere, it must be made distinctly manifest to the Investor that the return on his capital here [in Ghana] is superior to the return he may expect elsewhere. This means positively throwing benefits at him to make him move his resources from somewhere else to here.'

This was the neocolonial ideology that underlay the agreements. Thus behind the negotiations and agreements was a basic misunderstanding of the nature and objectives of multinational investment. Even a cursory study of the agreements should demonstrate the falsity of many of these assumptions. In the first place, except in a few cases the multinational companies had no interest in importing or risking their own capital to finance investments in Ghana. With the exception of Firestone, corporate capital directly invested in Ghana constituted only a fraction of the capital actually required to acquire and operate the assets of the joint venture. The main source of capital for the multinational takeovers was in fact local capital: in the form both of state capital, and of loans and credits advanced by Ghanaian commercial banks at preferential interest rates. This was expected to be supplemented by credit from metropolitan banks (Export–Import Bank, etc). Guaranteed access to local lines of credit was actually written into the terms of the joint-venture agreements. Capital contributions from the multinationals themselves mostly took the form of imports of plant, equipment and services, a practice notoriously conducive to overcharging and transfer-pricing.

It is, of course, no secret that MNCs finance the bulk of their third world operations from local capital sources, although the profits thus generated may subsequently be classified and repatriated as 'foreign investment'. For instance between 1957 and 1965 US MNCs operating in Latin America financed 83% of their investments from local capital sources, either from savings held by the local banks or from reinvested earnings generated largely from local sources. Of the manufacturing operations of these MNCs in Latin America between 1960 and 1970, 78% were financed from local capital sources; on the other hand between 1960 and 1968 these companies repatriated on the average 79% of their net profits out of the continent, with the highest levels of repatriation (83%) occurring in the mining, petroleum and smelting industries.[63] In Ghana this practice was facilitated by classification of reinvested (unrepatriated) profits as 'foreign investment' – as in the agreements with UAC to take over Juapong textiles in 1967 – irrespective of their initial source. Local banks, including state-owned banks such as the Ghana Commercial Bank and the Bank of Ghana, prefer to lend to large foreign corporate clients.[64] The preferential access to local credit allows these companies to expand their operations at the expense of smaller local companies and to dominate more and more of the national market. In addition the Ghanaian 'takeovers' occurred at a time when curbs imposed on outflow of investment funds under the US Direct Foreign Investment Program, and the high cost of borrowing on US domestic financial markets, had driven US companies to finance more and more of their overseas operations from the Eurobond market and from the capital markets of host countries.[65]

However, owing to the peculiar circumstances in Ghana, state capital played a crucial if indirect role in financing these foreign takeovers. Both the Abbott and Norcem agreements (as well as proposals advanced by UTC, Promoci and other companies during the negotiations) involved the state loaning assets to the joint-venture companies, or more precisely to the foreign partner, at generous interest rates. Much of the finance required for the acquisition of the assets by Abbott and Norcem would then have been derived from profits generated from operating these assets, with minimum investment of their own capital. At any rate, whatever capital was advanced by the foreign companies could hardly be described as risk capital. Both the original capital and return on it were guaranteed by extensive economic and political concessions: token rent, generous capital allowances, tax exemptions, remission of import duties, monopolistic conditions of production and pricing, etc., as well as state and USAID guarantees against expropriation. Risk was further reduced by heavy undervaluation of the original assets.

Secondly, the level of control conferred on the foreign companies could only work to maximize the return on corporate (as opposed to state) 'investment' and to facilitate the repatriation of corporate profits, through transfer pricing and other methods. 'Transfer pricing' refers to the procedure whereby by manipulating the prices on goods and services exported outside or imported into a country, a company is able to shift funds from one national territory to another, outside official channels and controls. This may be done in a variety of ways: by overpricing goods imported into the country, and then transferring the difference to the external account of the importing company ('over-invoicing'); or by quoting deliberately low prices on goods exported outside the country, with the difference between this and the real (higher) price again being credited to an account abroad ('under-invoicing'). As Tugendhat has rightly argued, 'the [multinational] companies' ability to manipulate transfer prices enables them to get around even the most severe [exchange] restrictions, at least partially'.[66] Transfer-pricing practices are optimized where transfers take place between affiliated companies, such as between a parent company and a subsidiary, or between two subsidiaries of the same company. In this case prices are all the more easily manipulated, taking advantage of brand naming and company 'special products', fees for know-how, interest on corporate loans, etc. Transfer pricing is routinely practised by multinationals in their Third World operations.[67]

Transfer-pricing has also been widely practised by foreign-owned companies to evade exchange restrictions in Ghana. Because of the structure of the Ghana economy, transfer-pricing usually takes the form of over-invoicing, although as the case of Union Carbide[68] demonstrates, some under-invoicing also occurs. Analysis by Government officials of a 'small selection' of 1971 imports revealed that ₵250,000 had been transferred abroad through overpricing on only 24 of the invoices on which irregularities were detected. The degree of invoicing in this sample ranged up to 30%, although in one case the price of the imports had been inflated by 1600%. According to no less a person than the Head of State, many local subsidiaries or affiliates of multinationals in Ghana had transferred millions in foreign exchange abroad through over- and under-invoicing and failure to repatriate commissions paid abroad.[69] These charges were confirmed by the government investigation into R.T. Briscoe, a subsidiary of the Danish multinational East Asiatic Company Ltd. (EAC).[70] According to the General Superintendence Company, a Swiss firm contracted by the Central Bank to check instances of over-invoicing, Ghana lost at least ₵60 million annually through transfer pricing. But General Superintendence itself was found to have colluded with Briscoe and EAC to evade Ghanaian customs and exchange regulations.[71]

This ability of the multinational companies to maximize returns and to repatriate profits through unofficial channels is further enhanced by the methods of accounting employed by the MNCs. These methods are designed to conceal rather than reveal the true state of company accounts; 'skilled obfuscation' by corporation accountants turns 'dividends into interest, and profits into losses',[72] thus minimizing the profit picture for the taxman, both at home and abroad. Further, as Barnet has correctly warned 'the interest of the [multinational] enterprises is *global* profit maximization, which may ... require profit *minimization,* in certain countries under certain circumstances.'[73] The process of ensuring global profitability hinges, to a large extent, on the power of the MNC to relocate 'profits' and 'losses' at any number of chosen points along its international structure to take advantage of most favourable tax systems or to facilitate profit repatriation as the case may be. Thus in joint ventures of the sort instituted by the Ghanaian agreements it cannot simply be assumed that profits for the multinational corporation would necessarily entail profits for the local subsidiary or its local partners. Yet the nature of the agreements gave maximum opportunity and incentive to the foreign partners to undertake both transfer-pricing and profit minimization. Complete control over management, accounting, etc., was granted to the foreign partner, ensuring the power to employ internal corporate accounting methods that would not be easily unravelled by outsiders. In the case of Abbott this control over accounting was cemented by sole power to place 'contracts for legal, accounting and auditing services', as well as to determine sources of raw materials and other inputs for the local firm.[74] In addition tax incentives for the joint-venture company (and in the case of Ghana Cement Works the length of the repayment period for the assets required) were tied inversely to the profitability of the local company, giving an incentive for the continued declaration of losses. Sawyer has argued that by employing transfer-pricing and a variety of other techniques, Firestone may have recouped its initial investment in the rubber and tyre scheme in the first three years of operation.[75]

It is worth stating again that the main problem posed by state industries was not that of simple profitability but of transformation of the neocolonial economy. The requirements for transformation are not necessarily the same as those for profitability (and vice versa), particularly for multinational companies, for whom maximum profitability often requires that the local economy be maintained in its dependent and disarticulated mould. While the original objective in all the socialist projects was industries completely owned and operated by Ghanaians, the effect of the NLC 'reforms' was to denationalize these industries, subordinate them to the world-wide structure and operations of multinational companies and thus further frustrate the possibilities of independent, integrated industrialization. This is the sense of the criticism that the agreements had turned state enterprises effectively into local subsidiaries of multinationals. Significantly Ghana was quoted as a reversal of the 'wave of nationalizations' sweeping the African continent in the late 1960s.[76] The enterprises transferred were by no means the 'problem' industries: these were retained in the state sector on the grounds that private capital was not interested in them. With minor exceptions (the so-called 'rural industries', the bakery, and the furniture and joinery factory) the promised sale of enterprises to Ghanaian businessmen did not materialize.

All the multinationals involved in the negotiations were essentially concerned to capture control of the most profitable aspects of the projects, leaving the Ghana Government with the heavy development and infrastructural costs required to integrate the projects (such as the rubber plantations in the tyre project, the limestone deposits in the cement project, and the cotton plantations in the Juapong textile mills). By the same token the MNCs had little interest in integrating their operations to a local resource base, nor could they logically be expected to, given their interest in the possibilities for transfer-pricing opened up by import-oriented activities and the fact that nationally integrated production naturally enhanced local control or the possibility of nationalization. Consequently projects that were originally planned as integrated production units (such as the textile and clinker mills) ended up as import-dependent semi-industrial processors.

The structural distortions that thus resulted from these arrangements were demonstrated by the cement industry. Ghana has the potential for an integrated cement factory, with proven limestone deposits at Nauli (400 million tons reserves), Buipe (100–200 million tons) and Bong-Da (15 million tons), as well as local charcoal for the production of clinker, which is then mixed with *gypsum* in small quantities in the final crushing and milling stage. At the time of the construction of the Takoradi factory it was envisaged that the industry would eventually be integrated backwards by exploitation of the Nauli deposits. The 1967 agreement committed Norcem to explore the feasibility of utilizing the Nauli deposits, albeit at the expense of Ghana Cement Works. However, a separate agreement negotiated at the same time contracted Norcem, a major clinker exporter, to supply the total clinker requirements of Ghana Cement Works for an initial period of two years (with the possibility of renewal). Norcem's feasibility study duly concluded that the Nauli deposits, which were located 80 to 400 feet underground, would be too difficult and expensive to mine and transport.

This was undoubtedly correct from the point of view of the *profitability* of Ghana Cement Works. Ghana Cement Works would have required state subsidies; but among the advantages of integration would have been considerable savings in foreign exchange (₡12 million annually by 1975). The later critical shortages of imported inputs that led to the collapse of the construction industry in Ghana would also have been averted. It is also worth noting that as early as 1967 Ghana's negotiators had concluded that Norcem had little real interest in tapping the Nauli deposits.[77] Thus, although by 1970 the Tema factory was producing at full capacity and the Takoradi factory at 50% capacity, the anticipated integration of the local industry had not occurred and appeared unlikely to materialize, although integration had already occurred within the corporate structure of Norcem. 'The existing cement industry only consists of the grinding of imported clinker with imported machinery and under a foreign management, into the form of cement', the government complained in that year.[78] This was only one instance of the conflict between the requirements for profitability and those for transformation in Ghana's industrial structure.

The Norcem case was made all the more remarkable by their curious relationship with the original sponsors of the Takoradi project, the Poles. Norcem itself obtained large quantities of its clinker under a supply contract from Poland. The training of Ghanaians in production technology under the Norcem contract was also carried out in Poland, followed by on-the-job attachment to Norcem facilities in Norway.[79] The Poles complained that Norcem had successfully utilized its monopoly control of the national cement industry to prevent them from establishing direct supply lines with Ghana.[80] Through the clinker contract Norcem was able to exercise a stranglehold over the industry. After 1974 the Ghana Government, indebted to Norcem, was to make a series of unsuccessful efforts to break the company's grip over clinker supplies.[81]

Some 20 enterprises (including most of the 'problem' ones) were retained in the state sector under a new holding company, the Ghana Industrial Holding Company (GIHOC). However, beyond this reorganization there was little serious attempt to tackle the operational weaknesses of these enterprises. Although the idea behind the Holding Company was that it would afford the enterprises a sufficient degree of freedom and ensure their efficient operation as commercial enterprises, in practice it did not run that way. Each enterprise was headed by a general manager, but responsibility for the most important aspects of the operation of each enterprise was centralized in the GIHOC headquarters in Accra, leading to overextension of the headquarters organization on the one hand and inadequate responsibility at the factory level on the other. Although there was improvement in some areas, many of the enterprises continued to be characterized by poor accounting control and non-preparation of accounts, bad management and planning, theft of funds and property, and heavy indebtedness. This report on the state Tannery Corporation emphasized once again the lack of progress:[82]

> Although large sums of money have been invested in factory buildings, staff growth and machinery and equipment at the factory sites, this Corporation has not started serious operations. The auditors' report for the years 1967, 1968 and 1969 enumerated a number of disturbing points which would have engaged the serious attention of the Ministry of Industries. The report indicates that boxes of machinery and equipment, some of them unopened, were still lying idle three years after delivery and that as the guarantee period has expired, it was doubtful whether any claim for suitability would be accepted under the guarantee. Reference may also be made to the corporation's inability to account for an amount of over N₵33,000.00 spent on the overseas training of 21 officers. The irony of the situation was that eleven out of nineteen trainees who returned home in 1966 have, for three years been engaged on no productive operation although each of them received a monthly allowance.

In a few cases, such as the State Electronic Products Division of GIHOC, deterioration appeared to have set in after a promising start.[83]

Performance of the Manufacturing Sector

In spite of the above, large-scale manufacturing industry recorded notable increases in production. This has been claimed as one of the most important achievements of stabilization. Between 1966 and 1969 gross output and value-added grew by 85% and 61% respectively at current prices, while employment (in contrast to other sectors) grew by 43%. Large-scale manufacturing establishments rose from 230 in 1966 to 346 in 1968. The most rapid expansion occurred in textiles, clothing, footwear and food, beverages, and tobacco. In 1968 textiles, clothing and footwear accounted for 21% of the increase in gross manufacturing output and 47% of the increase in value-added, while food, beverages and tobacco accounted for about 13% and 52% respectively. A closer analysis, however, reveals the limits to this 'growth'. First, although more efficient utilization of installed capacity occurred as a result of liberalization of imported inputs and spare parts, most of the expansion in gross production was due to new additions to capacity. This was particularly the case in the textile and clothing sector. Second, the operation of the new 'industries' merely duplicated the earlier pattern of industrialization, and was characterized by

Table 3 Textile, Weaving Apparel, and Footwear Industries: Imported Inputs as % of Total Materials in 1968

	S.I.T.C. Classification	% Imports
Textiles	2311	100
	2312	N.A.
	2319	90
	2320	100
	2391	94
Footwear and apparel	2411	94
	2430	98
	2442	95
	2443	69
	2444	100
	2449	100
	2451	46

Source: Bank of Ghana data

capital-intensity, import-dependence, and lack of backward or forward linkages. Again the textile and clothing industry was an excellent example of this. In 1968 most operations of this sector were heavily import-dependent (Table 1.3).

By 1972 local raw cotton provided only 3% of total cotton supplies, in spite of the fact that favourable soil and climatic conditions existed for cotton cultivation in Ghana and raw cotton could be cultivated and harvested in 4–5 months, while a similar period was required for its importation. Not surprisingly Ghanaian industry continued to maintain the dependent and disarticulated character so favoured by finance capital:

> Flour mills are devoted entirely to the grinding of foreign wheat. Flour bread and biscuits are almost exclusively derived from imported grains, yeast, milk powder and added nutrients. The GIHOC meat slaughtering, butchering and packing factory relies upon imported cattle for 98% of its output. All the hops, malt, concentrate and yeast, and most of the sugar used by the large-scale breweries, distilleries, and soft-drink manufacturers come from abroad. This is true of the milk-powder used for tinned milk and much of the oil which goes into margarine. Even the fish canning factory at the Tema Food Complex has required sardines and mackerel from foreign-owned vessels, as well as imported tinplate and oils.[84]

Conclusion

From this analysis it should be clear that the main objective of IMF stabilization in Ghana after 1966 was to destroy whatever fragile basis had been laid for local self-sufficiency and development. It is in this sense that 1966 may be regarded as a turning-point for Ghana. The question in 1966 was not whether or not a change was necessary. The CPP, immobilized by its internal contradictions, had shown itself incapable either of resolving the crisis in the economy, or of initiating a decisive advance to socialism. But the change required was one that would have *transcended* the CPP, accepting as a basis for further advance to socialist transformation and an integrated national economy the positive achievements already realized by the party. Instead, the military coup facilitated the repenetration of finance capital and the reintegration of the economy into world capitalism (see Table 4). In turn this required the destruction of precisely these positive aspects, both at the level of economic structures and (more important) the genuinely progressive and coherent content of Nkrumah's 'socialism'.

Neither of the two main benefits expected by the NLC for concurring in this process – a concessionary debt settlement and massive aid – materialized. The 1966 and 1968 debt agreements resulted in a direct increase of Ghana's total debt burden by ₵89.7 million in additional moratorium interest. Instead of debt 'relief', Ghana found her creditors, in the plaintive words of the Finance Minister, 'piling debt upon debt'. Ironically, in spite of anti-Soviet policies, the NLC received far more favourable terms from the socialist than from the Western creditors (see Document 54). Of the total 'aid' pledged in 1967 and 1968 by the Ghana Consultative Group (an association of Western creditors turned 'donors'), only 14% and 21% respectively were utilized. The most important reason for this was complex procedures tying 'aid' to procurement in the donor countries, a procedure designed to cultivate markets in the recipient country and enhance exports

Table 4   Direction of Ghana's International Trade 1965–69 (in %)

	Socialist Countries		United Kingdom		EEC		Dollar Area	
	Imports	Exports	Imports	Exports	Imports	Exports	Imports	Exports
1965	26.3	21.3	25.8	20.8	21.4	27.8	10.5	18.6
1966	13.2	21.0	28.8	25.0	21.2	22.0	17.5	17.0
1967	8.3	15.0	30.0	28.8	20.3	19.8	18.3	18.0
1968	7.7	9.2	27.6	27.8	20.3	25.8	21.5	20.6
1969	8.8	7.2	26.8	28.6	20.9	25.4	20.2	20.7

Source: Economic Survey, Issues 1966–69

for the donor. This kind of 'aid' could only have further underdeveloped Ghana: aid-tying results in the loss of at least 10% in the real value of the transaction and as much as 30% where the 'aid' (as in this case) consists of food and other agricultural commodities.[85] On the other hand both the formal debt conferences and Consultative Group meetings provided the creditor-donors with an ideal forum for dictating policy directions to Ghana.

For Ghana's economy the main effect of IMF stabilization was deepening stagnation and unemployment.[86] Public sector investment fell by 17% in 1966, 20% in 1967, and 3.5% in 1968, but the expected increase in private investment failed to materialize. A two-year development plan introduced to return the country to 'growth' at the end of the stabilization period in 1968 failed to stimulate the needed investment. Real per capita GNP fell from ₵142 in 1965 to ₵135 in 1969, mainly due to a fall in the living standards of the working poor. Even the most important achievement of stabilization, the reorganization and rationalization of state finances, proved temporary; the revenue base and tax effort of the state actually shrank in the period immediately following stabilization, with cocoa assuming once again an ever increasing role in state revenues[87]. In 1968, just after stabilization had been 'successfully' concluded, Ghana was caught in a renewed payments crisis and threat of bankruptcy. This was not in itself surprising, since the stabilization programme ignored the basic causes of the crisis in Ghana's peripheral economy – the stagnation of food agriculture, decline in export earnings due to the organization of external commodity markets, and the inherent limitations of dependent semi-industrialization. By artificially depressing the standard of living of the mass of the people, IMF stabilization was able temporarily to repress the symptoms of inflation, but without removing its fundamental causes.

The contradictions thus generated set the stage for the difficulties of the civilian government in 1969 and eventually for the second military coup in 1972. What *is* surprising is that these problems were not totally unexpected even within the Bank and the Fund. As early as 1967 the Hansen Mission had warned that with Ghana's domestic product stagnant for two years in a row while population increased at nearly 3% per annum, 'any stabilization policy based on a further decline in per capita consumption and investment would have undesirable economic and political consequences' (see Document 15). These 'undesirable consequences' were virtually guaranteed by the fact that even within the constraints of the stabilization programme far more attention was paid by both the Fund and the Bank to effecting public savings in order to repay foreign creditors and to justify tax concessions to foreign capital than to stimulating domestic production: thus while Fund expenditure ceilings and guidelines were strictly enforced, the Bank's 'development package' never left the drawing boards.[88]

Part I: The IMF, the World Bank and the West

Introductory Note

This chapter traces the course of the negotiations between the Ghanaian Government, the International Monetary Fund and the World Bank in 1965 and early 1966. These negotiations were initiated by Nkrumah's Government and completed by the military after his overthrow, following failure to reach agreement. Documents 1 and 2 contain summaries of the preliminary reports of the IMF mission of May 1965 and the World Bank mission of September 1965. The Fund mission report is extracted from open parliamentary records, but the Bank report is copied from confidential notes taken at meetings between the mission and high government officials on 22 and 24 September and subsequently presented to the government as the official preliminary report of the mission. Documents 3 and 4, also based on open sources, contain the initial response of the Nkrumah Government to the Fund and Bank reports; it should be noted, however, that the speech of the Finance Minister on 22 February 1966 responded to certain detailed recommendations made by the missions but absent from the preliminary reports reproduced here.

Two days after the Finance Minister's speech identifying certain areas of disagreement with the Fund and Bank missions, and while President Nkrumah was away in Hanoi, a military coup unseated his government. A military and police junta, the National Liberation Council (NLC), constituted itself into a new government. The NLC appointed a National Economic Committee and a Political Committee of civilians to advise on economic and political questions respectively; these two committees were the most important in the government but the Economic Committee was much the more influential committee. (Other major committees appointed were the Agricultural, Administrative and Publicity Committees). The Economic Committee was charged with the revision of the economic policy of the Ghana Government and with the conduct of crucial international negotiations on behalf of the Ghana Government. Its chairman was the government statistician, E. N. Omaboe, and its members were Albert Adomakoh, Governor of the Bank of Ghana (the Central Bank), R. S. Amegashie, the Director of the Business School at Achimota, two principal secretaries of the Ministry of Finance, and two officials from the Planning Commission.

Document 5 reproduces the minutes of the first two meetings of the Economic Committee in the first days after the coup, and provides some insight into the political and economic dimensions of the coup. The Economic Committee established urgent contact with the IMF and World Bank in Washington immediately after the coup. Documents 6 to 10 are the text of cables exchanged between the Ghanaian authorities and the IMF. The first formal approach to the World Bank was made by Governor Adomakoh on 4 March (Document 11); the response of Abderrahman Tazi, the Executive Director for Ghana, spelt out Bank conditionality for extending assistance to Ghana, viz: 'close collaboration' with the Fund and agreement on a standby arrangement, the preparation of a development programme to be 'appraised by the Bank', and negotiations on the external debts with creditors (Document 12). The Bank conditions reflected the position also taken by the Western creditors. The proposed 'Letter of Intent' dispatched by Omaboe and Adomakoh to Pierre-Paul Schweitzer, the Managing Director of the IMF, as the basis for negotiation (Document 13) closely reflected the recommendations of previous Fund–Bank missions. With certain modifications, this was accepted as the guidelines for the stabilization programme of the military government. In May 1966 the NLC followed this by sending a delegation of officials to the main Western capitals to solicit 'aid' from Western governments, the IMF and the Bank. The report of this delegation (Document 14) gives a fascinating insight both into the attitudes of the NATO governments, particularly that of the United States and Western Germany, to the 1966 coup, as well as the subservience of the new government. The report suggests that while sympathetic to political developments in Ghana, the Western governments had no necessary intention of extending either debt 'forgiveness' or large amounts of aid.

However, the delight of the World Bank with the new Ghana regime was unqualified. The report of the World Bank mission of November 1966, led by Hansen, expressed considerable enthusiasm for both the political leadership and economic policies of the officers (Document 15). The report also spells out the divergence between the World Bank's own philosophy of 'development' and that of Nkrumah, and indicates the 'performance criteria' expected of the military regime.

Document 1: IMF Report on the Ghana Economy
Parliamentary Statement by Minister of Finance, 10 September, 1965.

We have now reached a stage where our reserves cannot be run down any further without endangering the stability of the Cedi. It was for this and other reasons, particularly the catastrophic drop in the price of cocoa, that the Government decided recently to invite a mission from the International Monetary Fund, of which Ghana is a member, to come to this country and to assist us to prepare a programme which would enable us to re-negotiate some of the suppliers' credits which we have contracted. The object of this exercise is to re-negotiate with the foreign suppliers, through their governments, to extend the period of repayment of these credits and to reduce the burden of debt servicing. This would make it possible to use proportionately more of the revenues we are able to raise and the foreign exchange we earn in the further development of our country. The final report of the Mission has not yet been received, but before they left the Mission submitted a preliminary report in which they indicated certain lines of action for consideration. Mr Speaker, I am happy to inform the House that these preliminary recommendations were not essentially different from those proposed by Osagyefo the President and the Central Committee of the Party before the arrival of the Mission. These recommendations have therefore been accepted by the Government and action has already been initiated to implement them.

It was Government's intention to treat this preliminary report as a confidential document until the full report was received, studied and discussed with both the Fund and the International Bank for Reconstruction and Development otherwise known as the World Bank whose Mission is currently in the country at the invitation of the Government. In view, however, of the uninformed comments that are being made in certain sections of the world press with an axe to grind against Ghana, I propose, Mr Speaker, with your permission, to give Members a brief summary of the recommendations and to inform them of the steps being taken to implement them.

The report observes that the Ghana economy is severely overstrained and recommends a period of consolidation. This in no way means stagnation. We have to ensure that ministries we have set up or in the process of establishment are provided with the necessary tools to run efficiently. To achieve this the Mission recommends the following measures:

(1) Government expenditure, recurrent and capital, should be limited to an amount that can be covered by Government revenue and by non-inflationary borrowing.
(2) A temporary halt should be placed on the launching of new projects financed by suppliers' credits of a short or medium term nature.

(3) Steps should be taken to cut domestic demand, including a cut in the producer price of cocoa.
(4) The dependence of State enterprises on subsidies from the Central Government should be stopped.
(5) The control of the public purse and the commitment of public funds should be centralized and strengthened.
(6) The liberal attitude toward foreign investment found in the Capital Investments Act should be made more manifest in public policies.
(7) Import licensing should be based on a strict system of priorities. Some global quotas should be introduced, and licences issued should be honoured promptly by all relevant agencies of the Government.
(8) The present bilateral and barter arrangements should be reconsidered with a view to reducing their harmful impact on the Ghana economy.

Mr Speaker, the Party and Government see nothing wrong with these recommendations and have therefore started to implement them. The most delicate part of the recommendations, that is, the reduction of the producer price of cocoa has already been implemented, thanks to the realism and patriotism of our farmers who on their own initiative volunteered for a cut in the naked ex-scale price per load of 60 lb payable to them from ₡7.20 (£G3) to ₡4.80 per load. Osagyefo, the President, has also directed that the weight of the 1966 Budget should be shifted in favour of the productive sector; in other words, the total budget expenditure on the productive sector should be raised from 35 per cent to 55 per cent of the State Budget. A Master Budget is also in the course of preparation by which every effort is being made to rephase the rest of the planned expenditure in the Seven-Year Development Plan so that resort to borrowing from the banking system is reduced and 65 per cent of budgetary resources is used on economic or productive sectors by 1970.

No where in the report was there any specific mention of Ghana Airways, diplomatic missions or defence spending as a recent article in *The Economist*, a London weekly, suggested. Indeed the Fund report expressly stated and with your permission, Mr Speaker, I wish to quote:

> It would be impertinent for us to suggest which areas of expenditure might most appropriately be cut.

Document 2: World Bank Mission Preliminary Report
From 'Notes taken at meetings held between the World Bank Mission and the National Planning Commission and Ministers and Principal Secretaries/Secretaries on 22 September and 24 September 1965.'

General
1. The World Bank mission is impressed by the development effort in Ghana. There has been a notable achievement in construction, illustrated by the Tema Township and Harbour; the Akosombo Dam; the Universities of Ghana; and the overall transportation system.
2. The mission is also impressed by the high quality and dedication of the top management personnel, both in the Civil Service and in the State Enterprises.
3. The level of sacrifice of consumption income by the people of Ghana is also impressive. Ghana has achieved a relatively high rate of taxation compared to GNP and the level of per capita income, and compare favourably in this respect to any developing country anywhere in the world.
4. The mission believes, however, that Ghana has not obtained results in output commensurate with the level of investment. In short, Ghana has not achieved full value for its money, nor for the sacrifice made by its people.
5. The primary cause of this relatively low effective return to effort has been the overstraining of all of Ghana's resources. In turn, the latter is a result of the understandable desire to attain a very rapid rate of development.
6. Although top management is competent, its capacity has been overstrained by the rate of introduction of new projects. This rate has run ahead of the rate at which the middle and junior levels of management and technical personnel could be developed. The result has been an ever-increasing burden on top management; it has been spread ever more thinly. This explains much of the inability to achieve efficient utilization of Ghana's investment in farms, industries, and other facilities.
7. Financial resources have been similarly overstrained. Despite the rapid increase in taxation, recurrent development expenditures have grown at an even faster rate, resulting in very high levels of budget deficits. For example, although revenue is increasing significantly in 1965 as a result of the effort to reduce the deficit, the actual level of recurrent and development expenditure will result in a budget deficit that is approximately the same as in the past four years. These deficits have contributed to the obvious inflation in the country. In addition, the foreign exchange reserves have been mobilized for development, in part to finance the high budget deficit, and in part to finance the balance of payments deficit occasioned by the increasing excess of imports over export earnings. The result is that Ghana's foreign exchange resources are virtually exhausted. There is no doubt that the sharp decline in cocoa prices has contributed to this problem. But it should be noted that cocoa receipts increased in 1965; this suggests that demands for imports as well as the cocoa price movement

played a significant role in the weakening of the reserves position.

8. The result of this general overstrain of resources has been that Ghana has not achieved the rate of economic growth that would be indicated by the achieved level of investment; indeed, other countries less favourably placed have grown at faster rates with much less investment. In addition, Ghana now faces a very difficult financial and balance of payments situation.

9. It is the mission's preliminary judgement that the general overstrain of resources and the inflationary and balance of payments problems can only be remedied by a programme of consolidation. We are encouraged that the Government has adopted such a programme. The important thing now is to implement this consolidation programme as quickly as possible in order to preserve the development thus far achieved, and to avoid further deterioration in the outlook.

10. The mission wishes to emphasize the extreme importance of implementing the consolidation programme with a stern sense of urgency. The choice is no longer between consolidation and no consolidation, but rather between (a) consolidation organized under Ghana management and, hopefully, with increasing assistance from abroad, and (b) a rapid deterioration situation which will be highly unmanageable and, in the end, impose consolidation anyway, and however disorderly.

11. A consolidation programme means that the development programme must be reduced and reoriented to achieve greater value for Ghana's money. Fortunately, there is scope for obtaining a great deal of output for very little investment by bringing existing production facilities into full operation. This will require that high priority be given to the importing of raw materials and spare parts, and the most careful selection of the linking type of investment that would, for example, create the raw materials for existing factories.

12. The consolidation programme is also necessary to regain the confidence of investors from abroad, so that the assistance required by Ghana will be forthcoming. For example, the Government has expressed the desire to renegotiate a prolongation of existing foreign debt and to attract more long-term finance. This can be done only after having re-established confidence by demonstrating that firm steps are underway to control the economy and improve the management (of) resources. In short, this means the implementation of a carefully prepared consolidation programme. No assurances can be given that international or national agencies will provide assistance, of course; but the personal view of the mission members is that if Ghana successfully implements a consolidation programme, confidence abroad will quickly return and such assistance is likely to be forthcoming.

13. In order to get into a position to negotiate her foreign debt, it is most important that Ghana not sign any further pre-finance supplier credits, either under contracts or frame agreements. Ghana will not be able to convince outside agencies of the sincerity of her efforts if at the same time

she continues to sign pre-finance supplier debts. Moreover, to sign such credits would further burden the already serious balance of payments problem and make it that much more difficult to solve.

14. Preparation of the consolidation programme should focus on preparing the budget for 1966. This will be an opportunity to systematically review all on-going as well as potential projects to determine whether all such projects will return real benefits over cost to Ghana. In this review, it is important to apply carefully strict tests to determine that projects are viable; if they are not, they should be terminated. Some of the difficulties now being encountered are the results of taking decisions to invest before thorough feasibility studies by independent, objective experts have demonstrated real benefit over cost to the economy. No new projects should be undertaken until such thorough studies are in hand. This is particularly important with pre-finance supplier credits, where the supplier is interested in selling equipment rather than necessarily contributing to the growth of your economy.

15. When carefully selected projects are in hand, Ghana should seek more appropriate forms of finance for its development projects. Pre-finance supplier credits have their place in development, but only under special circumstances where the results will be achieved quickly. Where the gestation of a project is very long and the output will be long-term, supplier credit financing is not appropriate, as the earnings of the project will not come soon enough to pay for the credit. Of course long-term finance will be available only when careful feasibility studies demonstrate the viability of a project. This is particularly true of the World Bank whose member country stockholders insist on the most productive use of its limited resources among the many developing countries. The mission has, incidentally, been carefully looking for projects which when fully prepared might qualify for financing by the World Bank or other international or national agencies.

16. The preparation and implementation of this consolidation programme will be difficult for Ghana, as it has been elsewhere. It will be necessary that leadership and guidance come from the highest levels of authority. We are encouraged to hear that the President has established a committee, with himself as chairman, along with the Minister of Finance, the Chairman of the Planning Commission, the Governor of the Bank of Ghana and the Economic Adviser to coordinate and lead this effort....[1]

Document 3: Ghana Government's Response on Bilateral Payments Agreements
Parliamentary Statement by Minister of Finance, 16 September 1965.

The point was also raised that the existing bi-lateral agreements which have been entered into by the Government with the Centrally-Planned Economies of Europe and Asia should be re-considered. The Member who raised this point referred to a portion of the recommendations of the International Monetary Fund. Osagyefo, the President, in his recent Sessional Address[2] indicated that there was no question of our going back on our commitment under bi-lateral agreements with the socialist countries or with the Centrally-Planned Economies. I want to assure the House that as far as the Centrally-Planned Economies are concerned, the Government intends to foster our trade with these countries by continuing with these bi-lateral agreements. The capitalist countries of the West also trade with the Centrally-Planned Economies and most of them use the same method as we are adopting. There is no question of any outside body telling us that we should revoke our agreements with the Centrally-Planned Economies. We shall not accept such advice. Members are aware that the price of cocoa is not as high as it should be and this is so partly because of increased production. We can only hope to increase the price permanently, if we can increase consumption. If the Centrally-Planned Economies buy more of our cocoa, the present glut of cocoa on the Western markets will reduce. There is therefore no question of Government in any way revoking our bi-lateral trade and payments agreements. What we have to do is to ensure that these agreements operate to our advantage.

In the past, we accumulated credit balances under some of the agreements, but I can authoritatively say that on the whole we rather are today indebted under these agreements to our socialist partners. The agreements are now, strictly speaking, operating to our advantage.

Document 4: Finance Minister's Statement on IMF/World Bank Recommendations
Parliamentary Statement, 22 February 1966.

External Loans and Indebtedness on Suppliers' Credits
Mr Speaker, I would now like to make a few remarks on our external indebtedness on suppliers' credits and the impending negotiations which we hope will lead to the rescheduling of some of these debts.

87. By the end of 1965 total external loans received had gone up to ₡569 million (£G237 million) equivalent to £34 or $95 per head of our

population. Of this amount loans received in the form of suppliers' credits amounted to ₡491 million (£G205 million). This again indicates the extent of our reliance on foreign credit for our development following the sharp fall in the world market price for cocoa. But 68 per cent of these credits were from foreign private sources and of short maturities extending over 5 to 7 years. Only 20 per cent of the total loans were from foreign Governments while foreign financial institutions accounted for 12 per cent.

Table 4.1 External Loans

	₡,000	£,000	%
1. *Loans from Foreign Governments*			
(i) Suppliers' Credit	92,710	38,629	16.2
(ii) Volta River Authority	19,812	8,255	3.5
Total	112,522	46,884	19.7
2. *Loans from Financial Institutions*			
(i) Suppliers' Credit	11,138	4,641	2.1
(ii) Volta River Authority	38,080	14,200	5.9
(iii) IMF Drawings	7,414	3,089	1.9
(iv) Joint Consolidation Fund (Crown Agents)	13,829	5,762	2.4
Total	70,461	27,692	12.3
3. *Loans from Private Enterprises and Institutions*			
(i) Suppliers' Credit	387,511	161,463	67.5
(ii) 4½% Loan 1960–70	2,808	1,170	0.5
Total	₡390,319	162,633	68.0
Grand Total	₡573,302	237,209	100.0

88. As I remarked earlier, one of the greatest sources of the present pressure on our foreign exchange resources has been the extremely short-term nature of most of our external debts. The debt-servicing burden is now so great that we are finding it difficult, in the face of the very sharp fall in our export prices, to meet our obligations under these credits[3] as well as to meet our day-to-day foreign exchange requirements.

89. For this reason, it was deemed necessary first to review our Seven-Year Development Plan with a view to limiting our development expenditure within the scope of our resources. Secondly, to approach our creditors with a view to rescheduling instalment payments falling due.

90. Accordingly, the Government decided last year, to invite representatives of both the International Monetary Fund and the International Bank for Reconstruction and Development to hold

discussions with the relevant organizations with a view to giving assistance both in the renegotiation of the credits and in new long-term credits to finance certain approved projects.

91. The most important recommendation of the Fund–Bank team was that the size of the Budget should be limited to a cash expenditure of ₡391.2 million (£G163 million). This recommendation has been accepted in principle and indeed the current size of the Budget which includes suppliers' credits utilizations can be broken down as follows:

	₡M	£GM
Cash	391.2	163.8
Suppliers' Credits	51.8	21.6
	443.0	185.4

But whether or not the Fund–Bank team made this recommendation, it seems obvious that we had to reduce the rate of Government expenditure and it was done on the basis of financial prudence emphasized by Osagyefo rather than the dictates of the Fund–Bank team. However, in cutting down on expenditure we have attempted to keep in view some of the recommendations of the team.

92. But it must be made clear that although the Government accepts the preliminary report and recommendations of the team as a whole, certain aspects of the Bank recommendations cannot in our opinion be acceptable. In such cases it will be more because the Fund–Bank team failed to appreciate the special peculiarities and the basic principles of our social system or because we see certain inexplicable contradictions in the views of the Fund and Bank and the attitude adopted towards Ghana.

93. Mr Speaker, a case in point is the construction of silos for the storage of cocoa in Tema and also for storage of grain crops in the regions. With your permission I would like to quote a short piece from the document Number DM/65/71 dated 7 December, 1965, released by the Research and Statistics Department of the International Monetary Fund.

> The severe decline in prices of cocoa—from some 24 cents in December, 1964 to less than 12 cents in July reflected primarily the unexpected large African crops in 1964–65 which according to the latest estimates have exceeded the high level of the preceding season by more than one-third. An abortive attempt by the Cocoa Producers Alliance to support prices through its suspension of sales in mid-October precipitated a subsequent downward movement. Lack of suitable storage facilities in producer countries and relatively large stocks held by importers which enabled them to maintain a wait-and-see attitude were additional factors militating against the Alliance.

Again Mr Speaker, the World Bank Group is in the process of approving a soft loan for the construction of silos in Pakistan. Yet the World Bank experts denounced our silos construction programme in Ghana. We find it extremely difficult to reconcile these two attitudes.

94. However, as the Fund and Bank are aware, we can differ on the details of the recommendations without disagreeing on its major aspects. This is our view and we hope soon to be able to discuss the details of our plans with the Fund and Bank with a view to arriving at some positive results. As I have said earlier, we have had successful negotiations with the Governments of the centrally planned economies of Eastern Europe. We are now awaiting an opportunity to hold similar negotiations with our creditors of goodwill in the West through the intermediaries of the Fund and Bank. We are prepared to put our house in order and have indeed initiated the necessary measures to this end. We do hope therefore that the Fund and Bank will now show us their good faith by forgetting ideological differences and sitting at the negotiating table with us to see a solution to the problem to our mutual benefit.

Document 5: National Economic Committee Meetings
Minutes of the First Meeting of the Economic Committee of the National Liberation Council held on Friday, 25 February 1966.

Present: *Chairman*: Mr E.N. Omaboe
Members: Mr Albert Adomakoh
Mr E.N. Arkaah
Mr K. Gyasi-Twum
Mr B.K. Mensah
Mr S.E. Arthur
Mr R.S. Amegashie (out of the country)

The Chairman welcomed members to the meeting and congratulated them on their appointments. He explained that the Committee had been formed by the National Liberation Council to advise the Council on all economic and financial matters. He recalled that in the statement issued by the Council yesterday it was stated that there was need for a 'radical rethinking of our economic and financial policies' and said that this was the responsibility of the Committee. The Committee therefore had to work hard and to formulate plans which would assist the Council to cure 'our troubles within the next few days.' He added that the Committee's portfolio would include Trade, Finance, Industries, Agriculture and Planning....

Review of the 1966 Estimates
It was decided that an immediate review of the 1966 Annual Estimates should be undertaken and adjustments made where necessary.

In this connection it was decided that our Foreign Missions should be reduced and that the Ministry of Foreign Affairs should submit proposals for achieving this. Pre-finance contracts signed should also be reviewed.

On the revenue side it was decided that the Ministry of Finance should submit proposals for tax concessions for consideration by the Committee.

Imports: The issue of import licences was discussed. It was observed that some licences recently issued were not in the best interests of the country. It was therefore decided that Mr Arkaah should review the position and submit proposals for consideration. It was decided that as soon as possible, an approach should be made to the United States Government for assistance under PL.480. It was recalled that an application made by the former government was turned down.

State Enterprises: The future of State enterprises was discussed. It was felt that in some cases it might be necessary to hand over the enterprises to interested private persons. Mr Adomakoh undertook to submit proposals on this for consideration....

It was decided that the United Ghana Farmers Council should be abolished after its cocoa buying functions have been transferred to another organization. In this connection it was decided to request Mr Harry Dodoo and Mr Kwesi Hackman to submit proposals for setting up this organization.

Foreign Exchange: Mr Adomakoh was requested to submit a paper on the foreign exchange position and to make recommendations for ensuring that there is no run on the London Branch of the Ghana Commercial Bank.

General Economic Policy: The Chairman proposed and it was agreed that as soon as possible the National Liberation Council should be advised to make a statement on their general economic policy. In this connection members were asked to consider what the policy should be.

Minutes of the Second Meeting of the Economic Committee of the National Liberation Council held on Saturday, 26 February, 1966.

General
(1) The Chairman [E.N. Omaboe] reported that he had had useful and fruitful discussions with a representative of USAID Mission in Ghana on various foreign economic and financial assistance needed to see Ghana over the hump in the months that lay ahead.

PL.480: Ghana's previous application was for assistance under Title I. Such applications were usually for long-term aid and took several months to materialize. However, a short-term arrangement under Title II could be arranged for Ghana to cover items such as rice, flour, milk, maize and sorghum.

Delivery could be effected within six weeks.

IMF Loan: The climate in Washington appeared to be favourable to an IMF loan to Ghana to the tune of £15 million to £20 million. Dr Nikoi who is in Washington could be asked to restart negotiation on this.

Short-term Loan from US Government: It is reported that the US Government might feel disposed to offer Ghana a short-term loan not exceeding $5 million almost immediately to finance imports of food and/or essential machinery.

These preliminary offers were communicated to the National Liberation Council almost immediately and the Council gave approval for their implementation. USAID have therefore been told to help establish contact between Ghana and appropriate US agencies to pursue all these very important offers.

(i) *World Price for Cocoa*: Mr U. K. Hackman reported to the Economic Committee that the World Cocoa price appeared to be falling due apparently to rumours that the new Government in Ghana would cancel cocoa transactions with countries of Eastern Europe and would therefore have an extra 100,000 tons of cocoa on its hands to divert to Western markets.

The Economic Committee decided that it should advise the N.L.C. to issue a statement denying such rumours and reiterating its 24 February statement that it would honour all international obligations and agreements.

United Ghana Farmers Co-operatives Council: At the request of the Committee, Mr Harry Dodoo and Mr Hackman have each submitted recommendations for the reorganization of the UGFCC. The Committee may now wish to recommend to the NLC as follows:-

(a) that the present set up of the Council should be retained under a new Director, Mr Kankam Boadu, who would be required to reorganize the Council and to purge it of weaknesses and corruption (Hackman's view);

or

(b) The UGFCC should be taken over by the CMB and should be renamed part of CMB, to carry on its functions as before subject of course to reorganization of staff (Harry Dodoo's view).

(c) to abolish the UGFCC after its purchasing functions have been taken over by another organization.

Trade and Import Licensing: Mr Arkaah submitted a paper recommending that Ghana's bilateral trade agreements with Eastern Europe, USSR and China which would become due for automatic renewal this year, unless termination notices were given some stipulated months before the expiry of the agreements, should be renewed for a further period of only *one* year during which time the position should be reviewed. In this connection it was decided that the Government's import policy should be to buy from the most advantageous sources having regard to quality, prices and terms of payment.

It was further recommended in this connection that imports from the Eastern countries this year should be reduced. The monopolistic position given to these countries for the supply of crude oil and cement should also be reviewed. Mr Gyasi-Twum promised to have discussions with the directors of Ghaip,* Tema on this.

Ghana Peoples Trading Corporation: The Economic Committee decided to recommend to the NLC to cancel the establishment of the newly created GPTC. The GPTC had not been able to establish facilities and would just be dissipating the resources at the disposal of the State in distributive trade.

The GNTC as the only State distributive organ should be strengthened and expanded....

UAC Group of Companies: It was reported that the UAC group of companies would be prepared to finance a substantial amount of imports of essential consumer goods—milk, canned fish, corned beef, flour, sugar and rice—if they were assured that a proportionate share of the imports of other consumer commodities would be allocated to them.

The Economic Committee asked Mr Arkaah to get the UAC group to make their proposals formally to the Committee. If the proposals were acceptable part of the import licence allocation which would have been saved following the dissolution of the GPTC could be given to UAC.

---

*The Ghana–Italian Petroleum Company.—*Editor.*

Post-coup Contacts with the IMF and the World Bank
Document 6: Ghana Government's Request for IMF Consultations
Cable from Albert Adomakoh, Governor, Bank of Ghana, to P. P. Schweitzer, Managing Director of IMF, through Amon Nikoi, IMF Executive Director for Ghana, 28 February 1966.

... You are no doubt aware of the precarious position that as a result of the misguided economic and financial policies of the former Government of Ghana the country has found itself in[.] as was revealed in the report issued by the Fund staff after consultations with Ghana in May 1965 the economy has been severely over-strained with the result that the balance of payments has been in serious deficit[.] we take this opportunity to inform you that the new government of Ghana[,] the National Liberation Council[,] wishes to take up negotiations with the Fund immediately for drawing on the Fund's resources to the amount equivalent to our gold tranche and first credit tranche[.] Under the same urgency and especially since part of the causes of our present financial difficulties is attributable to the serious fall in the world price of cocoa particularly during the last two years we would also like to draw the twenty-five per centum of quota allowed under the Compensatory Finance Scheme[.] we desire also to arrange for a standby credit equivalent to the second credit tranche for a period of one year beginning from the date of drawing[.] we are sure that the Fund appreciates the urgency of our need and will give this matter due attention. If at all possible we would like to have concluded these transactions not later than end of March[.]

Document 7:
Adomakoh to Schweitzer, 1 March 1966.

Owing to critical shortage of foreign exchange the new Ghana Government wishes a drawing on the Fund soonest[.] The National Liberation Council has accordingly authorised urgent request for Fund staff mission to hold consultations and negotiate terms of drawing and standby[.] Grateful if you could expedite[.]

Document 8:
Schweitzer to Adomakoh, 4 March 1966.

In response your cable of March one we are prepared to send mission as soon as feasible[.] Will inform you later about date of arrival and composition of mission[.]

Document 9:
Ghana Embassy, Washington, to N. A. Quao, Secretary to NLC, and Adomakoh, 5 March 1966.

Mr Schweitzer, Managing Director of International Monetary Fund, has reported on a matter which is giving the Fund some concern regarding Mr Adomakoh's telegram about the foregoing mission.

Mr Schweitzer indicated a favourable response at appropriate time to be communicated soon.

He however expressed concern lest the image of the Fund as an impartial international organization be compromised if it appeared to be rushing in soon after widespread reports of expulsion of Russian and Chinese personnel from Ghana and alleged reports of government's intentions to de-nationalize certain projects in the public sector.

He feels it imperative that Ghana emphasizes continuity in Fund's policies towards Ghana and also that no undue publicity be given to the mission during its visit to Ghana. He requested Doctor Nikoi to report on this matter to me with a view to conveying the Fund's feeling on the timing and context of visit.

Document 10:
Adomakoh to Schweitzer, 8 March 1966.

Your cable March 4 received today[.] Grateful for favourable response and look forward to early mission[.] Meanwhile we understand Fund feels concerned about timing of mission which unfortunately coincides with current events[.] Am authorized to recall and emphasize that Article Fourteen consultations were due last year and would have been requested November[,] December or January but for ex-minister's travels and the budget preparations[.] Tis these routine consultations that we now request and in view of worsening balance of payments we have suggested negotiations for drawing at same time[.] Publicity will be minimal and refer only to routine consultations[.]

Document 11: Request for World Bank Assistance
Letter from Adomakoh, Governor, Bank of Ghana and Member, National Economic Committee, to A. Tazi, IBRD Executive Director for Ghana, 4 March, 1966.

You are no doubt aware of the change of Government that has taken place in Ghana. The new Government—the National Liberation Council—assumed the powers of government of this country with effect from 24 February 1966. The Council is served by a National Economic Committee of which I have the honour to be a member.

The new Government shows, more than the old regime, a better awareness and understanding of the problems facing this country; both short-term and long-term. Their economic policy was enunciated yesterday—2 March,[4] in a broad policy statement of which [sic] I enclose a copy for your information.

You know very well the problems of this country. I can tell you that the short-term foreign payments problem is a very acute one now, and the National Economic Committee feels greatly concerned about the imbalance. We are determined to look for adjustments in all directions, particularly by a critical review of public expenditure.

It is clear, however, in fact urgent, that we should secure every available support for our balance-of-payments position while the measures being taken to treat the imbalance have time to work. We have accordingly invited the International Monetary Fund to send a staff mission for consultations leading to a drawing by us on the Fund's resources.

But a drawing on the Fund may by itself alone not be adequate for our immediate needs. I remember that when you were here last year we had useful discussions on the various forms of short-term to medium-term assistance that may be explored with the IBRD in conditions such as we find ourselves in at present. I have in mind particularly the possibility of our getting immediate Bank assistance to finance part of our imports of raw materials and spare parts.

I believe that the Bank has given this assistance to other member countries in the past, and we would like to make an approach for similar facility.

I shall be grateful if as a matter of utmost urgency you would look into this and advise me both as to the possibilities and the procedures.

For our longer-term requirements, the National Economic Committee is at present undertaking a review of our needs and we plan in the near future to approach the Bank with a programme in accordance with the understanding reached last October at my meetings with Mr El Emary and the Heralz/Hansen staff mission.

Document 12: World Bank Position on Aid to Ghana
Letter from Abderrahman Tazi, IBRD Executive Director for Ghana, to Adomakoh 23 March 1966.

In view of Ghana's determination to take quick and courageous action to tackle its financial problems, Mr [George] Woods [President of the World Bank] believes that the Bank should continue in the effort begun last summer to assist Ghana in re-establishing the basis for sound economic growth. The Bank, as you are no doubt aware, has taken immediate steps to associate Mr Hansen with the IMF mission which is currently in Ghana. Mr Woods considers maintaining the closest collaboration with the [International Monetary] Fund of major importance in helping Ghana work out appropriate policies to support and justify extensive foreign assistance.

Until we have established direct contact with the new authorities and reviewed what next steps seem appropriate, Mr Woods can do no more than indicate in a general way what the Bank's approach would be. However, Mr Woods will continue to consider sympathetically any request from Ghana for technical assistance, as was done last year when the Bank sent a very strong mission to Accra on short notice. Mr Woods agrees with you that the most urgent task for Ghana is to negotiate a Fund drawing based on an agreed programme. He also knows that you will appreciate the urgency of Ghana's entering into a renegotiation of its external debt, a matter on which I understand the Fund has already indicated its willingness to assist.

Mr Woods sympathizes with your request for Bank financing of a short- or medium-term character for imports of raw materials and spare parts, but you must know that, even if the Bank thought that there was no other way of tackling the problem, it is ill-placed to provide quick short-term financing of general commodity imports. The Bank would not only have to identify the concrete projects which would use such imports, but also be able to judge the priority of the projects in the context of a development programme appraised by the Bank. Ghana does not have such a development programme. It would in any case take considerable time to prepare the necessary justification for such a request. As Ghana is seeking immediate import financing, such time delays would defeat the purpose of the request.

Mr Woods assumes that similar requests for import financing have been sent to bilateral donors and believes that Ghana would be well advised to concentrate on that approach.

In connection with your reference to approaching the Bank in the near future about longer-term requirements, Mr Woods assumes you refer to the understanding reached with Mr El Emary in October 1965 that, subject to effective action on stabilization and debt reorganization, the Bank would move quickly on project identification and preparation in 1966 in order to be ready for possible negotiations of loans when the necessary conditions for Bank lending had been established. I am pleased to inform you that this position still prevails.

When Ghana has revised her development and recurrent expenditure programmes, successfully negotiated agreed programmes with the Fund and carried through negotiations with her creditors, she would be in a position to negotiate for long-term capital assistance. The Bank realizes that considerable effort will be required to carry through these steps but stands ready to give what help and advice it can, so that effective action can be taken in the shortest possible time.

I am happy indeed to be the bearer of such encouraging remarks from Mr Woods and would like to assure you that I shall personally give you all the assistance it is in my power to bring.

Document 13: Proposed Letter of Intent, IMF Standby Agreement

Letter from E. N. Omaboe, Chairman of the National Economic Committee, and A. Adomakoh, Governor, Bank of Ghana, to P. P. Schweitzer, 26 April 1966.

Following the change of government on 24 February 1966, the National Liberation Council has found the Ghana economy to be critically overstrained. Essential food-stuffs are in short supply, domestic prices have risen very rapidly, the productive capacity of the economy is seriously impaired by the lack of imported raw materials and spare parts, and domestic and international confidence in Ghana's economic prospects is undermined. The cause of all this difficulty is not only the fall in the price of cocoa in recent years, but also the excess of total governmental spending. The previous government placed excessive emphasis on investment in prestige and low priority development projects as well as on the provision of services which were beyond the ability of the economy to sustain.

2. Confronted with this situation, the National Liberation Council has decided to embark on a national programme of economic rehabilitation and financial reform. As part of this programme, a thorough review of government expenditure has been initiated, the findings of which are to be reflected in a new budget to be introduced in July 1966. To enable us to effect savings, a number of measures have already been implemented, including the abandonment of the Seven-Year Development Plan and the cessation of work on prestige projects. The programme of action envisaged by the Government falls into three stages. The first, and the most immediate problem is to alleviate the present emergency characterized by critical shortages of foreign exchange and of essential commodities required for the efficient functioning of the economy. The second stage, beginning with the new budget in July 1966, is envisaged as a period of stock-taking during which the Government will endeavour to eliminate the distortions that have emerged in the economy and to prepare a new development programme for the balanced and orderly growth of the economy. The third and final stage shall begin with the implementation of the aforementioned programme, hopefully towards the middle of 1968.

3. The task of rehabilitation is rendered extremely difficult by the state in which the National Liberation Council finds national finances; foreign exchange reserves, which totalled ₡357 million ($416 million) at the end of 1960, are now virtually depleted and, instead, a national debt of more than $1 billion [sic] has been accumulated. This includes nearly $600 million of suppliers' credit, nearly four-fifths of which mature in the next five years.[5] Debt service payments already account for about 28 per cent of current export earnings. The foreign exchange stringency which this situation imposes is compounded by the fact that, under the impact of declining international prices, export receipts have remained virtually stagnant for a number of years despite a substantial rise in cocoa output.

4. To implement its programme of financial reform and to avoid any disruption in its trade and payments in the very difficult period ahead, the Government of Ghana would like to be assured of the Fund's support. We therefore request a one year standy-by arrangement with the Fund for the equivalent of $36.4 million to be augmented by the amount of any repurchases in respect of purchases under the proposed stand-by arrangement. The Government will discuss with the Managing Director the currencies to be purchased from the Fund prior to any purchase under the proposed stand-by arrangement. The policies which the Government of Ghana intends to pursue during the period of the stand-by arrangement are set forth below.

Although the new Government has been in office for only a short time, it has addressed itself from the outset to making a thorough reform of public finance in order to eliminate waste and restore financial discipline. The Government has already called a halt to new suppliers' credits and has cut back expenditure in several important areas. The Workers' Brigade is being reorganized, the number of Government Ministries has been sharply reduced, and expenditures on the national airline and diplomatic representation abroad are being reduced. Work on a number of projects of a prestige nature has been stopped, and that on others has been suspended pending a review of their economic desirability. The Government will operate through June of this year on a modification of the 1966 budget introduced in February by the old regime and the effects of the new economic and financial policies contemplated by the National Liberation Council will be fully reflected only in the new budget which will be introduced in early July and will cover the period 1 July 1966 to 30 June 1967. On the basis of the 1966 budget, the uncovered deficit for the first half of the year was estimated at about ₡21.0 million.

5. This, however, did not take into full account a number of bills outstanding in respect of subsidies to the State Mines, the National Airline, and debts owed by various State organizations or various Government commitments in respect of continuing projects. The actual deficit for the whole year would have mounted to over ₡70 million if full provision had been made in the Estimates for these commitments.

We expect to make savings amounting to about ₡13.5 million between now and the end of June. The actual deficit finance will therefore not exceed ₡60 million.

The Government will make every effort to reduce this deficit, and hence reliance on Central Bank financing for the fiscal year 1966/67. The Government will firmly endeavour to ensure that total expenditures are limited to an amount that can be financed through domestic revenues and other internal and external sources that do not have inflationary consequences.

6. The Government will press forward with the reorganization of the operations of state enterprises as a matter of national urgency with a view to improving their efficiency and terminating their dependence on budgetary subsidies. A detailed study of these enterprises is currently in progress and some steps have already been taken to improve their operations. Steps have already been taken to recruit technical assistance in this work.

7. A major objective of monetary and credit policies for some time to come will be to avoid, as far as possible, further additions to the large monetary demand that exists in the economy as a result of heavy past reliance on inflationary financing of the budget and the increasingly stringent application of import and exchange controls. To this end, apart from the special arrangements that have been made for clearing payment arrears of the treasury of up to ₡34 million, the Bank of Ghana's net credit to the Government (total loans and advances to the Government plus holdings of government securities minus government deposits which amounted to ₡149 million as of 31 March 1966, will not exceed ₡149 million during the period up to 31 July 1966. The limit on net credit to the Government for the remaining period of the stand-by arrangement will

remain at this figure unless and until agreement on a different figure is reached between the Government and the Fund following the review mentioned in paragraph 12 below. The Bank of Ghana's total loans, advances and rediscounts to the private sector and commercial banks, with the exception of credit to finance cocoa exports (which fluctuates seasonally and with the size of the crop) will not exceed ₡13.3 million during the period of the stand-by arrangement; they totalled ₡103 million as of 23 March 1966.

8. The Bank of Ghana does not intend to allow any large increase in commercial bank credit during the period of the stand-by arrangement. To this end, the Bank's rediscount rate was raised from $4\frac{1}{2}$ per cent to 7 per cent with effect from 15 January 1966 and the commercial banks were advised to reduce the level of their credit outstanding on 31 December 1965 in selected fields by $25-33\frac{1}{3}$ per cent. The Bank will not reduce the reserve requirement against commercial bank liabilities and the 'cash margin' requirements below their existing levels. It will ensure that total commercial bank credit other than for cocoa financing which totalled ₡213 million at 31 January 1966 (the latest date for which data are available), does not exceed ₡218 million during the period of the stand-by arrangement. Should total commercial bank credit exceed the above mentioned margin, the Government of Ghana will consult with the Managing Director of the Fund regarding the cause of the increase and any corrective measures that might be necessary.

9. While the objective of the Government is to work towards the eventual abolition of import and exchange controls, any significant liberalization will depend upon the availability of adequate foreign assistance to alleviate the present critical shortage of foreign exchange. Nonetheless, in operating the existing licensing system, the Government will endeavour to be as liberal as is compatible with the country's balance of payments situation, and will ensure that the limited foreign exchange earnings of the country are utilized in accordance with carefully considered priorities. Commercial banks no longer have to refer to the Bank of Ghana before opening letters of credit in accordance with import licences. It is planned, as soon as some additional foreign assistance is assured, to liberalize the imports of selected spare parts, raw materials and fuels under the open general licence procedure. The Government will work towards eliminating discrimination in its import and exchange policies. Effective immediately, import licensing from convertible currency countries will not distinguish as between sources of import, except insofar as it is found necessary to utilize foreign loans and grants on a tied basis. The possibility of placing all imports on a global quota basis is also being given consideration, but such a step again is contingent on the adequate availability of convertible currency resources. The Government has initiated a review of its bilateral trade and payments arrangements and will undertake negotiations with its bilateral partner countries with a view to eliminating the restrictive features of these arrangements. The Government

has already announced the termination of two of the three special 'barter' agreements; the third is being allowed to run its course as it contains certain favourable features. If during the period of the stand-by arrangement Ghana should consider introducing further restrictions or increasing the present restrictions or discrimination, Ghana would enter into prior consultation with the Managing Director in order to obtain the Fund's approval where such approval is required, and, if the Managing Director deems it necessary, would agree on new terms with the Fund before a request for drawing under the stand-by arrangement is made.

10. The Government will limit its foreign borrowing for new capital projects to such terms as are consistent with its debt repayment obligations and the Government's future overall debt service capacity. The Government believes that an appropriate long-term stretch-out of its debt is of vital importance for the successful implementation of the economic and financial policies outlined above. It plans soon to undertake negotiations with its major creditors to resolve this problem and will appreciate your assistance in this matter.

11. The Government will not incur any new external debt obligations or guarantee any foreign borrowings which have a final maturity of less than 12 years except:

(i) normal trade credits of up to 360 days maturity,
or
(ii) after agreement with the Managing Director of the Fund.

12. The Government undertakes to review with the Fund staff before the end of July 1966 the economic and financial situation and the specific policies and measures which the Government plans to undertake in connection with the 1966/67 budget, and in the foreign trade and payments field. On the basis of this review, the Government undertakes to agree with the Fund on the ceiling of the Bank of Ghana's net credit to the Government for the remaining period of the stand-by arrangement, and for such revisions as might be necessary in the ceiling on the Bank of Ghana's credit to the private sector and commercial banks and the limitations on total commercial bank credit.

13. If at any time during the period of the stand-by arrangement, the limits on the credit operations of the Bank of Ghana specified in paragraph 7 or as subsequently modified in paragraph 12 are exceeded, or the undertakings in paragraphs 8 and 11 are not adhered to, or if any new bilateral payments agreements are concluded with Fund members, Ghana will not request any further drawings under the stand-by arrangement except after consulting the Fund and agreeing with it on the terms on which future drawings may be made.

14. We have been directed by the National Liberation Council to convey to you the foregoing statement as the basis for our request for a stand-by arrangement.

Document 14: Report of Ghanaian Delegation to the West
E. N. Omaboe, 'Report to the National Liberation Council by the Economic Delegation on their discussions in the United States of America, Canada, United Kingdom and West Germany' (n.d.).

At the request of the National Liberation Council a delegation of the Economic Committee left Ghana on Friday, 13 May to attend a meeting of the Executive Board of the International Monetary Fund (IMF) in connection with Ghana's application for a standby arrangement and to explore the possibility of further economic aid to Ghana from the four countries mentioned above.

2. The delegation was made up as follows:

Mr E. N. Omaboe,	Chairman of the Economic Committee, Leader.
Mr A. Adomakoh,	Governor, Bank of Ghana.
Mr S. E. Arthur,	Ministry of Finance.
Mr J. H. Mensah,	United Nations Adviser to the Economic Committee.

Preliminary Meeting with United Kingdom Officials
3. The delegation spent the night of 13 May in London and held informal discussions with Commonwealth Relations Office officials headed by Mr Norris. It was clear from these informal discussions that the United Kingdom was not in a position to offer any substantial assistance to Ghana mainly because of her own financial difficulties although she appeared to sympathize with us. The officials also hinted that the United Kingdom would favour a unilateral decision by Ghana to default in the payments of the instalments in respect of suppliers' credits rather than agreeing to our request for a temporary suspension of these payments.

Discussions in the United States of America
4. The delegation left for Washington, USA the following day. On Sunday, we held discussions with the International Monetary Fund Mission which visited Ghana recently and agreed with them the statement which we were to make at the Executive Board meeting of the Fund the next day. We were assisted in these discussions by Dr Amon Nikoi, Ghana's Executive Director on the Fund.

Meeting with IMF
5. On Monday 16 May two members of the delegation namely, Mr Omaboe and Mr Adomakoh appeared before the Executive Board of the International Monetary Fund to put forward our case for a stand-by arrangement. In our statement we made it clear that Ghana was passing through a very critical period in her economic history as a result of the mismanagement of the old regime, but that the National Liberation Council had taken certain positive measures which, with the assistance of

friendly countries and such international institutions as the Fund and the World Bank, would made it possible for the country to get out of her present difficulties. After some discussions the Board approved our application for a standby arrangement. Under this arrangement Ghana is entitled to a drawing of $36.4 million between now and the end of February next year. As part of the arrangement we had to give certain undertakings, the main one of which was our determination to reduce Government expenditure and therefore reduce substantially Government dependence on central bank financing. We also agreed to restrict total bank credits. The aim of these undertakings is to reduce the inflationary pressures in the economy, to improve the balance of payments position and to restore balance to the Central Government budget. To ensure that these undertakings are respected the Fund agreed to our request to station their representative in Accra during the period of the stand-by arrangement. We also undertook to review with the Fund the 1966/67 budget which will be introduced in July. In this regard the Fund agreed to give us two experts to assist us with the preparation of the budget. We are happy to state that the Fund representative and the two budget experts have since arrived in the country and are working with us.

Discussions with IBRD (World Bank)
6. On the next day we had a meeting with the World Bank. We apologized for the broken promises of the old regime and assured the Bank that the new Government would honour all promises that will be made. We then discussed with them projects in respect of which Bank assistance was required.... We also asked for technical assistance, particularly with regard to the preparation of the development plan estimates for the review period and the new development plan to be launched in the middle of 1968. The Bank agreed to offer technical assistance and in this regard undertook to send out two missions, the first one to assist with the preparation of the 1966/67 budget and the second one late in September to prepare a list of projects which would qualify for Bank loan. Here again we are happy to observe that the Bank's experts are already in the country and are helping with the preparation of the development estimates for the 1966/67 budget.

Preliminary Meeting with Ghana's Creditor Countries
7. On the same day, under the auspices of the IMF, a preliminary meeting was arranged for us to meet with representatives of Ghana's principal creditor countries which are members of the IMF. At this meeting we made it quite clear that although the National Liberation Council is anxious to honour all obligations entered into by the old regime Ghana was finding it increasingly difficult to do so. This was because in the past we had been meeting all maturing instalment payments under supplier's credits at the expense of payments for our current imports. As a result we have now accumulated large arrears on current payments for imports some of which have been outstanding for a long time. This state of affairs could not be

allowed to continue because otherwise we would not be able to import essential commodities to keep the economy going. For this reason we asked for another meeting to take place in Europe to decide on what temporary relief Ghana could get from payments under suppliers' credits. After considerable discussion it was agreed to hold this meeting in London on 1 and 2 of June.

Discussions with the State Department

8. In the afternoon of the same day, that is 17 May, we had discussions with officials of the State Department under the Chairmanship of Mr Hutchinson. At this meeting we went through the *aide-mémoire* which had already been sent through the Ministry of External Affairs to the United States authorities. The items discussed were:

(i) *Supplied under PL.480:* The United States authorities noted that discussions were going on in Accra and gave us an assurance that as soon as a firm decision was reached the necessary agreement would be signed to enable supplies to come in 1967.

(ii) *Soft Loan:* We asked for a soft loan of $20 million a year for the next two years to enable us to undertake certain essential development projects during the stabilization period. The United States authorities sympathized with our request but suggested that this should await the outcome of the debt re-scheduling exercise. They did not want to give us a loan at this time because they feared that this might be used to pay our existing debts.

(iii) *Financial Assistance to the National Investment Bank:* The United States authorities expressed willingness to provide financial assistance to the National Investment Bank but they would prefer to corraborate [sic] with the International Finance Corporation (IFC), one of the affiliates of the World Bank.

(iv) *Assistance to the Agricultural Credit and Co-operative Bank*: The United States authorities agreed to send two experts to come and appraise the organization and operations of the Bank and to advise on measures for making the Bank more efficient and effective. These experts have since arrived in the country.

(v) *Assistance under the Executive Corps Scheme:* Under this we asked for technical assistance for our state enterprises. This was agreed to in principle although the general feeling was that this could probably best be done by bringing private participation in the state enterprises concerned.

(vi) *Kaiser Irrigation Scheme*: We asked whether in view of our present financial difficulties the US Government would be prepared to pay for the contract which Ghana had already entered into with Kaiser. The US authorities undertook to consider this request.

9. On the following day, that is 18 May, we had discussions with the

Peace Corps authorities under the chairmanship of the Director of the Peace Corps programme. We asked for more teachers in our secondary schools and teacher training colleges. We also asked for Peace Corps volunteers for the Geological Survey Department to replace the Russians who have left the country, as well as volunteers for the Department of Social Welfare and Community Development in connection with the Volta River Project resettlement scheme. We were assured that consideration would be given to our request and that 50 volunteers had already been lined up to come to Ghana in January 1967. We also raised the question of the payment for these volunteers and it was explained that the general policy is that the host country should make a contribution towards the cost of the volunteers. We were assured, however, that in view of our present financial difficulties, the US Government would be prepared to consider making modifications to this general principle. In fact we were informed that negotiations on these lines had already started in Accra and that the Local Director here had been given authority to negotiate and agree on a figure which he thought was reasonable. We were therefore asked to contact him as soon as possible on our arrival back in Ghana.

10. We later saw Mr Palmer the new Assistant Secretary of State for African Affairs, Ambassador Tremble and Mr Bell, the Head of USAID and had informal discussions with them. In all our discussions with the State Department we found nothing but a genuine desire on the part of the US Government to help Ghana.

Discussions in New York

11. We then left for New York to continue with our discussions. Our first meeting was with Mr Frank Pace, Head of the International Executive Corporation of AID. He also showed a keen interest in the affairs of Ghana and assured us of the US Government's readiness to help.

12. In the afternoon we were invited to lunch by the African-American Chamber of Commerce. This was our first contact with the business community in the US and we seized the opportunity to appeal to US investors to come to Ghana.... [Our] statement attracted considerable interest and it was obvious from the discussions that followed that American businessmen are now desirous of looking for investment possibilities in Ghana....

14. We also had discussions with the banking community. The Chase Manhattan Group showed very great interest in Ghana and undertook to send their Second Vice-President, Mr H.D. Martin to Ghana to see things for himself. Mr Martin has since been in the country.

Meeting with UNCID

15. While in New York we also took the opportunity to have discussions with UN Agencies. We met Mr Abdel Rahman, Commissioner of the United Nations Center for Industrial Development (UNCID), and his staff and had very useful discussions with them. We wish to explain here that

shortly before the delegation left for the US the UNCID had, at our request, sent a team to investigate some of our state enterprises. This mission had made a thorough study of the Fibre Bag Factory at Kumasi, the Match Factory at Kade and the Paper Conversion Factory at Takoradi, and had made certain recommendations. In New York we discussed these recommendations and it was agreed that for the Fibre Bag Factory in Kumasi three experts namely a managing director, a maintenance engineer and a factory manager should be found by the CID to take charge of the factory. With regard to the Match Factory at Kade it was agreed that UNCID should assist Ghana in finding and engaging a management firm which would be charged with responsibility for running the factory for a stipulated period. The UNCID undertook to promote and finance the negotiations which would lead to the appointment of the firm. With regard to the Paper Conversion Corporation it was agreed that, as a first step, the accounts of the Corporation should be verified as it was not clear at present what the Corporation's financial position was. When the accounts have been verified the UNCID would consult us on the next step to take.

16. The UNCID also agreed to send out, at their own expense, four experts to strengthen the State Enterprises Secretariat. These would be Director of Industrial Production, Director of Financial Planning, Director of Industrial Planning and Director of Marketing Development. These four experts will also study the other public enterprises and make appropriate recommendations to the Government. In addition the UNCID agreed to send experts to advise on the future organization of the State Enterprises Secretariat itself. It is our view that if our state enterprises are to operate properly as industrial concerns then the State Enterprises Secretariat itself must first be reorganized so that it may be better able to cope with its functions.

17. We later met Mr Hoffman, Managing Director of UN Special Fund who undertook to made funds available for financing the schemes agreed with the UNCID. We also discussed with him Special Fund Assistance for detailed drawings in respect of the Accra–Tema Sewerage Scheme which has since been granted.

Discussions in Canada

18. We left for Ottawa on Monday 23 May. Our first meeting was with Mr Crandy, Assistant Deputy Minister of Finance. Here too we went through the items included in our *aide-mémoire*. These included surplus food, soft loan, balance of payments support and technical assistance. We had a general discussion on these items but we did not come to any definite decisions. In the afternoon we had a meeting with Senior Government officials from the Ministries of Finance, External Affairs, Economics and the Central Bank of Canada. We also had discussions with Mr Moran, Director-General of External Aid. In all these discussions one fact was clear and that was that Canada was willing to help as much as she could. Agreement was reached on the points raised as follows:-

(i) *Surplus Food:* Although Canada does not normally provide gifts in the form of food the Government would be prepared to consider repeating next year the food gift they offered this year if the need arose.
(ii) *Soft Loans:* Canada would be willing to consider our formal application after the debt re-scheduling exercise. Such a loan might be for a period of up to 50 years.
(iii) *Technical Assistance:* Canada was pleased to note that we regarded the Trade Training Centre at Accra, now almost completed, as of great value to the country and they expressed willingness to build one or two others in the immediate future. With regard to the financing of these centres the Canadian authorities undertook to take into account our financial position at the time a request is made.

Canada also agreed in principle to provide technical assistance to study the pulp and paper project, to assist in the implementation of Ghana Groceries and to help establish a Seed Multiplication Scheme. All these would be provided within the frame of an annual grant of $2 million to Ghana but the priorities would have to be established by Ghana herself.

In this connection the Canadian authorities informed us that for the fiscal year 1966/67 Ghana had been allocated a total of $2 million in aid grant and that $1,675,000 out of it had already been committed leaving a balance of $325,000 to be used. We were also assured that for purposes of planning we could take it that we would obtain not less than $2 million annually from the Canadian Government in the form of aid grant.
(iv) *Balance of payments support:* It was agreed that a successful debt re-scheduling would ease our balance of payments position. Nevertheless the Canadian authorities agreed to consider our request after the debt re-scheduling exercise.
(v) *Spare parts for military aircraft:* We were assured that the ECIC would be prepared to examine with the De Havilland Aircraft of Canada Limited the possibility of financing these spares. As a result of this assurance we met representatives of De Havilland and arranged with them for a 360 day credit. This was to be confirmed later by De Havilland.

19. It was quite clear from our discussions, both formal and informal, that there is plenty of goodwill in Canada for Ghana under the new regime and that, provided we make the necessary approaches, we would get considerable assistance from the Canadian Government....

Discussions in the United Kingdom
21. We then left for London on the night of 25 May arriving at London in the morning of the next day. We started our discussions the same morning

with Mr Norris and Mr Miles of the Commonwealth Relations Office. These discussions centred mainly on the debt re-negotiations.

22. In the afternoon there was a larger meeting at which were representatives from a number of Ministries including the Commonwealth Relations Office, the Foreign Office and the Ministry of Overseas Development. At this meeting we discussed the points made in our *aide-mémoire*. The subjects discussed were:

(i) The re-scheduling of debts under suppliers' credits.
(ii) Unspent balance of Volta loan.
(iii) Overseas development aid.
(iv) Technical assistance.

The United Kingdom authorities dwelt at length on the debts re-scheduling exercise and asked us for assurances (a) that this will affect only suppliers' credits; (b) that there will be no discrimination in our treatment of creditors; and (c) that the re-negotiations will affect only suppliers' credits entered into before 24 February 1966. We have these assurances....

Meeting With Our Creditors

25. On Wednesday, 1 June 1966 we had a meeting in Church House, Whitehall, with representatives of Ghana's creditor countries which are members of the IMF. All but the United Arab Republic and Yugoslavia were present. In addition there were representatives of the IMF and the World Bank. Sir Arthur Snelling of the CRO (Commonwealth Relations Office) and former United Kingdom High Commissioner to Ghana was the Chairman for the meeting.

26. In the statement which we made we stressed that although we were very anxious to meet all our obligations we could not do so without serious consequences to ourselves and appealed to the countries to help us to avoid taking a unilateral decision to default in the payment of our debts. We therefore asked the meeting to agree to a temporary suspension of our debt repayments, both interest and principal, in respect of all suppliers' credits for a temporary period until an appropriate rescheduling could be organized. We also asked the creditor countries to agree to meet us again in August or September to arrange the re-scheduling. After our statement a number of countries made their preliminary remarks from which it was clear that although many of them were sympathetic to our position they could not legally agree to the suspension of the payments as this might make them liable to court action by the individual firms whom we are owing. At this stage we were asked to retire to enable the creditor countries to discuss the matter among themselves.

27. When we rejoined the meeting later the Chairman informed us that firstly, the government representatives at the meeting could not legally agree to a suspension of any payment by Ghana because they had not the mandate of the individual creditors to agree to this; secondly, the meeting attached great importance to the principle of non-discrimination and

expressed the hope that this principle would be scrupulously observed by Ghana when dealing with various creditors irrespective of whether the debts were insured by state insurance agencies or not; thirdly, the meeting wanted us to appreciate that the re-scheduling of the debts itself constituted a substantial balance of payments support and therefore the countries could not commit themselves at this stage to making available to us any further balance of payments support. Fourthly, it was the view of the meeting that not all the creditor countries assembled there could participate in the consortium which we asked for, and for this reason the consortium could better be considered separately and in a different forum. After some discussions we agreed on a communiqué which was issued at the end of the meeting. This communiqué gave *de facto* recognition to our intention to suspend payments of all debts under suppliers' credits for the next three months. We have since stopped these payments. ...

Discussions With West German Authorities
29. We left for Bonn in the evening of Thursday, 2 June. The next day we had a meeting at the Foreign Ministry with representatives of the Ministry of Finance, the Ministry of Foreign Affairs and the Ministry of Economic Affairs under the chairmanship of Dr Harkort. The meeting went through the points contained in our *aide-mémoire* which had already been submitted to the German authorities. The points covered were: [Balance of payments support, technical assistance, insurance cover for German imports, loan to the National Investment Bank and minor financing for Volta power distribution].

Points raised by the German authorities:

(i) *Shipping:* The German authorities alleged that Ghanaian authorities were clausing import licences to the effect that the imports should be carried only by Black Star Line ships and they thought this was discriminatory.

(ii) *German properties in Ghana:* They also raised the question of German properties which were confiscated during the Second World War and asked whether they could be released.

(iii) *Landing rights in Accra for Lufthansa*: The German authorities stated that an application was submitted to the Ghana Government some time ago but that there had been no reply. We informed them that as matters stand at present the reverse was the case and that Ghana was in fact waiting for Lufthansa to respond to a request to start negotiations.

(iv) *Guarantee of foreign private investments:* It was stated that the German Government submitted to the Ghana Government the draft of an agreement to safeguard the investments of German citizens in Ghana but that so far nothing had been heard about it. It was suggested that if we could dispose of this matter this might encourage German private investors to come to Ghana. We assured them that this was receiving attention and undertook to look into the other points raised.

General Comments
30. On the whole our mission proved to be worthwhile. Our initial success with the IMF in getting the stand-by arrangement strengthened our hands in all our subsequent negotiations. We also found considerable goodwill in all the capitals we visited and provided we do the right things and continue to have the support of the IMF and the World Bank we will succeed in getting the external assistance we need....

Document 15: World Bank Assessment of the Military Regime
Report of the World Bank mission of November, 1966.

1. The new military Government that replaced Kwame Nkrumah in February 1966 found itself confronted with a major economic and financial crisis, the solution of which has since predominantly concerned the new regime. Given the dimensions of the crisis, the need for important structural adjustments on almost all fronts will continue to dominate economic policy for a long time to come. Ghana is presently going through a period of severely interrupted economic growth which is all the more disappointing since Ghana, in spite of these difficulties, still is in many aspects one of the more promising countries in Africa. It has had a long history of favourable economic development and its per capita income of nearly US$200 million [sic] reflects a standard of living for its 7.7 million people which is well above the African average. Ghana has the human and natural resources to resume this economic growth and to strengthen its comparative position in Africa. It has an infrastructure which for some time will require only supplementary investments and it inherited considerable assets in manufacturing capacities which if vitalized properly will help economic growth to swiftly regain momentum. But at present Ghanaian authorities have to cope with the consequences of an economic policy which, though full of good intentions, proved to be quite unrealistic, especially in the face of a sharp fall of cocoa prices and which led by 1965 to stagnating growth, surging prices and an unmanageable balance of payments gap.

2. One of the outstanding characteristics of Ghana's effort in 1960–65 was the continuously rising investment which in 1965 reached a ratio of 21 per cent of GDP. In this year the public sector accounted for almost two-

thirds of gross capital formation as compared with an average of 20 per cent in 1958 and 1959. The Government's ambitious development effort was motivated by the idea that firstly an increase in agricultural productivity called for large-scale mechanized farming which could only be brought about by direct Government investment in state farms, cooperatives and equipment pools. Secondly, in order to turn Ghana from a primary commodity producing country into an industrialized economy, again state enterprises were considered essential to guarantee both quick and sizeable results. However, most of the investments in both sectors were poorly conceived and badly administered once in operation. This policy was paralleled by fiscal and other measures which discouraged private investment and private activity generally. As a result the growth rate of real output started declining in the early 1960s and was down to zero in 1965. The Government made serious efforts to mobilize resources commensurate with its investments. It increased revenue from 15.9 per cent of GNP in 1957/58 to 18.1 per cent in 1965. In the latter year alone current revenue was raised by 38 per cent. But current Government expenditure rose even faster, reducing savings to an average of 13 per cent of Government investment in the period 1960–64. In 1965 the percentage was increased to 45 per cent due to the almost reckless levy of revenues combined with the introduction of the social security scheme and a reduced cocoa producer price. The rate at which both current and capital expenditures were increased resulted in budget deficits averaging 10 per cent of GNP over 1960–65. This figure does not include annual deficits of the Cocoa Marketing Board. Such expansion of public claims on resources could only be realized by suppressing private consumption. In addition the supply of domestically produced foodstuffs suffered both from disincentives to private production and from failure of the public ventures in agriculture, which together with deficit financing of the budget resulted in decreasing real consumption and inflated prices. As a result, private savings decreased even faster than those of the public sector.

3. In an effort to finance its growing external deficits, the Government first ran down reserves, by ₵387 million (US$450 million) between 1957 and 1965. In February 1966 Ghana's net reserve position was virtually negative. In the period 1962–65 it also made increasing recourse to medium term suppliers' credits, which only resulted in a rapid accumulation of debt service, and which often had adverse effects on both cost and quality of investments. By early 1966 Ghana had contracted more than 200 separate commitments involving a contract value of ₵610 million (US$710 million). With the exception of the Volta Dam and a bridge across the same river, Ghana did not finance any development projects on a long-term basis in this period. Total debt service would have absorbed 24 and 25 per cent of current account earnings in 1966 and 1967. This, however, became known only in 1966 after the new Government undertook an inventory of all its obligations.

4. Since taking power one year ago the new Government had made

substantial progress in regaining control of domestic and foreign economic affairs. It has cut back substantially on both current and capital expenditures; it has begun to deal energetically with its difficult external debt problems and has adhered to credit policies which permitted a moderate improvement in exchange reserves during 1966 with practically no growth in the money supply. In fact the retrenchment of non-productive public expenditures initially for March–June 1966 and then in the new fiscal year 1966/67 is one of the major achievements of the new Government. Recurrent expenditures are budgeted at the actual level realized in 1965 which required, because of automatic growth features such as salary increments, an average of close to 10 per cent reduction in ongoing recurrent expenditure programmes. The Central Government's current surplus is now estimated at ₵47 million for the current fiscal year which would cover 70 per cent of its development expenditures as compared with 9 per cent and 45 per cent in 1964 and 1965. Surpluses of the Cocoa Marketing Board (₵28 million) and the social security scheme (₵22.5 million), which was created in 1965, will add up to a significantly improved public finance picture.

Table 15.1 Public Finance

(₵ million)

	1963	1964	1965	1966/67 (Estimate)
Central Government Current Surplus	28.5	74.4	83.5	47
Surpluses (–Deficits) of State Enterprises				
Social Security and others	–	–	–	+23
Marketing Board	+8.0	–52.0	+12.0	+29
Statutory Corporations	*+6.0*	*+7.0*	*+6.0*	*+9*
Total Public Sector Savings	42.5	29.4	101.5	108
Public Sector Development Expenditure	144.9	194.4	197.0	76
Domestic Financial Gap (+Surplus)	–102.4	–165.0	–95.5	+32

5. The reduction of public sector development expenditures from ₵197 million in 1965 to the estimated ₵143.2 million before debt re-scheduling and ₵76 million after debt re-scheduling in 1966–67 reflects the Government's efforts to implement the advice of several Bank missions and to rid the public sector of a variety of non-viable projects. A number of suppliers' credit financed projects have been cancelled, reducing obligations under these credits by ₵64 million or 13 per cent, and

negotiations are under way to cancel a further ₵90 to ₵100 million. On other projects, construction has been either stretched out or halted completely while advice is sought on whether remedial action could make them viable or whether to close them down.

6. In agriculture for example, the large cocoa marketing and mechanized farming activities of the United Ghana Farmers' Council have been dissolved; 68 of 115 state farms have been designated for closing, of which 23 are already closed and about 12,000 workers retrenched; the Workers Brigade has retrenched 9,000; some 12 non-viable fishing trawlers have been sold or chartered to private Ghanaians and contracts for 12 not yet constructed have been cancelled; work on the cocoa silos is suspended and contracts for a tractor assembly, 8 large urban food storage centres and milk and sugar processing have been cancelled. In industry, contracts for diamond mining, wood processing and quarries have been cancelled and 20 state enterprises have been designated for sale in whole or part, of which sales terms for 4 have reached final negotiations. Government is actively seeking consultants' services to assist in further sales or preparation of remedial programmes for state enterprises. To this end it has obtained a team from the UN Center for Industrial Development to help reorganize the State Enterprises Secretariat as well as to provide management assistance for three viable public enterprises; obtained the direct services of a consulting firm to advise on possible private participation in other state enterprises; and obtained externally financed consultants of the National Investment Bank for the same purposes. In transportation, contracts for two ships under construction for the Black Star Line have been cancelled; Ghana Airways has abandoned unprofitable routes, returned 6 Russian aircraft, cancelled the contract for a third VC-10 jet aircraft and chartered the second VC-10 to a foreign airline, and changed the senior staff and retrenched other staff; cancelled the extension of the Accra–Tema super highway; and is negotiating a foreign private management and possibly participation in the large dry dock. Finally, the new Government is seeking to sell a new frigate warship recently completed but not yet delivered.

7. In general Government is aware that excessive public sector expansion in the past has overstrained its manpower capacity and is therefore undertaking retrenchments in development expenditures also with a view to reallocating staff to support viable programmes, especially in agriculture. The new Government has refrained from including any new projects in the 1966–67 development budget except for a special contingency programme and the Bank mission which participated in the preparation of the budget is satisfied that only projects with obvious merits were continued. Altogether retrenchments made so far have led to significant unemployment, although there is evidence that some part of it has been absorbed by the traditional pattern of rural agriculture....

10. In summary, the new Government has made an impressive start in managing its economic affairs in a responsible manner, especially considering the small margins of manoeuvre open to it and the degree of

sacrifice accepted in implementing its stabilization programme. The period 1966–68 is intended to be a stabilization period during which the foundation for future growth could be laid. The substantial progress already made with the stabilization programme resulting in growing public sector surpluses along with sizeable unemployment indicates that the Government should now aim at well prepared and moderate expansion in the last 18 months of this period, beginning with the new fiscal year 1967/68....

11. In assessing Ghana's investment and capital inflow requirements for the next eighteen months the Bank has been guided by the fact that Ghana's domestic product has not grown for two years in a row and that with the population increasing at a rate of 2.6 to 3.0 per cent per annum, *any stabilization policy based on a further decline in per capita consumption and investment would have undesirable economic and political consequences.** But with output in agriculture stagnating and manufacturing capacities seriously idled due to lack of spare parts and raw materials, any increase in production for consumption and investment will initially result in higher demand for imports. External financial requirements for 1967 and 1968 as suggested by the mission imply a major structural change in imports by increasing the share of raw materials to 26.9 and 33.6 per cent of total imports in the two years compared with an average of 15.4 per cent for the period 1959–65. Spare parts imports also increased consistent with the increase in production made possible by increased imports of raw materials. Both imports of spare parts and capital goods are consistent with an investment ratio reduced to about 12 per cent of GDP compared with an average 18 per cent in 1959–65. This reduction reflects a sharply curtailed public sector programme but takes into consideration a policy for increased private investment. Food imports have been increased while other consumer goods, except textbooks and pharmaceuticals have been based on a minimum import concept. Suggested import levels should allow a 2–3 per cent increase in real consumption in each of the two years provided that important raw materials and spare parts are sufficient to permit increased domestic output. On balance the mission concluded that total imports should be about ₡353 and ₡371 million in 1967 and 1968 as compared with an annual average of ₡320 million in 1962–64 and ₡384 million in 1965....

16. The Government thus faces a delicate economic problem. On the other hand, steady progress is essential in rationalizing public sector expenditure programmes, but together with existing public savings, this will result in increased public sector surpluses. If further unemployment and reduced consumption is to be avoided, selective expansion of credit to the private sector and of priority development projects will be required, but selected in ways that will not aggravate the balance of payments problem.

*Emphasis added—*Editor.*

The mission, therefore, suggests the following to allow an orderly transition from the period of stabilization to resumed economic growth in 1967/68 and the next several years in general:

(a) *Public Sector Savings.* Current revenues amounting to more than 18 per cent of GNP in 1965 reflect an adequate tax effort. However, the present structure of rates has a depressing effect on productive private sector investment, and, therefore, the structure of revenue should be given more attention than the total yield. There is room for rationalizing the tax system with a view to encouraging private enterprises in the primary and secondary sectors, but this will require further study before major changes are introduced.

(b) Considering the role of the cocoa producer price both in generating public savings through the Cocoa Marketing Board and its effect on replanting, maintenance and output of cocoa, the mission recommends that the price increases should not exceed 5 shillings per load per year up to a maximum of 60 shillings by 1969.

(c) In order to establish an adequate public savings record, Ghana should be expected to contain the growth of recurrent expenditures well below the historical rate of 13.7 per cent per year. The mission tentatively recommends a ceiling of 5–6 per cent per year subject to more detailed studies of the implications of further reductions in educational expenditures, introducing increased user fees, and the recurrent requirements of the new contingency programmes. Within the total of recurrent expenditures a shift in current expenditures from defence and education to essential programmes like agricultural extension services, road maintenance, etc., would be desirable.

(d) *Public Development Expenditures.* The Government would be well advised to abstain from any new investments in industry except when joint participation with private investors is the only practicable way of realizing high priority investments. Instead it should aim at steady progress in acquiring technical assistance to recommend and implement remedies for state enterprises which are in difficulty or otherwise not in line with standards of proper industrial management. Output from existing industrial facilities should be considered one major source of economic growth in the near future and provision of adequate working capital for state enterprises should be given priority.

(e) The development of an incentive programme in peasant agriculture, especially through appropriate price policies, extension services and credit should be pursued energetically. In addition the speed with which assets of state farms, Workers' Brigade and Young Farmer League farms are dissolved or converted into productive public or private propositions will be an important performance criterion.

(f) The mission assigns crucial importance to a strengthening and diversification of Ghana's exports. Urgent policies should be considered to improve conditions of existing industries, particularly for timber and minerals. In addition Ghana will have to embark on a long-term programme to develop more agricultural exports. There are immediate prospects in fishing and tree crops, such as rubber and palm oil.

(g) Ghana should not embark on major expansions in education before a replanning effort is completed.

(h) *Policies for the Private Sector.* The mission endorses considerations to give the private sector a larger role in the future development effort. To this end Ghana should be expected to improve the staffing and management of its incentive legislation administered by the Capital Investment Board and the Ministry of Industry.

(i) The Government should support an expanded role of the National Investment Bank.

(j) The Government should encourage private credit within the framework of the agreements with the IMF.

(k) *Import Licensing.* Ghana should aim at continued progress in improving import licensing including implementation of a coherent framework consistent with the budget, balance of payments and the requirements of the private sector. Allocation of licences should follow economic priorities as suggested in Annex B of this report.

(l) In general the mission recommends that efforts be continued to attract technical assistance to strengthen the planning and executing capacity of the public sector. UNDP and WHO assistance to analyse the feasibility of road and water supply projects, the establishment of a Harvard Advisory Group to prepare a new development plan and efforts to obtain AID assistance for sector studies, are some of the positive steps already taken to approach Ghana's future development in a sound and reasonable manner.

17. As soon as the stablization problem is solved, Ghana can resume a sustained development effort. Successful growth of exports and agricultural output will be essential to regaining a growth rate comfortably above the anticipated population growth rate. There are good prospects in both of these sectors, and implementation of the sector and project studies now getting under way will lay a firm foundation for the new development plan. Improved investment productivity and domestic savings will also be essential if future resource gaps are to be kept within manageable limits. Here success in stimulating and supporting private investment will be important and, as noted above, will require increased re-channelling of public savings into private sector investment. Successful future development will, as with other developing countries, also depend upon new external capital and technical assistance and, given the external debt problem in Ghana, the terms of new external borrowing will be a major consideration over the foreseeable future. However, a Ghana with increasing levels of output, exports and domestic savings will have both diminishing external capital requirements and an increasing debt service capacity while maintaining a steady expansion of per capita consumption. Conversely, a Ghana without increasing output and exports would be

unable to generate the savings and balance of payments capacity to either service existing external debt or increase per capita consumption.

18. It appears that the new Government's assessment of past economic policy coincides with the views expressed in this report. The Government is aware that *Ghana's voluntary exclusion from accepted approaches to economic development has proved detrimental to growth.** It is determined to reverse this policy and has shown skill and success in initiating and mobilizing corrective domestic actions as well as external technical and financial assistance from a variety of bilateral, regional and international sources. The new Government deserves commendation for taking decisions based on technical and economic reasoning with often difficult but unavoidable political and human implications. The chances are good for this to continue and the mission has gained the impression that Ghana, under the new Government, is embarking on a course of sound and realistic economic development.

Background
. . .

3. Even though Ghana became fully independent only in 1957, participation of Ghanaians in the government of the then Gold Coast was constitutionally provided for as early as 1951. At general elections in February 1951 Kwame Nkrumah's Convention People's Party (CPP) won a decisive victory and Nkrumah himself became the Gold Coast's first prime minister in 1952. The CPP repeated this success in two subsequent elections enabling it to proceed with its plans for complete independence from British control. This was achieved in 1957 when the Gold Coast became one of the first independent states in Africa and changed its name to Ghana. The country's political scene thereafter was more and more dominated by Nkrumah and his party. Organized opposition was neutralized and many of its best elements left the country. The range and depth of party penetration and the personal authority of the party leader went further than in any other state in Africa.

4. In February 1966, the army and police took control of the country while Nkrumah was abroad. The Government was transferred to a National Liberation Council (NLC) comprising an equal number of army and police leaders. General Ankrah, chairman of the National Liberation Council, has since been head of state. The members of the NLC appear to be a dedicated and unified group and prospects are good for it to remain so. The new Government has concentrated its efforts on solving domestic economic problems, the re-establishment of good relations with neighboring African states, and the restoration of Ghana's name abroad, both politically and economically. It has declared its intention to lead the

---
*Emphasis added—*Editor.*

country back to civilian rule under a constitutional democratic government and has appointed a constitutional commission to work out procedures to this effect.

5. Because the military overthrow of the Nkrumah regime came after a long period during which the once lively Ghanaian spirit of political controversy had been systematically suppressed, the new Government is faced with a political vacuum. While the chances of Nkrumah's return to power are very remote, it is impossible to say at the present time just who will emerge as the new political leader or leaders. Since tribalism is not a political issue in Ghana, they are not likely to be chosen on tribal lines. Moreover, irrespective of politics, there is a good chance that the present civil service will continue in the day to day management of the government's affairs, giving continuity to the implementation of policy during the difficult period of stabilization. While the positive aspects of the situation are strong and many, it will, however, require skill and some luck to reconcile the radicalism of the young, the liberalism of the rehabilitated refugees and the conservatism of the latent traditionalists in the political sphere.

Part II: From 'Socialism' to the 'Welfare State'

Introductory Note

Documents 16 and 17, both drawn from early working papers of the National Economic Committee, set forth what was probably the fullest statement of the economic ideology of the NLC regime. An earlier and shorter version of Document 16 formed the basis to General Ankrah's statement on economic policy of 2 March 1966. The paper reproduced here enunciates the concept of the 'Welfare State' and discusses the role of the state, joint state/private, and private and cooperative sectors in this 'Welfare State', as well as measures to be taken to promote industry, agriculture, and private enterprise in general. Policies towards foreign private capital, and the development of Ghanaian private capital in dependent relationship with foreign capital, are discussed in Document 17. A particularly strong source of pressure to expand the foreign capital sector came from the World Bank; Document 18 reproduces an excerpt from the report on the World Bank mission of June 1966, recommending measures to be taken to attract foreign capital.

Far more than the World Bank, the Political Committee was preoccupied with the development of indigenous capitalism. However, it saw this development occurring, not at the expense of North Atlantic capital, but of Indo–Levantine capital (Document 19). (Unfortunately the report of the 'Committee on Promotion of Ghanaian Enterprises', on which the comments of the Political Committee were based, was not available to the Editor. This together with the recommendations of the Political Committee formed an aspect of the background to the 'indigenization' measures of 1968 and 1970.)

Document 20 offers the most extensive critique by NLC advisers of the agricultural policies of the Nkrumah Government. It also shows how the state farms and other large-scale public sector agricultural projects of the CPP period were disposed of. However, the Agricultural Committee of the NLC, from whose report this document is drawn, made few suggestions on an alternative agricultural policy. This deficiency was the subject of a critique in a Minority Report written by two members of the Committee (but not included here), who made extensive and interesting recommendations on agricultural policy. However, these recommendations were never implemented by the NLC.

The next document originates from the World Bank. Document 21 was from a Bank mission to the National Economic Committee and contains the recommendations of the mission on the 1967–68 development budget. It emphasizes once again the main features of Fund–Bank stabilization: reductions in state spending, cuts in social services and new investment, tax concessions to foreign capital etc. While confirming that on almost all of these counts the mission took a more rigid line than Ghanaian officials, the memorandum contains important admissions of the limitations and contradictions of the stabilization programme.

Document 16: Military Government's Economic Policy
'Draft Memorandum on the Economic Policy of the Ghana Government', National Economic Committee Draft Paper (n.d.—March or April 1966).

The Fundamental Objective and Basic Characteristics

The fundamental objective of the Ghana Government is to establish, in Ghana, a strong and progressive welfare society in which no one will have any anxiety about the basic needs of life, about work, food, health and shelter; a society in which the individual Ghanaian will be able to enjoy a modern standard of living based on gainful employment. The National Liberation Council regards the well-being of the people as the supreme law and its policies will be directed to the attainment of that end.

2. The welfare state is not a mere ideological concept; it is a real indicator of economic policy. In pursuance of this, the Government will manage the economy in such a way that the opportunities for honest and gainful employment are steadily expanded and will ensure that this employment yields increasingly higher returns to the worker and his family. The Government will also pursue a policy that will promote such a rate of economic growth as will ensure that enough reserves are available to modernize progressively the services which the Government provides to the worker and his family to improve radically their standard of living.

3. The welfare society which is the Government's pressing target, can be achieved only on the basis of further significant economic development – by substantial development of the country's economic potential, especially in agriculture and industry. Our economic policy is based on a constructive partnership between the public and the private sectors which is designed to promote the fastest possible rate of economic development so that the standards of wealth and welfare of the people can be rapidly improved. All measures of the Government and all activities of individual Ghanaians should be directed to realizing this goal. The concept of the *welfare state*,

therefore, serves as the basis for the Government's economic policy.

4. The National Liberation Council, unlike the former regime, does not seek to base its economic policy on any doctrinaire preconceptions and assumptions. It recognizes the variety and diversity of economic and social problems, and the equally manifold and different solutions which can be applied.

We have rejected any hard and fast ideas about the sphere of the public or the private sector based merely on ideological or simple theoretical considerations. The policy of the National Liberation Council would, therefore, be to find the best possible solution to economic problems. The over-riding policy objective of the National Liberation Council is the successful application of economic measures designed to restore and stabilize the country's economy, secure well-balanced development and a more efficient utilization of resources, and to induce the maximum effort from the people of Ghana to enhance their standard of living as fast as possible. In this endeavour, the National Liberation Council believes that *all sections of the community and the major sectors of the economy have a legitimate, recognizable and very important contribution to make*. The Council will direct its economic policy in a manner that will virtually [*sic*] assign definite tasks to the various groups in the economy and ensure their fulfilment. In brief, Ghana's policies will be so designed as to obtain the maximum contribution from each sector towards the over-all growth of the economy. It is only through these measures that a progressive welfare society can be built in Ghana.

5. The economic policy of the National Liberation Council shows some basic characteristics, distinguishing it conspicuously from the former regime's economic policy. The most important characteristics are the following:

> the significant change in the relation between different social sectors;
> the difficult task of consolidation of the country's economy and preparation of further development;
> the serious endeavour of improving the allocation of economic resources and their utilization.

The aims, means, methods and measures of the Government's economic policy are strongly influenced by these characteristics.

II. The Government's Sectoral Policy

In Ghana *four* major sectors of the economy will be recognized. These are:

1. the Private Sector;
2. the Joint Private/Government Sector;
3. the Government Sector; and
4. the Cooperative Sector.

It would be emphasized at the very beginning that there will be fair treatment between the four sectors of the economy. Healthy competition will be encouraged to the advantage of the national economy. The various sectors will have equal chances; belonging to particular sectors will not confer any special privileges or attract any discriminatory treatment. The fact that the State gives such prominence to the Private sector as stated below does not mean that the State intends to withdraw from the economy... [the Government will build up – and maintain – solid political and institutional foundation, by securing real democracy and freedom of action, by providing opportunity of individual initiative and by abolishing over-centralization and bureaucracy. It will offer a large – but not unlimited – scope for the forces of market mechanism, making use, at the same time, of the advantages of economic planning on national levels.] We are simply trying to institute a system of genuine partnership between Government and private interests. Government must share with the private sector the task of increasing production and employment under a rational division of responsibilities....

(a) The Private Sector

8. The *Private Sector* will remain the largest sector in terms of number of persons engaged and gross output. This sector will be open to both Ghanaians and non-Ghanaians, but every effort and encouragement will be given to Ghanaians to organize themselves better and more efficiently so that they will be able to assume an increasingly large share of the sector. Controls of a general nature will be introduced to ensure that the workers in this sector are not exploited by the owners of the various business concerns.

9. As a permanent feature of our policy for the economic development of the country, the National Liberation Council intends that the primary responsibility for running and developing certain sectors of the economy should predominantly belong to the private sector. In particular: agriculture, commerce and housing will be activities in which the principal responsibility for management and for expansion will be assigned to private initiative...

The activity and development of private industrial enterprises could be promoted by the following incentives provided:

(a) Encouragement of fair competition between the four economic sectors;
(b) Assurance that nationalization and arbitrary interference are not contemplated;
(c) There shall be no restriction
   (i) on the remittance of capital, including repatriation, to the country of origin of an investment in the event of a sale or the liquidation of the approved project;
   (ii) on the transfer of profits to the country of origin of the

investment after the payment of any tax due in respect of the investment;
  (iii) on the transfer of payments in respect of principal, interest, and other financial charges where a loan has been granted to a project by a non-resident for the purposes of the project in accordance with the approved conditions of the loan;
 (d) Reasonable facilities should be provided to expatriate personnel employed or engaged in an approved project for making remittances abroad in respect of the maintenance of their families and other contractual obligations such as insurance premiums and contributions to provident and pension funds.

The application of these principles will, however, become more meaningful after the correction of our present unfavourable foreign exchange position.
 (e) The Capital Investment Act, administered by the Capital Investment Board, offers generous fiscal incentives to foreign private investors. These incentives comprise for instance, tax holidays up to 10 years, various tax exemptions like exemptions from import and excise duties, deferment of registration fees and stamp duties.
 (g) The Capital Investment Board will remain the main centre where information on the prospects for investment may be obtained by overseas investors. The Board will be well-equipped to assist foreign investors in the implementation of their projects.
 (g) The Administration of Government agencies which handle project proposals will be streamlined so that (a) the processing of project proposals may be effected expeditiously, (b) investors will no longer be plagued with vexatious controls.
 (h) The Government will strengthen the Economic Section of our missions in order that information on investment opportunities in Ghana may be effectively disseminated.
 (i) The Reduction of the present tax on profits from 50% to 45% and that on dividends from 15% to 7.5%....]

(b) The Joint Government/Private Sector
12. Besides the private sector, *the Joint Government/Private Sector* will play an important role in the country's economy. . . .

13. Ghana's attempts at joint state/private undertakings have been rewarding. All the joint state/private enterprises existing in November, 1965, were found profitable. In contrast with wholly state-owned enterprises, the balance sheets of the joint enterprises revealed that they were able to keep costs at a minimum, while plant was utilized to the fullest capacity. The management was generally more efficient; they undertook better pre-planning studies and the accounting and recording systems were more complete and up to date than those of most of the state-owned enterprises. . . .

15. The establishment of joint private/government business enterprises will be purely on a voluntary basis. No private enterprises will be forced to accept government participation. At the same time every application from a private enterprise inviting the government to participate in the enterprises will be considered on its own merits....

17. It is a well-known fact that the majority of state enterprises is operating with losses. In order to disburden the budget and to promote more profitable production, the National Liberation Council had decided to invite private participation in or turn over to private enterprise, certain state enterprises. In deciding which enterprises were to fall in either of these categories, the following factors were considered:-

   (a) the strategic nature of the enterprises;
   (b) the suitability or otherwise of each enterprise for private operation as against state operation;
   (c) the ability of the enterprise to earn revenue to support itself or otherwise;
   (d) the need for additional capital;
   (e) the need for efficient management and technical know-how.

18. The decision on the purchaser of, or participant in, a particular enterprise would depend on negotiation but due consideration should be given to the following factors:

   (a) the price offered;
   (b) the percentage down-payment to be made;
   (c) the period of repayment of the balance;
   (d) the credit worthiness of the purchaser;
   (e) the availability of technical know-how to the purchaser, and
   (f) the experience of the purchaser himself in the particular industry.

It has been decided that:

   (a) in the case of selected state enterprises to be sold to the private sector, preference should be given to Ghanaians,
   (b) the valuation of a team of experts appointed by the National Liberation Council should form the basis for negotiation; but in case of dispute a joint valuation team may be appointed to re-value the enterprises;
   (c) as a general rule private participants should be given up to 49% of the shares, although serious consideration should be given to offering majority share to private interests, if this is found desirable;
   (d) only new investments from abroad and on profits eligible for remission abroad should be used in financing participation;
   (e) the National Investment Bank will assist as many Ghanaians as possible to participate in this exercise.

It is emphasized again that, although Government has already offered for sale those public industrial concerns which, in its view, can be more efficiently and profitably managed by private enterprise, Government is by no means withdrawing entirely from the field of industrial development. Most of those enterprises which have not been retained in the Government's portfolio will remain there until, in the process of review, it is established that any of them should be transferred to the private sector.

(c) The Government Sector
21. In general the National Liberation Council recognizes [that] *active State participation in economic activity* will be necessary to promote a vigorous rate of economic growth. The justification for this is that private capital may not always be available for certain important enterprises. Active State participation will, however, be limited to certain basic and key projects....

23. The delimitation of the scope of the Government's activity is one of the most intricate problems of economic policy. There can be no doubt about the fact that, especially under the present circumstances, dynamic economic policy and the planning of development are indispensable. The Government must act as the defender of the public interest and has to perform several duties in the field of social and economic infrastructure, as well as in various economic branches....

(d) The Cooperative Sector
30. The National Liberation Council recognizes the vital role which a properly organized *Cooperative Movement* can play in our economic development. It is therefore proposed to promote an efficient and *truly cooperative movement*. Its activities will be purely economic and it will not be allowed to get itself involved in politics....

V. The Government's Policy on Various Economic Branches

...(a) Agriculture
(i) Agriculture will be open to both domestic private, and foreign private capital. Every attempt will, however, be made to maintain the local *private farmer* as the central unit of agricultural practice. His position will be further strengthened by increasing the central services and facilities offered him.
(ii) The operation of the foreigner in the agricultural sector will be governed by regulations to be drawn up later; but the principle of fair competition vis-à-vis the local farmer will be observed....
(iv) Henceforth, active *state participation* in agriculture will be limited to the production of industrial raw materials, such as rubber, oil palm, sugar-cane, cotton and non-apparel fibres, livestock and livestock products where large-scale organization has decided advantages in production; introduction of new crops

and proven techniques and opening up uncultivated, rather than already farmed areas. However, public agricultural agencies, e.g. the Agricultural Wing of the Workers' Brigade, might be requested to produce some food-crops of high cash value on a crash programme basis....

(b) Industry
... Industrial development during the consolidation period should therefore, aim at the following economic objectives:

  (a) The production of import substitutes for consumer staples like soap, textiles, clothing, sugar, footwear, cereal and cereal preparations, fish and fish preparations and meat and meat preparations, for which there is a large demand at present and the demand for which is likely to increase in future with increase in population and gainful employment and with growth in incomes.
  (b) The processing of agricultural and mining commodities – cocoa, timber, gold, bauxite and manganese that are presently exported mostly unprocessed, before exporting them, and increased exports of other agricultural products like bananas and kolanuts....

Document 17: Further Aspects of Military Government's Economic Policy

'Ghana's Industrial Policy', National Economic Committee Draft Paper (n.d. – March or April 1966).

Role of Foreign Capital

... 11. To dispel some doubts and misconceptions about foreign private enterprise, it is important to comment on its role, and its costs and benefits to our economy in the process of industrial development. All private enterprise, whether domestic or foreign, in a developing country like Ghana expects to make substantial profits. The reason is that the risk of investing in such countries is greater than that of placing an investment in the developed economies where the determinants of profitability are better known and more easily controlled. Also, from the point of view of industrial development what is important with [*sic*] profits is not how large they are but how much is repatriated from the country. Many foreign capitalists automatically re-invest some of their profits, and indeed there is no reason why they should not do so if Ghana continued to offer them opportunities for economic expansion....

14. There are four major reasons why Ghana will for a long time have to rely on a net inflow of foreign private capital. First, such capital is necessary for closing the trade gap which is largely related to the import demand resulting from economic development. Second, partly on account of the mounting pressure of current consumption needs, and for other reasons, the rate in domestic savings cannot be raised to the point where it would be adequate for carrying out a sufficiently high rate of investment. Third, foreign capital can assure a stream of modern industrial technology into Ghana. Finally, foreign private enterprise in Ghana constitutes a medium through which those practices of labour and management which make for a high level of productivity in advanced countries can be imported into Ghana.

15. Since the test of economic maturity of an industrial system is the extent to which its own nationals can run local industries, the most valuable contribution which foreign enterprise makes to the economy is the training in management and new skills accorded to the indigenous people. The Government of Ghana considers it a most desirable objective that foreign private enterprise endeavours to give opportunities to Ghanaians for capital participation, and superior employment in skilled, technical and managerial positions in industry. In this connection, the Government looks most favourably upon the recent action taken by one sizeable foreign firm* in selling shares to the Ghanaian public....

Joint Ventures

18. There are also certain instances where the state would seek to encourage joint ownership of industrial schemes. These may be outlined as follows:

(i) In view of the significant shortcomings of Ghanaian enterprises – such as lack of intcrpreneurship, and capital, inadequacy of managerial and technical expertise, etc. – and thc need to carry...on industrial development and at the same time to preserve some important investment opportunities to potential Ghanaian industrialists at a future date, the Government may consider it advisable to continue holding equity interest in joint schemes which under normal circumstances may not be considered of special or strategic importance to merit state investment. This principle applies to most of the existing joint schemes, and also the new Government projects seeking foreign private participation. Under normal circumstances the state... would leave commercial and technical management in the hands of the experienced private partner. In view of the likely competing demands on the limited resources of the state, the

*UAC – *Editor*

Government may not find it possible to invest substantially in most of such industries.

(ii) The state may also consider it advisable to promote new joint schemes as pioneering ventures. This may be sought in instances where the government considers that the scheme would be successful but private enterprise is reluctant for various reasons, to take the lead. Once the pioneering stage is over and it can be demonstrated that the schemes could be run profitably, Government expects to withdraw from the industry and sell its interest to private Ghanaian enterprise.

Government Sector

19. Full ownership and operation of industrial schemes by the state will be kept at an inescapable minimum. There are three cases in which the Ghana Government may apply the principle of public ownership. These are: (a) public utilities, (b) industries of strategic importance, and (c) pioneering industries....

22. In view of the risks involved in investing in a developing country, private investors when presented with a variety of opportunities often, though not always, pre-select those which offer the best opportunities for short-term profit while involving the minimum investment, the least organizational effort and the least technological difficulties. Thus industries of *key importance for development* process, and which are likely to succeed, may be neglected by private enterprise. The Ghana Government considers that wherever important industries with chances of successful operation are, in spite of promotional effort and fair inducements, long neglected by private enterprise the state should be prepared to pioneer temporarily and to hand them over to private interest when they become going concerns.

Section III—Special Encouragement to Small- and Medium-Scale Ghanaian Industries

23. It has been indicated already that while in the private sector there will be no discrimination against foreign industrialists, every effort will be made to encourage Ghanaians to organize themselves more efficiently and to assume an increasing role in the industrial development of the country.

24. In this country there are very few top Ghanaian managers and businessmen. Among the existing entrepreneurs there is general inadequacy of managerial ability in organization, of skills, finance and experience. Furthermore, the Ghanaian entrepreneur generally lacks overseas business connections which foreign enterprises tend to command.

The development of industry and rapid introduction of new technology in recent years has introduced more complex technical and management problems associated with factory operations. Industrial opportunities in small- to medium-scale industries in which some Ghanaian industrialists are likely to compete successfully have been increasingly taken up by non-Ghanaians with greater capital, expertise and better foreign business connections essential in modern industry.

Consequently the majority of Ghanaian enterprises are confined to farming, small- to medium-scale retailing of manufactures and primary commodities, and other services, notably transportation.

25. The traditional import–export trade, in which Ghanaians' business had flourished, has undergone major structural changes over the years. The emergence of larger and better financed international trading companies has led to increased efficiency of import trading, lowering of administrative and transportation costs and a decline in profit margins. The attainment of high profits has depended increasingly on larger volumes of business at lower profit per unit of sales. The increasing sophistication and larger scale financing and organization of import trade have operated against Ghanaian import–export traders and led to a decline in their overall share of international trade.

26. As a long-run objective, Government will provide potential Ghanaian industrial investors with opportunities for capital formation and pursue general policies which would enable Ghanaians to take an increasing share of industry and trade.

27. *As and when the general economic conditions improve,* Government will positively promote and give substantial encouragement to Ghanaian enterprises particularly in small- to medium-scale industries. The forms of encouragement envisaged would include the following:

(i) Credit facilities and technical assistance to Ghanaian entrepreneurs in small- to medium-scale industries will be substantially increased. Funds from Government and financial and technical aid from international sources for this purpose will be channelled to a special scheme to be set up under the National Investment Bank and the Small Industries Section of the Ministry of Industries.

(ii) Specially favourable tax treatment will be accorded to royalties and other incomes which Ghanaian small- and medium-scale industries (or such size of foreign private projects with substantial Ghanaian participation) pay for licensing arrangements providing for a flow of technology and generally for technical and management assistance contracts with firms in developed economies.

28. But sometimes the supply of know-how is indeed a better business if combined with the introduction of a product into an overseas market. Again, simple provision of know-how can be unsuccessful if the company that provides it has no stake in the business of the receiving company. Hence an important element of Government policy will be the systematic

promotion of partnership between private foreign and private domestic investors, particularly in the small- to medium-scale industries.

It is known that in certain cases the self-interest of the foreign private investor often induces him to look for local private partners. A variety of motives impel him to do so, such as special knowledge of domestic markets possessed by nationals, the easing of relations with Government and the desire to reduce the risk of political discrimination. However, Government appreciates the fact that there are many difficulties in joint ventures. It is often difficult to find a local private partner willing to invest in a joint foreign local private scheme. Sometimes the varying interests of shareholders and subsidiaries of a foreign company may make it difficult to promote a joint venture.

29. While for various reasons the Government does not declare participation of Ghanaian private capital mandatory in small- to medium-scale industries, the Government *will provide additional incentives for associations between national and foreign capital so that in certain cases the balance may be tipped in favour of partnership in the decision making process of the foreign investor.* The existence of such incentives might at any rate stimulate potential investors to examine ever more seriously the possibilities of operating in Ghana in a manner that will be conducive to the emergence of domestic private enterprise. The further inducements are outlined as follows:

(i) In addition to the general conditions specified under the Capital Investment Act, private schemes with capital investment of less than N₵200,000.00 may be eligible for benefits under the Act if not less than 40% of equity is held by Ghanaians. If such benefits are granted under the Act, the sale of Ghanaian interest to non-Ghanaians can be effected only after reasonable attempts to sell such shares to other Ghanaian interests through the Capital Investment Board and National Investment Bank have failed.

(ii) In respect of loans from the National Investment Bank to private industrial projects with investment of less than N₵200,000.00, the Bank might consider a reduction of the normal interest rate, if the scheme is either wholly owned by Ghanaians or not less than 40% of its equity is held by Ghanaian investors. The special loans scheme to be set up under the National Investment Bank and the Small Industries Section of the Ministry of Industries will be reserved specifically for private Ghanaian schemes and joint private foreign and Ghanaian projects.

(iii) For small- and medium-scale projects a reduced land rent may be charged for Government industrial land if Ghanaian equity interest does not fall below the prescribed minimum.

(iv) The Government, through the National Investment Bank, might consider to build [*sic*] industrial estates where standard factory buildings would be leased on reasonable terms to joint schemes or wholly owned Ghanaian projects, of small to medium size. If the whole or part of an operating small- or medium-sized industrial scheme already wholly owned by a foreign private interest is to be sold, reasonable attempts should be made through the National Investment Bank and the Capital Investment Board to sell not less than 30% of the offer to Ghanaian interests....

Document 18: World Bank Recommendations on Private Foreign Investment

Excerpts from Recommendations of World Bank Mission of June 1966 on the 1966/67 National Liberation Council Budget.

If Ghana is seriously interested in attracting foreign and domestic private investment, the present burden of company taxation should be reduced, and treatment of income tax relief should be made more equitable among taxpayers. It is believed that certain revisions can be made without significant loss of revenue, which will nevertheless improve the inducements offered to private investors and thus stimulate productive investment.

The principal measure to be considered is elimination of the 15% tax on repatriated profits. As noted in an earlier report this tax puts the total burden well above levels prevailing in those countries from which it is hoped to attract investment capital. Businessmen and officials at both NIB [National Investment Bank] and CIB [Capital Investment Bank] have stressed emphatically that the repatriated profits tax adversely affects foreign investor interest. To the extent that relief is granted under the Capital Investment Act, of course, the discouraging influence of the tax is diminished. As agreed before, however, selective treatment in itself poses administrative difficulties and may exercise a damping effect on investor interest.

Under present circumstances the revenue effect of the tax is subordinated to the scarcity of foreign exchange, which has led to restrictions on the repatriation of profits. This situation is likely to continue over the near future and a decision eliminating the tax will have to await clarification of the balance of payments effects. The mission believes that both the ability to repatriate profits and equal tax treatment of all companies will be required to attract and sustain a significant inflow of foreign private capital.

Other measures for consideration would be a small reduction in the companies tax (say to 45%) accompanied by a reduction in the tax holiday for three years, applied uniformly to all new investment over a certain magnitude. The decrease of companies tax would diminish government revenues by about ₡1.5 million on the basis of 1965 actuals and by about ₡2 million on the basis of 1966 estimates. The stimulus given to productive activity might, however, offset the revenue decline.

The Bank draft report,* Annex II, discussed the problem of discretionary tax holidays. Essentially they open the possibility of discriminatory treatment and increases investor uncertainty. With a lower repatriated profits tax and/or a slightly lower companies tax, incentives should be sufficient to outweigh the disincentive of the shorter tax holiday. The mission understands that certain small investors make very high returns and (what is the same thing) have short pay-back periods. For this reason the three-year holiday might be automatically extended to all investments over a certain size in new industrial enterprises.

Capital Investment Board

In view of renewed emphasis on domestic and foreign private investment, it is anticipated that the Capital Investments Board will play an increasingly important role in the promotion and authorization of new enterprises.

To date in 1966 ten requests for approval under the act have been received, well above the level of private interest shown during the same period in the preceding year.

In particular, the mission recommends that CIB assume primary responsibility for general programmes of investment promotion and for providing liaison between investors and the various agencies in government with whom they deal. This role should not conflict with the responsibilities assumed by NIB; indeed, the two organizations should work closely together. Industrial promotion should not, however, be a prime responsibility of other government agencies. While it is not clear that there can ever be too much promotional activity, to the extent that it is an official undertaking it should be coordinated with the activities and programmes of CIB.

Earlier mission suggestions with respect to consistency in the treatment of productive investment continue to apply. The mission believes that to the extent possible discretionary concessions and prerogatives should be avoided. The administration of the Capital Investment Act will be more successful in accomplishing its stated objectives the more consistent and general is the application of the provision of the act.

---

*IBRD, *Public Sector Development Policies and Programmes in Ghana*, Washington: 14 March 1966 (11 volumes) – *Editor.*

National Investment Bank

Increase in Investor Interest

Over the past three months there has been an increase in investor interest in NIB-sponsored industrial investment projects. Among Ghanaian individuals and firms it has been found that there is greater readiness to invest local currency resources. In particular there have been serious proposals for participation with NIB on a starch processing factory and an electrical appliance factory. Foreign private investors have become more seriously interested in

    (a) tinned reconstituted milk (Fan Milk)
    (b) dry cell batteries (Union Carbide).

It is anticipated that (a) and (b) will be finalized over the coming six months. NIB is also proceeding as rapidly as possible with the Ghana Groceries Scheme and the Ceramics factory.

Diminished Government Role

Government is prepared to see its share in most new projects reduced... This policy will decrease the pressure on public capital expenditure while increasing the need to seek funds from other sources.

Financial Resources of NIB

Uncommitted and unutilized funds are presently invested in government securities paying on the average about 5%. On its loan portfolio most repayment commitments are being met on schedule. Exceptions appear to be the Government-guaranteed fibre bag loan and the State Fishing Corporation loan (£375,000). On private loans difficulty was encountered when a poultry producer lost his flock and had to be refinanced. Otherwise obligations are being met.

Future Requirements

NIB management states that it is likely to require more funds in the future. As private investor activity picks up, it expects existing resources to be insufficient. The present strategy is as follows:

    (1) Request government subsidy to fibre bag corporation to repay its commitment to NIB.
    (2) Request additional government loan.
    (3) Request from USAID local currency PL480 counterpart funds.

(4) Begin arrangements for increased private participation, both domestic and foreign, with view to eventual IFC participation. Negotiations with IFC to begin in earnest at fall Bank–Fund meeting.

The mission believes that NIB should play an increasingly important role in the development of Ghanaian industry. With past and continuing feasibility studies (presently being undertaken by a West German study team) and preparation in depth of project proposals, results in terms of productive new investment should begin to be achieved. Present loan and guarantee commitments total about £2.5 million while paid in capital is $3.25 million (£2.5 million government, £150,000 private). Disbursements are, however, only about one-fifth of total commitments. NIB's plans to increase financial resources over the coming year appear advisable and consistent with earlier recommendations. Over the intermediate run efforts to strengthen the capital structure and to seek international assistance and participation should be continued.*

Document 19: Recommendations on Promotion of Indigenous Business

Political Committee of the National Liberation Council, Memorandum PC/M.84/67: 'Comments on the Report of the National Liberation Council Committee on Promotion of Ghanaian Enterprises', 15 June 1967.

.... The industrialization of the country and the present attempts to resuscitate the economy are the responsibility of Ghanaians first and foremost. The Government therefore owe a special duty to Ghanaian businessmen to provide facilities that will encourage them.

The recommendation in the Report that larger trading firms, presumably UAC, SCOA, UTC, etc., should withdraw from retail trade is laudable, but this will create a vacuum which will most certainly be filled by Lebanese, Syrian and Indian Traders, thus defeating the object of the whole exercise. We may mention the Nigerian petty trader who is a constant source of danger in the retail trade, though perhaps one might describe him at the village level as a useful intruder. It is obvious that even at present the Lebanese, Syrian and Indian traders are exploiting and controlling the retail trade in many commodities and are gradually squeezing out the Ghanaians. As a matter of policy, therefore, the

---

*See Document 38.

Government must embark on a definite, bold and effective plan to meet this field of our commercial activity within a target period of between 4 to 5 years. This exercise would aim first and foremost at eliminating them from the retail trade as follows:

(a) 1st year: Exclusion from the sale of provisions.
(b) 2nd year: Exclusion from the sale of textiles.
(c) 3rd year: Exclusion from the sale of spare parts.
(d) 4th year: Exclusion from the sale of drugs and pharmaceuticals.
(e) 5th year: Exclusion from the sale of retail of other items.

This plan, however, cannot succeed without a decree or legislation and this should also make it an offence for any Ghanaian to allow himself to be used by such foreigners in the 'protected retail trade' of the items to be listed. Such an offence should be punishable by very heavy fines as a deterrent. The total withdrawal of import licences regarding the items concerned might also be considered and effected by a graduated plan over a similar period but it is suggested it should be longer in this case.

Similarly, this policy should be extended to declare certain industries exclusively for Ghanaians. For example, food cannery, animal husbandry, garment manufacture, printing, timber and ammunition. In this regard perhaps exception may be made to the few very large timber concerns employing say over 250 to 300 men, with at least N₵500,000.00 investment and paying about N₵100,000.00 in tax and revenue to the Government. Again the following should also be left exclusively to Ghanaians: distillery, laundry and dry cleaning, bakery, polythene, film extrusion, and plastic moulding. Foreigners who are already operating in these reserved industries may be permitted to remain under certain conditions only, viz:

(i) That they furnish evidence of actual transfer of capital into Ghana for the setting up of the particular industry in which they are engaged;
(ii) That they employ at least 100 Ghanaians;
(iii) That they own plant, equipment and machinery;
(iv) That they have been engaged in the industry for at least 5 years by January, 1967 or 1968;
(v) That they employ qualified Ghanaian accountants and managers;
(vi) That the taxes they have paid within the last three years of their existence come to an average of £6,000/-/-or N₵12,000.00 per year.
(vii) That they do not own retail shops.

Another field in which the Lebanese and Syrians exploit the Ghanaian is in the taxi service, and it is advised that this should be reserved to the Ghanaian.

The question of finance must not be overlooked in this regard. It is accepted that Ghanaians have a very little capital to enable them to embark on certain industries. There is very little doubt that considerable assistance is needed in this direction. It is believed that the foreign commercial banks in Ghana are more willing to advance facilities to Lebanese, Syrian and Indian businessmen than to Ghanaians. The assistance given by the Ghana Commercial Bank, though considerable, is not adequate, and the Investment Bank, Agricultural Loans and Credit Bank and similar institutions should be advised to assist more.

Lastly, it is generally accepted that investment in retail trade by the Lebanese, Syrians and Indians in Ghana is the cause of the country's most serious problem of bribery and corruption. This was common in the former regime and the exclusion of these foreigners will undoubtedly reduce considerably, if not eradicate completely, this detestable practice in our country.

Document 20: Agricultural Policy

'Report of the Agricultural Committee of the National Liberation Council' (November, 1966).

(I) Terms of Reference

1. The Agricultural Committee was appointed by the National Liberation Council on 16 March 1966, with the following terms of reference:

2. 'To look into the agricultural problems facing the country and to make recommendations to the Economic Committee for the Council's consideration. This Committee could also advise on the feasibility of some of the agricultural projects now being undertaken in the country and recommend whether they could be improved or scrapped altogether.'

3. The Committee did not consider it necessary to formulate plans for the implementation of specific projects but felt that the planning of such projects and their execution should best be left to the agricultural production and services organizations of, or associated with the Ministry of Agriculture which should be guided by the broad policies outlined in this report. ...

13. It has been found necessary, in the light of past events, to propose a new structure of production and economic activity in agriculture which is designed to enable each of the four sectors of the economy; namely, the State, Joint State/Private and Cooperatives, to have clearly defined areas of operation in order that each may play its full role in ensuring maximum national output. The services which should be provided by the educational institutes, research and the Ministry of Agriculture to promote the work of these sectors are also outlined. ...

III Agriculture Under the Old Regime

(1) Ministry of Agriculture

26. The reorganization of the old Department of Agriculture in 1959 into General Agricultural Services, Scientific Services, Cocoa Industry and Economics Divisions, each with its own Head and complementary staff, marked the first major step in the execution of certain policies of the old regime which called for radical changes in the development of existing manpower resources and other facilities of the Ministry of Agriculture. Prior to this, the old Department devoted its energies to the problem of cocoa rehabilitation, soil conservation in the Land Planning Areas, as well as research and agricultural extension. The agricultural stations formed the bases from which other extension activities were launched for the development of coconut, oil palm, coffee, tobacco, rubber and banana industries, and the use of improved techniques in food and livestock farming. Training courses for both departmental staff and farmers were also regularly organized.

27. The General Agricultural Services Division, which became the extension arm of the Ministry of Agriculture was handicapped, from the start, by shortage of staff with the result that no effective liaison could be established between the Division and farmers. Thereafter, a new concept based on the so-called socialization of agriculture led to the abolition of the four Divisions in 1962 and eventual disorganization of the Ministry itself. The State agricultural organizations entered the agricultural scene. The Ministry virtually lost its technical leadership over the agricultural industry, and its most important function, that of providing mechanized, advisory and other services to farmers, passed into the hands of the erstwhile United Ghana Farmers' Cooperatives Council.

(2) State Farms Corporation

28. The State Farms Corporation was established in 1962 as a government operated enterprise with the aim of using modern techniques of farming in the production of sufficient foodstuffs to cope with the demands of the increasing population as well as of raw materials for the developing industries and export. To achieve this objective, the Corporation took over the old agricultural stations and converted them into production units. In addition, it established large-scale farms and livestock projects all over the country. By the end of 1965, a total of 123 farms had been set up, with approximately 64,300 acres, planted to such crops as rice, maize, groundnuts, millet, sorghum, cashew, yams, vegetables, fruits, bananas, sugar-cane, oil palm, rubber, cotton, tobacco and kenaf. These farms commanded a total labour force of about 20,000. Considerable sums of money had to be spent on these enterprises. Nevertheless, the total acreage cultivated represented an insignificant fraction of what the peasant farmers are able to farm.

29. Some farm lands were illegally acquired in order to establish these

farms and many of the dispossessed owners were absorbed into the labour force of the Corporation. Thousands of workers were also dumped on these farms through political pressure and consequently the number of workers employed on a project was economically unrelated to the actual returns from the project. In fact, as the farms were directed from the head office, no proper accounts were kept of the expenditure and returns from each farm. In addition, farms were sited in some areas to satisfy political interests rather than the basic agronomic requirements of the crops cultivated. Farm Managers who lacked the managerial experience and initiative required for the work they were entrusted with, were appointed obviously for political reasons. In view of these circumstances, the returns from these projects were significantly low in comparison with the investments made and the viability of most of the farms was questionable.

(3) Other Corporations
30. In its bid to promote agricultural development and the rapid industrialization of the country, the old regime embarked upon the establishment of a number of other enterprises. For instance, the Sugar Products Corporation, the Fibre Bag Manufacturing Corporation, the Vegetable Oil and Textile Mills were all set up to process locally produced agricultural raw materials, the State Fishing Corporation to develop the fishing industry and the State Tobacco Products Corporation to organize the production and marketing of tobacco. However, the tempo of development was such that many difficulties were encountered. The successful operation of these Corporations was hindered by lack of qualified technicians and competent managers, nepotism, over-staffing and inadequate supply of raw material, coupled with unavailability of foreign exchange for the importation of other items essential to the production and manufacturing processes.

31. Some factories were established when no provision had been made for the production of the raw materials required to feed them. One reason for this was the desire of the old regime to satisfy certain political interests and demands; consequently, the supply of the raw materials was considered of secondary importance. In other cases, poor feasibility studies before the execution of a project and lack of effective coordination at the planning stage among the various agencies concerned with the establishment of the enterprise contributed to this unfortunate situation.

(4) United Ghana Farmers' Cooperatives Council
32. The Council was formed ostensibly to organize farmers and fishermen into cooperatives and to provide them with direct services, but in actual fact, it was designed to obtain the support of the farming community for the disbanded Convention People's Party. It was also made solely responsible for the internal marketing of cocoa for which it received an annual subvention from the Cocoa Marketing Board.

33. The agricultural production programme of the Farmers' Council

placed much emphasis on mechanized farming, though more than 80% of its producers' cooperatives had to depend on traditional farming, with the aid of the cutlass, axe, hoe and mattock. The very few farms which were partially mechanized ignored all soil conservation practices, leaving the surface soil exposed to the elements with consequent loss of fertility.

34. In furtherance of its mechanization programmes, it entered into a number of contract agreements on credit terms with foreign trading firms for the supply of large quantities of machinery and agricultural implements, most of which turned out to be unsuitable to farming conditions in the country. Among these contracts was one for the construction of two Tractor Assembly Plants in Kumasi and Nsawam and for additional supply of 1,400 crawler tractors and 1,500 wheeled tractors respectively, at a total cost of ₡24,256,890.00. The Farmers' Council also borrowed over ₡7,200,000.00 from the Ghana Commercial Bank to finance other agricultural programmes.

35. There were about 870 recognized cooperative societies under the Council by the close of 1965, with a total membership of 15,300. In addition to the rearing of livestock, these societies cultivated a wide variety of crops: rice, maize, cassava, yams, plantain, groundnuts, sugar-cane, oil palm, citrus, coffee, rubber and so on, under both mechanized and traditional farming. In spite of the large number of machinery at its disposal, the Council was only able to mechanize partially a small percentage of the cooperative farms. The total acreage cultivated was about 18,400.

36. Though the United Ghana Farmers' Cooperatives Council was encouraged by the old regime to incur heavy financial expenditure in its production operations, it was unable to make any impact on the national agricultural output and very few cooperatives derived any benefit from the services which it offered. In fact, the Council did not operate as a union of cooperative societies since it disregarded all the basic principles of cooperation.

(5) 'Old' Cooperatives
37. Prior to 1961, there was a strong cooperative movement in Ghana operating successfully under the Department of Cooperatives. About 500 produce-marketing societies which had been affiliated to the 16 Cooperative Unions were in existence. After this period, however, almost all of these cooperatives were compelled by circumstances to come under the control of the erstwhile United Ghana Farmers' Cooperatives Council. Those which continued to function as private cooperatives had to do so under extremely difficult conditions.

(6) Agricultural Wing of the Workers Brigade
38. The Workers Brigade occupied a peculiar position in the agricultural structure of the old regime. The objective was to train the unemployed in various skills to enable them to secure gainful employment. It was made up of four divisions, namely: Agricultural, Constructional, Industrial, and

Training and Administration (including social and cultural) Wings. However, the original aim was lost sight of and the intakes became permanent unproductive salaried employees in a para-military set-up.

39. By 1965, the Agricultural Wing of the Workers Brigade had a strength of over 10,000 workers which represented more than 50% of the entire labour force of the Brigade. It established officially 47 farms in various parts of the country, out of which about 19,140 acres were cultivated to food crops, oil palm and rubber. As in the case of the State Farms Corporation, the Brigade could not operate these farms profitably.

(7) Young Farmers' League

40. The Young Farmers' League started as a voluntary organization with the primary objective of encouraging and training middle school leavers to take up settled farming as a career. It was expected that the youth, with their educational background, would easily acquire modern techniques of farming.

41. After the League was amalgamated with the United Ghana Farmers' Co-operatives Council in 1959, its praiseworthy ideals immediately became subordinated to the political doctrine of the Council. Most of the organisers were political agents who had established private farms of their own and were only interested in collecting their daily allowances and salaries. The League was therefore unable to show any results which could justify its existence. By the end of 1964, its 1,824 settlers had established 39 farms and cultivated approximately 1,630 acres, mainly for food crops. None of the farms was, however, organised as an economic enterprise...

(8) Private Farmers

42. Whilst the old regime continued to spend considerable sums of money on the production organisations, the private farmers and fishermen who produce about 98% of the food in the country were denied every assistance; even cutlasses and fishing nets were hard to come by. It is therefore not surprising that peasant farmers and fishermen became disillusioned and alienated and many of them who could not survive under the trying circumstances were compelled to drift to the urban areas in quest of alternative employment in industries and State sponsored enterprises where their monthly earnings were assured. Consequently, labour in the rural areas particularly on the farms became scarce. Food production decreased and with the restrictions on the importation of essential commodities, the cost of living rose sharply to an unprecedented high level.

43. In the course of the Committee's meetings with farmers' representatives in the Regions, repeated requests were made for the provision of adequate feeder roads, irrigation facilities, veterinary drugs, agricultural chemicals and fertilizers, marketing and storage facilities, improved seeds and planting materials, efficient mechanization services and so on. The representatives of fishermen, on the other hand, emphasized

the need for fishing nets, spare parts for out-board motors, fishing vessels, cold storage, marketing and transport facilities.

Recommendations[2] ... (3) Projects and Production Organisations

General
52. The organization of the various production enterprises should be geared to providing the basic food necessities of the population and raw materials to feed existing factories having direct bearing on the improvement of the country's balance of payments position. (p. 42)...

54. The State should invest particularly in projects requiring large investments with long pay-off periods, which the private entrepreneur may not be inclined to undertake on a fully commercial basis. (p. 43).

55. Corporations should engage in the cultivation of certain raw materials whose production must always be dependable and geared to the requirements of factories already established to process them. To effect economies in the transportation and management of raw materials, factories should always be located near the site of the farm enterprises. (p. 43).

56. Each farm project must be operated as an economic unit under very competent management and experienced technical personnel. (p. 43).

57. All unqualified and inexperienced employees in the State production organizations and the Ministry of Agriculture should be removed or placed in other positions commensurate with their qualification. (Interim Report).

58. The salaries in the Corporations should be analogous to those in the Civil Service, but workers in the production organizations should be paid bonus for extra productive work done which increases the profits of the organization.

State Farms Corporation
59. The State Farms Corporation should be abolished forthwith, and uneconomic farms scrapped and the affairs of the Corporation taken over by independent organizations to be established under competent management. (Interim Report)

60. The tobacco farms and barns of the Corporation should be given to private and cooperative farmers and the State Tobacco Products Corporation on terms to be decided by the Ministry of Agriculture and the Department of Cooperatives of the Ministry of Social Welfare. (Interim Report)

61. Out of 125 farm projects of the Corporation, 47 should be retained and assigned by the Ministry of Agriculture to the following organizations: (i) Oil Palm Corporation to take over 4 major oil palm projects; (ii) Rubber Corporation to take over 9 rubber projects; (iii) Fibre Corporation to take over 10 fibre projects; (iv) Extension Services Division to allocate 3 rice schemes to farmers; (v) Animal Husbandry Division to operate 7 livestock

projects for supplying improved breeds to farmers, and (vi) Cocoa Division to recover its 12 cocoa stations for use as seed gardens and in conducting experiments. (p. 45)

62. The remaining 78 farm projects should be disposed of as follows: 37 of these are to be reallocated to the Divisions of the Ministry of Agriculture; 20 should be given back to the landowners or farmers and the remaining 21 offered for sale (p. 45)

63. Redundant labour of the State Farms Corporation should be given priority consideration in the apportioning of abandoned farms to farmers and when staff for the new corporations are being recruited. Responsibility for the reallocation of the farms to landowners should be entrusted jointly to the respective Chiefs and Administrative Officers in the Regions. (p. 46)

64. On the liquidation of the Corporation, its movable assets, machinery, vehicles, etc., should be offered for sale on hire-purchase terms to the new corporations and to farmers and other organizations who have acquired interests in the abandoned farms. (p. 46)

65. The new corporations should be financed entirely with loans from the Banks on a long-term payment basis at special low interest rates. The Government should not grant any subsidy to support these corporations. (p. 46)

State Tobacco Products Corporation

66. The State Tobacco Products Corporation should be redesignated State Tobacco Marketing Board to reflect its marketing function. It should continue to operate under the direction of its new management. (p. 47)

67. Tobacco farmers should be encouraged to expand the production of tobacco by both the Ministry of Agriculture and the State Tobacco Products Corporation through the provision of extension and direct services. (p. 47)

68. The new barns constructed by the Corporation in the hope of their embarking on tobacco production should be sold to farmers on a long-term payment basis and farmers should be assisted by the Corporation in the curing of the tobacco leaves. The Corporation may, however, continue to operate the old barns taken over from the Pioneer Tobacco Company. (p 47)

State Fishing Corporation

69. The entire organization of the State Fishing Corporation should be overhauled with a view to removing redundant and unqualified employees and replacing them with experienced and qualified administrative technical personnel. (p. 48)

70. The Corporation's fleet of Japanese, Norwegian, British and Russian trawlers should be reduced and its operations limited to those it can efficiently manage, especially the Norwegian vessels; the surplus is to be sold to private fishing concerns preferably Ghanaians. Negotiations

must also be initiated to cancel some of the additional orders of Japanese, British and Yugoslav makes of trawlers.

71. Owners of fishing boats should be encouraged to recruit suitable personnel to replace those who have been repatriated. (Interim Report)

Fish Processing Factories
72. The two fish processing factories being constructed at Tema should be placed under one management and efforts should be made to reduce the cost of operating these factories. (p. 48)

State Boat-Yard Corporation
73. The State Boat-Yard Corporation should be reorganized with a view to removing redundant and unqualified employees and replacing them with experienced and qualified administrative and technical personnel. (p. 48)...

State Fibre Bag Manufacturing Corporation
74. The State Fibre Bag Manufacturing Corporation, in collaboration with the Ministry of Agriculture, should organize the production of urena lobata and kanaf at suitable areas and near sources of water to meet the requirements of the factory. The Irrigation Division of the Ministry of Agriculture should construct dams at suitable sites for retting the crop. (p. 49)

76. Farmers should be encouraged, through guaranteed prices and assured markets and other incentives, to achieve the level of production required by the Corporation. The system of extension work for the production of the fibres should be based on that formerly employed by the Pioneer Tobacco Company for tobacco. (p. 50)

Ghana Food Marketing Corporation
77. The Ghana Food Marketing Corporation should be abolished and its function and assets taken over by marketing cooperatives which should be properly organized and encouraged by the Department of Cooperatives and the Ministry of Agriculture. The marketing cooperatives may engage those of the staff of the Corporation qualified and experienced in food marketing. (p. 50)

Young Farmers' League
78. The Young Farmers' League should be abolished and its assets taken over by the Ministry of Agriculture, and the present members sincerely interested in farming should be encouraged to do so along the following lines:

(i) The farms should be kept by the present settlers who should continue to receive the allowances of 48 pesewas per diem up to the end of January 1968;

(ii) Farm lands should be acquired and allocated to groups of these settlers, farm supplies and services being provided free of charge;
(iii) Proceeds from the farms should be properly accounted for and given back to the settlers at the end of the 1967 cropping season, after which they will farm on their own and pay for all services provided, and
(iv) the Extension Services Division of the Ministry of Agriculture should be responsible for organizing and executing this programme. (p. 51)

79. The whole concept of settling young farmers should be reviewed at the end of 1967 on the basis of the results of these interim proposals. (p. 51)

Sugar Products Corporation
80. Adequate import licences should be made available to the Sugar Products Corporation for the importation of essential materials, such as processing chemicals and spare parts for tractors and vehicles, which would ensure the smooth operation of the project. (p. 52)

81. The manpower wastage resulting from the lack of transport to convey workers from their homes to the fields should be prevented by the provision of more vehicles. A more effective solution to the problem would be to provide living quarters on the site at both Asutsuare and Komenda for the workers. (p. 52)

Agricultural Wing of the Workers Brigade
82. The Workers Brigade should give up farming and undertake feeder road and dam construction. However, those brigaders who sincerely wish to engage in farming should be assisted by the Ministry of Agriculture to settle as private farmers. (Interim Report)

83. In order not to prejudice the report of the Kom Commission which is enquiring into the functions of the Brigade, it is expedient not to make further comments on the redeployment of the brigaders. (p. 53)

State/Private Sector
84. The production enterprises should be allowed to invite foreign or local participation, wherever necessary, either in the form of capital investment or management. (p. 53)

85. Foreign capital contribution to production enterprises should be limited to such sectors and to a percentage which would not permit investors to have undue domination over the country's strategic sectors of the agricultural industry. (p. 53)

Private Sector
86. The individual farmers who contribute the greatest percentage of the country's food production should be encouraged through provision of agricultural services, incentives and advice to improve their farming techniques. (p. 53)

87. A special Development Committee, composed of representatives of the Capital Investment Bank, Ministry of Agriculture and the Agricultural Research Institutes, should be set up to provide technical information to private investors. (p. 54)

Cooperative Sector
88. Private farmers should be helped to organize themselves into politics-free cooperatives with a view to availing themselves of mechanized services, storage facilities and other farm supplies. Marketing cooperatives should particularly be encouraged. (p. 54)
89. The Agricultural Production and Marketing Cooperatives should be reorganized by and function with the assistance of the Department of Cooperatives of the Ministry of Social Welfare. Technical advice and assistance should be given to these cooperatives by the Agricultural Extension Services Division and other agencies of the Ministry of Agriculture (Interim Report).

Document 21: World Bank Recommendations on Stabilization Policy

'Memorandum to the Economic Committee of the National Liberation Council from the World Bank Mission', 6 June 1967.

1. During the last five weeks we have received the 1967/68 development budget requests in the context of Government finance and prospects for the economy. Members of the Mission have consulted the officials of the ministries and agencies dealing with the principal development programmes, and the Mission recommendations have already been discussed with these officials and the budget review committee. The purpose of this memorandum is to report briefly on our recommendations regarding the 1967/68 development budget, and to discuss the financial and economic issues involved in framing budget and economic policy for 1967/68.
2. Budget and economic policy in our view, must be shaped in a manner that is consistent with growth and investment requirements of the consolidation period, balance of payments prospects, the likely outcome of Government finance and public savings policy, and its implications for monetary policy. We should like to elaborate on each of these aspects.
3. The economy in 1966/67 appears to have achieved a fair amount of domestic equilibrium with prices stable or declining. This appears to be the result of a relative decline in Government demand and increased supplies from domestic production and special imports of essential foods and raw materials. There has been, however, an appreciable increase in urban

unemployment, and the balance of payments continues to be under pressure despite relief obtained through external assistance and debt rescheduling. In these circumstances, the Mission supports continuance of Government's stabilization policy with emphasis on public savings, and in regard to development, utilization of existing assets rather than new investment. New investment in exports and agriculture where high returns are demonstrated, is a desirable exception to this consolidation policy, and efforts to shift resource use to maximize the use of labour and minimize the use of imports have obvious merit. This time is also one to initiate actions to prepare new investment projects for implementation when circumstances permit, as well as to build up a pipeline of projects suitable for external finance in order to facilitate financing the balance of payments. The Mission has used these guidelines in evaluating progress made in 1966/67 and to recommend development policy for 1967/68.

... Against estimated 1966/67 recurrent expenditures of N₡212 million, the Mission recommends a ceiling of N₡225 million for 1967/68. This recurrent expenditure ceiling permits a 6% increase in recurrent expenditure which is the maximum consistent with establishing a viable long-term public savings capacity. The mission... concluded that a development budget of N₡75 million would be feasible in terms of sectoral balance, productivity and executive capacity.... In summary:

	N₡ million
Resources	326
External debt service	23
Recurrent expenditure	225
Development expenditure	75
Total Expenditure	323
Unallocated balance	3

5. Balance of payment considerations will continue to be important determinant of the size and composition of Government investment. It will be recalled that we estimated that external public capital inflows of about N₡82 million in 1967 and N₡117 million in 1968 would be required to sustain 1967/68 Government expenditures of N₡285 million (net of external debt) while at the same time permitting a small aggregate increase in private investment, minimal private consumption imports and a large increase in imports of raw materials and spare parts. The analysis of the Bank of Ghana now indicates that the likely capacity to import will fall far short of these estimates. On the one hand, export receipts from cocoa and timber are less than anticipated, and on the other, higher exports to and reduced imports from bilateral countries had reduced import availabilities. Special efforts to use bilateral country imports could partially offset this gap in capacity to import. Furthermore and of particular importance, it

appears that new external financial commitments although impressively large in 1967, will clearly not be as large as originally estimated as required, and it is only prudent to plan on commitment levels in the range of N₵58 to N₵65 million in 1967 and 1968. Assuming external financial commitments of N₵65 million per year, and special efforts to use bilateral imports, the capacity to import might be about N₵230 million (c.i.f.) in 1967 and N₵266 million in 1968.

As these estimated import levels are clearly below the originally estimated requirements (by N₵58 million in 1967 and N₵44 million in 1968), the question arises as to where imports and the concommitant private and public investment and consumption are to be reduced, or to what extent a structural shift away from import use could be effected. In regard to the latter, our review of the development programme revealed that at present relative prices, it is cheaper to use machines than labour in construction, and cheaper to use imported cement and steel than domestic wood and tile. Indeed the effects of these relative prices combined with pressure on Government savings, have largely frustrated the attempt to shift to labour intensive methods in Government development. Administrative directions could induce such a shift, but the higher Cedi cost of construction given Government finances, would require a proportionate reduction elsewhere in the recurrent or development budgets....

9. ... The Mission suggests that the budget review attempt more of the shift from imports than reductions in Cedi allocations, and further suggests the following guidelines:

(i) All staff housing, dormitories and office blocks be deferred except where commitments have been made to external aid agencies or compelling need can be demonstrated;

(ii) The building and house construction that goes forward be given to the most labour intensive tender allowing in the budget for the extra Cedi cost;

(iii) Acquisition of new vehicles and machinery be ruthlessly restricted;

(iv) Programmes with high import content but no foreign aid prospects (health, defence, foreign affairs) be restricted to essential ongoing schemes;

(v) Programmes with high import content but with good foreign aid prospects, to not go ahead unless commodity or project aid is in hand (Railways, Ports, State Transport, P & T, Civil Aviation, Electricity);

(vi) and on the recurrent side, to restrict transport, office equipment and uniforms to the barest minimums except for priority areas of agriculture, industry, road maintenance and health....

11. ... Successful adherence to these budget guidelines will permit a reduction in taxes or increase in the cocoa producer price. The Mission attaches first priority to increasing incentives for exports and confirming a

positive environment for private investment. We, therefore, suggest substantial reduction in diamond marketing fees and mining royalties; elimination of marketing fees and export duties on timber; reduction in other mining royalties; elimination of all export duties except on agricultural products; and elimination of the surcharge on company taxes earned in the future and remitted abroad. We estimate that a 60% reduction in timber and mining royalties, elimination of export duties on these commodities and the company tax surcharge would involve about N₵4 million of revenue. This would still leave a surplus of N₵4 million after Government expenditure.

13. Implementation of this type of budget and fiscal policy would, in our judgement, not require special monetary adjustments to compensate for Cedi counterpart funds provided private credit is expanded consistent with the import programme and private investment.

15. The essential features of the Mission's recommendations on the 1967/68 Development Budget are:

(i) The Mission programme of N₵75 million net of debt service compares with the 1966/67 development budget of N₵76 million on the same basis. It is estimated that 1966/67 actual expenditures will be of the order of N₵60 to 65 million whereas the 1967/68 actual after shortfall might be about N₵70 million. The 1967/68 programme in terms of real work put in place will be marginally higher by about 8%.

(ii) The sectoral balance shows a continued improvement. The economic sectors is N₵80.7 million (including debt) in 1967/68 compared to N₵61 million in 1966/67. The social and to a lesser extent, administrative sectors show a proportionate decline. Although this comparison is distorted by annual changes in external debt service and allocation of contingency programmes, the direction of the change is clear.

(iii) The 1967/68 sector allocations features holding administrative and social sector programmes to ongoing projects except for health (0.5 million) and low cost labour intensive housing (N₵4.3 million). Selective expansions characterize the economic sectors....

(v) Agriculture features continued closure of State Farms and Young Farmers' League Farms; substantial reductions in farm settlements and mechanization; and expansion of extension and farm supply services, credit, tree crops, pilot irrigation, and new crop programmes (cotton). Industry shows an expansion only in respect of loan and equity contributions to National Investment Bank; the emphasis on remedial actions and creation of joint ventures continues. Mining allows for a new diamond dredging programme, and remedial efforts for the State Gold Mines.

(vi) Transport and communication features continuing projects plus

a few new projects if foreign aid is obtained, e.g. railways rehabilitation and signalling; tugs and ferries; telephone maintenance; and vehicle replacement for State transport. Electricity plans are a major expansion of distribution.
(vii) Education features no expansion at primary and secondary levels; completion of only ongoing University and research projects; and a small expansion of technical education. Water can expand urban distribution schemes if foreign aid is obtained, but health has only a marginal expansion. Only low cost housing schemes of a labour intensive type will go forward.
(viii) All other programmes are reduced to ongoing programmes.
(ix) The Mission recommendations differed most markedly from Ministry requests in respect of agriculture and education, and implicitly by reducing administrative and other social sector programmes to ongoing projects.

Part III: Economic Relations with the East

Introductory Note

Document 22 discusses the complications introduced by the expulsion, in March 1966, of personnel from the Socialist countries engaged on public sector projects. The fate of some of the projects mentioned here has already been analysed in the Introduction. One curious incident resulting from the expulsion of Soviet personnel was the attempt to get UAC to recruit crews for the Soviet fishing vessels (Document 23).

The next three papers (24–26) reopen the controversy about the bilateral trade and payments agreements with the socialist countries. The evidence presented here challenges the dogmatic view that the agreements were necessarily detrimental to the interests of Ghana. The large debit balances accumulated by Ghana under the agreements would on the contrary tend to support the assertions of Finance Minister Amoako Atta (see Document 3). It is true, however, that the revival of the cocoa market after the coup (to £218 per ton in July 1966) had tended to make the fixed price of £172 per ton negotiated by Amoako-Atta in November 1965 (when the price had fallen to about only £147 per ton) for Soviet deliveries less attractive.[1] Under these circumstances the new Ghana Government did not hesitate to divert stocks from the Soviet deliveries to Western markets.

The last document (27) incorporates the report of a trade and economic mission to Yugoslavia and the USSR, in March 1967, to negotiate the rescheduling of Ghana's debts and new Trade and Payments Agreements. This was the first formal contact between representatives of these governments after the expulsion of socialist personnel from Ghana in March 1966. It should be noted that no similar renegotiation of Ghana's debts was undertaken with the GDR, China and Hungary; the NLC unilaterally rescheduled these in accordance with the terms of the Soviet rescheduling.

Document 22: Fate of Soviet and Eastern Projects
Memorandum to National Economic Committee by Secretary to CECEC (Committee for Economic Cooperation with Eastern Countries), 10 March 1966.

Members are aware by now that according to an order from the National Liberation Council through the Ministry of Foreign Affairs, all Chinese and Soviet Experts have had to leave Ghana. 9 March 1966 was the date line and one could presume that all those affected have left. The GDR Mission, although only a Trade Mission, has also been ordered to pack up.

There may be good reasons for the Ministry of Foreign Affairs' action, but I submit that in the interests of the country, the National Economic Council considers appealing to the National Liberation Council to consider allowing some handful of experts to stay on and help to finish some of the projects started by them.

The Chinese Government signed in 1962 and 1964, two Economic and Technical Aid agreements in which they offered Ghana an interest free suppliers' credit of £15 millions or ₡36,000,000. The agreements to provide for utilization of the credit from 1961–71, and repayments to start from 1971–81. In other words, the credit was for 20 years. In a subsequent Protocol the Chinese Government agreed to pre-finance the Civil works of the projects by converting part of the loan as Counterpart funds. That is part of the loan was converted into consumer goods and the proceeds of which, when sold used in meeting local expenses. The Protocol covering this Counterpart fund made provision for a yearly ceiling of up to £2 millions. Under this Economic Agreement the Chinese offered to build a Textile factory at Juapong in the Volta Region and a Pencil factory in Kumasi. Civil works of both projects started in September last year and progress has been very satisfactory. In Juapong, one could assess civil works as 50% of expected works completed, and about 20% of those in Kumasi. As regards supply of machinery in both places, 70% of materials have already arrived in Juapong and about 40% in Kumasi. The schedule of works showed that both projects would have been completed before the year was out. The total cost of the two projects is ₡5.6 million, and since more than 50% of this is in the form of structures or materials and equipment on the site it would be uneconomical to abandon them. It might be advisable either to invite some other Textile experts from any other country... who can interpret the technological [sic] documents to help in the installation of the machines, or appeal to the same Chinese to send down some limited number of experts to complete the works. The Civil works of the Juapong mill which were being done by the Chinese themselves can be given to any local contractor to complete. The works in Kumasi were being done by Ghana National Construction Corporation. I would like to stress that, if action is not taken almost immediately in the handling of machinery and equipment exposed to the elements on the site, damage to Government property would be considerable. Ghana is now faced with the problem of meeting local expenses connected with these works; it will therefore be necessary to look for funds from somewhere to meet the local expenses. There were, before works came to a halt, as many as 620 Ghanaian workers at Juapong and 100 in Kumasi. These workers were paid by the Chinese from the special Counterpart funds referred to above.

As I have indicated earlier on, not all the machinery and equipment are in and it may be necessary to appeal to the Chinese to send in whatever is left, in order to get a complete mill, or threaten not to honour our obligations under this agreement should they refuse to send in what will constitute a complete factory. This refers particularly to the knitwear machinery, 50% of which has been delivered.

The Textile factory is to be an integrated one, and under the circumstances one could suggest that the State Farms could be asked to take on the farming side. The two projects are both economically viable and every effort should be made to get them completed.

USSR

The Soviet Union, like the Chinese Government, offered Ghana in two Economic Agreements signed in 1960 and 1961 a total suppliers' credit of ₡10,476,190,00. Out of this an amount of ₡19,064,400 was converted into Counterpart Funds.

The credit as a whole is payable in 12 years at an annual interest rate of 2.5%. The Counterpart funds are on the same rate of interest, but payable in 8 years. Repayments according to the agreements should start a year after completion of projects or services.

Under the agreements the Soviets are building the following projects:

(a) *Reinforced Concrete Panel:* This has been completed, at a cost of ₡2.3 million, in machinery and equipment and ₡1.5 million in civil works. The factory now needs working capital to start operations. Unfortunately no capital has as yet been provided and so the factory is standing idle. The first projects to use the products of the factory are the two proposed residential areas in Accra and Tema which together will cost anything up to ₡36,000,000. These could be built in stages and might take at least 6 years to complete. If the factory is to be useful, then provision must be made for it to start producing the panels for the Ministry of Housing. The cost of houses alone might be in the neighbourhood of ₡13 million.

(b) *The Gold Refinery:* The total cost of the project is just over half a million pounds. About 85% of the works are completed, and according to the schedule of works the factory should be completed by June this year. The plant is a *specialized* one and since the machinery is all Russian, it will be advisable to allow at most 3 top technicians to remain and help with the installation of the technological [sic] equipment. The Civil Works which are more than 88% complete, are being undertaken by A. Lang. Here again, not all the machinery is in, and the Russians are being asked to supply whatever is left with them.

(c) *The Fishing Complex:* which, when finished will cost £1.3 million in machinery and equipment and almost ₵1 million in Civil works, is just about half way through. Almost 20% of the machinery and equipment are on the site, and one could assess the civil works as 45% of estimated works. Here again Ghana stands to lose, if we should abandon it or look to other sources for completion.

(d) *The State Farms:* can go on I suppose without the Russians.

(e) *Geological Survey:* Although the Director of Geological Survey believes there are some specialized assignments which can be undertaken by the Soviet experts, I feel Ghana can get experts of similar calibre from other countries to satisfy the Director.

(f) *Training Centres:* Two Training Centres are being built by the Soviets in Tema and Accra. In Tema progress has been satisfactory and almost 50% of works have been completed. About 90% of the equipment has arrived. Ministry of Education, I am sure, can go ahead without the Russians.

(g) I have nothing on record for the Atomic Reactor and the Tamale Air field.

German Democratic Republic
The German Democratic Republic offered Ghana, in an Economic Agreement signed in July 1966 a supply credit of ₵17,280,000. The credit goes with an interest rate of 2.5% and repayment is to be spread over a period of 12 years starting 6 months from the date when the agreed efficiency of the plant will be proved. Under this agreement the GDR won a tender for a Pulp and Paper Mill which will cost C10,511,694 to build. This GDR will build on a 'Turn-key' basis. Although under the contract Ghana is due to pay 5% of the total contract cost (i.e. ₵525,585), no payment has been made yet. The Mill was to use as raw material Bagasse from the Sugar Factories, and at a later stage, Rice straw from the State Farms. The project is very viable economically, and if Ghana can only afford it, one feels that there is every justification in going in for it.

The GDR has already built for Ghana a Printing Press at Tema at a cost of ₵1,992,897.60. This was finished in 1963. The credit element in the cost of machinery and equipment is ₵1,395,028.32 and is repayable in 5 years. At the moment there are 3 GDR technicians working with the Printing Press on a Ghana/GDR Technical Assistance programme and it might be advisable to continue with their services until Ghanaians are sufficiently trained to take over.

I may mention that the agreements signed with the GDR do not in any way recognize GDR politically, and therefore there is no harm in allowing them to continue.

Although other socialist countries were not affected by the order, I submit that it might be useful to review some of the existing contracts.

I may refer to

(1) UGFCC contracts for the assembling of tractors from Yugoslavia and Czechoslovakia.
(2) The Hungarian Incandescent [sic] Lamps Contract, for which a down payment of ₵73,920.00 has already been made. This particular contract was signed on the 21/6/61, and has since been shelved.

I therefore appeal to the National Economic Committee to consider appealing in turn to the National Liberation Council to consider asking the Governments involved to send over some experts to finish the following projects started by them:

(a) Chinese – (1) Textile Factory at Juapong
             (2) Pencil Factory at Kumasi; and
(b) USSR   Gold Refinery and Fishing Complex.

I also suggest that a Committee be formed to consider the best use [to which] the products of the Prefabricated Panel can be put.

Document 23: Recruitment of Crew for Russian Boats
R. S. Amegashie, member of NEC, to A. R. Wood, Chairman, UAC of Ghana Limited, 12 April 1966

A few days ago I called on you and Mr Anderson who was then here from your London Office and asked if you could get some technical personnel from your organization to look at the Russian boats, property of the State Fishing Corporation, which are now tied up at Tema, with a view to advising the Economic Committee of the NLC on the recommissioning of these vessels as soon as possible. My request was followed up by the submission to you of drawings and specifications in connection with these vessels by Mr J N Adjetey, Chief Fisheries Officer.

I am anxious to know what progress has been made on my request. Please let me know when I may expect an answer to this request.

J. M. Tiddy, UAC of Ghana Limited, to Amegashie, 13 April 1966:

Mr Wood has asked me to reply to your letter of the 12th April concerning the provision of technical personnel to survey and man the Russian trawlers, the property of the State Fishing Corporation. On the 31st March I contacted Mr J. N. Adjetey, Chief Fisheries Officer, and gave him the following message over the telephone.

1. UAC would be unable to undertake the recruitment of 70 personnel as the Company has no experience in this field of operation.
2. The Ministry of Overseas Development have been contacted who advise that the Crown Agents should be approached.
3. Mr L. H. V. Piarcey of the Crown Agents in charge of Appointments Department has expressed willingness to undertake necessary recruitment.
4. If this suggestion is acceptable to the Ghana Government an approach should be made to Mr Piarcey direct.
5. Understand standard fees for this service are £25 per vacancy with maximum of £100 if several recruits required for same job: in addition $7\frac{1}{2}\%$ of first year's salary of anyone actually appointed.
6. Crown Agents will undertake all advertising, interviewing, medical examination and drawing up of contracts, etc.
7. A possibility that Unilever might be able to provide an expert to survey trawlers, such an expert might be of a West German origin.

I am sorry that you have not received this information earlier, at the same time I am surprised that Mr Adjetey has not informed you that the information was passed to him on the 31st March.

Document 24: Bilateral Trade and Payments Agreements Recommendations

'Renewal of the Bilateral Trade with Socialist Countries of Eastern Europe, USSR and China': Memorandum from the Ministry of Trade to the National Economic Committee (n.d.).

All of the Bilateral Trade Agreements signed between Ghana and the Socialist countries of Eastern Europe, USSR and China are due for automatic renewal this year unless notices to terminate them are given three months before their expiry and in the case of the agreement with the USSR, six months prior to the expiry of the Agreement. Each Agreement has been in force for almost five years. A schedule giving details of the date of signatures is attached.

2. The IMF has recommended the review of all bilateral trade and

payments agreements with a view to removing their harmful effects on the economy. In the main, the continued operation of these agreements will not be in the interest of Ghana and it is proposed that consideration should be given to the renewal of these agreements for a further period of one year only, during which time arrangements could be made to settle our debts with these countries on the clearing accounts both by an exchange of goods and by currency.

3. It is proposed, however, that during the current year, a definite move should be made to reduce substantially our imports from these sources. It is further proposed that the monopoly position given to these countries in the supply of crude oil and cement should be discontinued in order to avoid any undue reliance on them.

Document 25: Bilateral Trade and Payments Agreements Recommendations

'Report of the Committee Appointed to Review Ghana's Bilateral Payments Agreements', 23 June 1966.

In response to the request of the Economic Committee of the National Liberation Council, reference letter No. SCR/EC/32 of 4 May 1966, the Committee appointed to review the Bilateral Trade Agreement resumed sitting and considered the Bilateral Payments Agreements with Communist China and the Eastern European Countries including the USSR.

During the examination of the Agreements the Committee noted the following features which either (a) did not serve the best interest of the country or (b) were potential sources of misinterpretation and of difficulty in implementation. The Model Agreement attached hereto* sets out to eliminate such undesirable features of the Agreements.

1. **Language Difficulties**
   The Committee observed that the existing Payments Agreements, like the Trade Agreements, are liberal translations from their original non-English expressions which could easily lead to difficulty and confusion in interpretation.

2. **Diplomatic Service**
   Under the existing Bilateral Payments Agreements, Diplomatic Missions resident in each other's country could be financed through the Cedi Clearing Accounts established under the respective Agreements.

*Omitted—*Editor*

Whilst the Diplomatic Missions representing the Trade-pact Countries in Ghana are financed in accordance with the provisions of the Payments Agreements, Ghana's Diplomatic Missions in the respective countries are financed mainly from convertible currency sources. It is estimated that about 60% of the total expenditure on Ghana's Missions in the Trade-pact countries is in convertible currency.

The reason for this is found in the trade pattern existing in the Trade-pact Countries. There are diplomatic, as distinct from ordinary, shops in these countries. The diplomatic shops sell imported goods which can be purchased only with convertible currency while the ordinary shops sell locally produced goods which can be purchased with the respective local currency. Ghana's Missions in these countries could therefore use funds transferred to them through the Cedi Clearing Accounts to purchase such locally produced goods.

The requirements of Ghana's Missions in these countries are to a large extent, however, obtainable from the diplomatic shops and therefore the Missions require convertible currency funds.

The pattern of trade in Ghana which does not make distinction between shops selling imported goods and those selling locally produced goods allows the Diplomatic Missions of the Trade-pact Countries in Ghana to finance their operations in Ghana, including purchases of goods from the Cedi Clearing Account. Since the shops in Ghana sell goods imported, to a very large extent, from convertible currency countries it is considered that the existing practice is not in the best interest of Ghana. The Model Agreement therefore seeks to introduce a system of financing the Diplomatic Missions in each other's country from convertible currency sources.

3. Currency of Account

In its review of the Trade Agreements the Committee noted that some Trade-pact Countries had, unofficially, expressed the wish to the Chairman of the Committee to pay for all their purchases from Ghana in convertible currency.

It is now considered, however, that it would not be in the best interest of Ghana to pursue this suggestion at this stage. Ghana's net position under all the Payments Agreements together is a debit balance of nearly ₵27.6 million as at 31 May 1966. Ghana's debtor position has developed over the period since 1963. In addition to this trade balance Ghana, as at the same date, owed a total of about ₵46.6 million under the Long-term Credit Agreements. Repayment of long-term liabilities is made through the clearing account.

The Appendices A and B show the positions of the clearing and of the Long-term Credit Accounts respectively, as at 31 May 1966.

In view of this sizable debit balance against Ghana and also of Ghana's present balance of payments difficulties the Committee does not consider it advisable that the wish expressed unofficially by some of the Trade-pact Countries, as indicated above, should be pursued at this stage.

Recommendations

In conclusion, the Committee wishes to submit the following specific and general recommendations for consideration:

(1) The draft Payments Agreement which is attached is recommended for adoption as a model for negotiating the Payments Agreements with all the Trade-pact Countries.

The Payments Agreement in each case should cover the same operational period as the respective Trade Agreement i.e. the Payment and the Trade Agreements should be operative from, and expire on, the same respective dates.

(2) The existing arrangement regarding operations through the Cedi Clearing Accounts should be maintained *except* that financing of Diplomatic Missions should be made from convertible currency sources. In effect the Diplomatic Missions in each other's country should operate convertible currency accounts.

(3) As in the case of the Trade Agreements all the Payments Agreements should be renewed on a yearly basis. Notice of intention to terminate or review the Agreement should be given at least three months before the date of expiry of the Agreement.

(4) In view of Ghana's net debtor position under the Agreements and also of the increasing volume of trade developing under the Trade Agreements in the past two years it is recommended that Ghana negotiates for increased levels of swing limits as the existing limits have all nearly been drawn on fully by Ghana.

Table 25.1

APPENDIX 'A'
Clearing Account Balance as at
31 May 1966

Swing Credit Limit, ₡	Country	Cr. ₡ Owed to Ghana	Cr. ₡ Owed by Ghana	Over Swing Credit
72,000	State Bank of Albania	38,805		
1,200,000	Bulgaria Foreign Trade Bank	—	1,295,865	95,865
1,200,000	Statni Banka Ceskosloveska	—	5,273,743	4,073,743
9,600,000	China A/c. 1962/63	854	—	—
	China A/c. 1963/64	—	870,740	—
	China A/c. 1964/65	—	2,318,009	—

continued

Swing Credit Limit, ₵	Country	Cr. ₵ Owed to Ghana	Cr. ₵ Owed by Ghana	Over Swing Credit
	China A/C. 1965/66	—	2,508,795	—
1,800,000	Deutsche Notenbank	—	2,724,061	994,061
	Egypt Account	1,106,374	—	—
1,200,000	Guinea Account	134,977	—	—
600,000	Banco Nunez Havana	133,077	—	—
1,920,000	Hungary Account	414,266	—	—
480,000	Israel	—	1,763,781	1,283,781
856,000	Banque de La Republique du Mali	—	4,028,337	3,172,337
1,200,000	Polish Account	—	3,687,540	2,487,540
360,000	State Bank of Roumanian People's Republic	—	617,456	257,456
1,200,000	Upper Volta	—	—	—
24,000,000	Bank of Foreign Trade of the USSR	—	2,937,465	—
840,000	Yugoslavia Account	—	569,392	—
1,200,000	Dahomey Account	—	—	—
	China Local Account	—	755,759	—
		1,828,353	29,350,943	12,364,783

		29,420,943
Balance	₵	27,592,590
	£	11,496,913

Table 25.2

APPENDIX 'B'

Ghana's Indebtedness on the Long-term Credit Accounts with the Trade-pact Countries at 31 May 1966

USSR	29,161,024
Czechoslovakia	9,790,390
Yugoslavia	1,874,000
Hungary	1,452,903
Poland	3,925,762
China	112,374
Bulgaria	291,604
	₵46,608,057

Document 26: Bilateral Trade and Payments Agreements Recommendations

'Bilateral Payments Agreements': S. Ohene-Nyako, Executive Director, Bank of Ghana, to the Secretary, NEC, 25 August 1966.

With reference to your letter No. NEC. 19 dated 4 July 1966 in connection with the report on the above-mentioned subject we comment as follows:

Diplomatic Service
(i) Ghana's Missions in the Trade Pact Countries spend about ₵9.6 million annually, 60% of which is said to be in convertible currency. It seems, however, that the Missions of the Trade Pact Countries do not spend as much per mission on purchases in Ghana. Their main items of expenditure include rent and local fruits and vegetables which may not amount to much.

Further, the 60% spent by Ghana's Missions in convertible currency, is on goods from outside the countries in which these missions are located. In fact, it is spent on purchases from 'Diplomatic Warehouses', there is therefore no question of the countries in which the Missions are located benefiting, there might of course be occasional purchases from local 'diplomatic shops' but it is our experience that this is not the usual practice.

Since all diplomats can and do know that with convertible currency they can buy at diplomatic prices which do not include taxes, from 'Diplomatic Warehouses', it seems to us, therefore, that members of missions would, if they have to make local purchases in convertible currency, prefer to import directly their requirements and the number of special Unnumbered Licences issued in favour of these Missions seem to bear this out. *It thus seems to us that not much will be gained by implementing the suggestion that the Missions of our Trade Pact Countries be made to pay for their local expenditures in convertible currency.* In fact, the method by which convertible currency funds are transferred to our Missions has been the cause of a substantial loss. Although the convertible currency funds sent to the Missions are not mainly used for local purchases, exchange costs and transfer charges arise as a result of the transfers in and out of these countries. These receipts of course, accrue to the countries concerned but we can avoid such payments by issuing Ghana's Missions with Sterling Cheques and by holding all their convertible currency funds in London. This will save us some of these unnecessary payments.

In addition, we have technicians from these countries working in Ghana and paid by the Ghana Government. Their earnings are currently paid partly in local currency and partly in the currencies of their home countries through the Clearing Accounts; the prospect of these countries requesting that their technicians working in Ghana be paid partly in Local currency and partly in convertible currency should not be lost sight of (Ref. USSR reaction to NLC request to reduce the size of their diplomatic mission), i.e.

anything affecting their diplomats equally affects their technicians and Ghana will be the looser.

(ii) Nothing has been said in the Report about Ghana's Economic Cooperation Agreements with these countries. According to these Agreements, amounts due on projects are credited to a 'Special Account' attracting interest at the rate of 2½% per annum. Balances on such accounts are utilized in the purchase of goods from Ghana and until they are so utilized earn interest.

Currently, Ghana's position with regard to the Clearing Accounts is anything but satisfactory but perhaps it would be desirable to try to negotiate, for future purposes, for any excesses over the swing in favour of one trading partner to be set off against what is owed another on the 'Special Account'. Should the trend turn in Ghana's favour, this would save us the payment of interest on the balances that would otherwise be standing against us. In our present circumstances the acceptance of this suggestion will have no adverse effects on Ghana since there are no special Accounts in favour of Ghana.

Swing Limits

(iii) As a result of negotiations completed by the Amoako-Atta* [Finance Minister under Nkrumah] delegation to some of the Trade Pact countries in December 1965, the following arrangements were concluded *even though they have to date not been ratified by either side:*

(a) The USSR Government agreed to a moratorium of 1 year after completion or 2 years after final delivery, and in addition a repayment of 50% of all matured bills during 1967–1970.

(b) The German Democratic Republic Government accepted a moratorium of 2 years after the completion of projects and increased the swing limit from ₵1.2 million to ₵1,800,000.

(c) The Czechoslovakia Government accepted a moratorium of 2 years after final delivery. This covers instalment repayments whose maturity dates were to be fixed after the date of the protocol of 31/12/65. An increase from ₵600,000 to ₵1,200,000 in the Swing Limit Agreement was also agreed to.

(d) The Hungarian Government accepted the proposal that repayments should start 24 months after final delivery, and agreed to the proposal that all instalment payments due in the years 1966–1967 should start 2 years from their due dates. They have also agreed to an increase in the swing limit from ₵480,000 to ₵1,440,000.

(e) The Polish Government agreed to a moratorium of 2 years after final delivery or 1 year after completion of project and to an increase in the swing limit from ₵.2 million to ₵2.4 million.

*See Document.

(f) The UAR Government also agreed to an increase in the swing limit from ₵360,000 to ₵1,200,000.

Ghana's Association with CMEA
(iv) The above delegation also took the opportunity to inform the USSR Government of Ghana's intention in the near future to seek association with the International Bank for Economic Cooperation which operates a multilateral clearing system among the socialist countries and to seek the support of the Soviet Union for Ghana's application when it is submitted. The Soviet Union promised to support Ghana's application when it is submitted.

The Bank for International Cooperation has since 1 January 1964 been operating from Moscow. It provides for multilateral clearing in respect of all trade and service payments between the bilateral trading partners who are members. Each member-country has an account with this Bank into which amounts due from the others are paid and from which all obligations, that is, trade, services and credit payments are met.

Instead of eight different varieties of non-transferable clearing roubles, the new system has introduced transferable roubles as clearing currency for the payment of liabilities of member countries.

The Bank may, subject to the consent of its members, extend clearing in transferable roubles to dealings with other countries. This applies both to the Socialist countries which are not members of CMEA and to non-Socialist developing or other countries. Yugoslavia and China are not members of this Bank.

The Bank also grants credit to finance trade between member-countries, such credits are granted in the first place with a view to ensuring the execution of settlements in due time, and also with a view to stimulating the expansion of member-countries' trade. Interest payable on such transactions does not exceed 2 per cent per annum. On funds held on current account or on deposit, the bank pays from 0.25 per cent to 1.5 per cent interest per annum.

We hope the above points might be useful in coming to a decision on the Bilateral Payments Agreements.

Document 27: Report of Ghanaian Delegation to USSR and Yugoslavia:

E.N. Omaboe, 'Report of the Trade and Economic Mission to Yugoslavia and the USSR,' 31 March 1967.

The National Liberation Council at its meeting on 7 February 1967, approved that a Trade and Economic delegation under the leadership of Mr E.N. Omaboe, Chairman of the Economic Committee of the National Liberation Council should visit Yugoslavia and the USSR to discuss trade and economic matters with the governments of Yugoslavia and the USSR.

Terms of Reference

The delegation were to discuss the following matters:

(a) *Yugoslavia*
  (i) The re-scheduling of debts under suppliers' credit.
  (ii) The negotiation of a new Trade and Payments Agreement and the Protocol for the exchange of goods and services for the current year.
  (iii) All other outstanding economic matters, especially the issues raised by the Yugoslav Government on the Tractor Assembly Plant.

(b) *USSR*
  (i) The re-scheduling of debts under suppliers' credit.
  (ii) The negotiation and conclusion of a new Trade and Payments Agreements and the Protocol for the exchange of goods and services for the current year.
  (iii) All other outstanding economic matters, especially:
    the Fish Processing Plant in Tema;
    the Gold Refinery;
    the Atomic Reactor;
    the Reinforced Concrete Panel Factory; and
    the Training Centre.

Accomplishments

A. Yugoslavia

Negotiations started on 11 March 1967...
 At the first Plenary meeting, definitions on general principles were arrived at. Two Committees were appointed.

The IMF and Ghana

Committee I to deal with the Trade and Payments Agreement and the Trade Protocol

and

Committee II to deal with the re-scheduling of debts.

Technical co-operation was discussed at the Plenary Session.

With regard to the Tractor Assembly Factories, it was decided that arrangements be made for the Ghana delegation to meet representatives of the Agencies concerned to discuss the problems. These agencies are:

Agrovojvodina
Bratstvo
Rudnap (Import and Export)
14 Oktober.

Trade and Payments Agreements and Trade Protocols
Full agreement was reached on all matters connected with the Trade and Payments Agreements and the Protocol for the exchange of goods for 1967.

The draft Trade Agreement prepared by Ghana was accepted as the basis for the new agreement subject to slight amendments by the Yugoslav side and the shortening of the duration from 5 years to one year, with provision for automatic renewal annually, unless 90 days' notice of termination is given by either side.

The Yugoslav side insisted on having balanced trade between the two countries. Lists 'A' and 'B' were therefore prepared, the level of each being fixed at N₵10,000,000 or £5 million.

As members of the GATT, it was found inadvisable to conclude a new Payments Agreement. It was therefore decided to amend the 1961 Agreement to meet the demands of Ghana. The Swing Credit was also raised to ₵2 million...

Re-scheduling of Debts
The economic difficulties facing Ghana were very clearly explained to the Yugoslav authorities, with a request that even though the Yugoslav Government did not find it convenient to send representatives to the London meeting of Ghana's creditors,* the Ghana delegation would wish to negotiate the deferment of the debts on similar bases as those agreed at the London meeting, the terms to be finally agreed upon to be as favourable, if not more favourable than those agreed upon in London.

After a very long discussion of the issues involved, the following agreement was reached:

(a) the re-scheduling was to cover all debts including loans with

---

*See Document 51

maturity exceeding one year but not exceeding twelve years and for supply of goods and services from Yugoslavia concluded before 24 February 1966.
(b) Payment of the debt was due or will fall due between 1 June 1966 and 31 December 1968.

It was agreed that in respect of each debt due or falling due on or before 30 June 1967 an amount equal to 20% of that debt in two equal instalments shall be transferred to the Yugoslav Government on 1 July 1967 and on 31 December 1967.

In respect of each debt falling due between 1 July 1967 and 31 December 1968, an amount equal to 20% of that debt shall be transferred to the Yugoslav Government on maturity.

In respect of the outstanding balance of 80% of the debt, there shall be transfer payments in sixteen equal half-yearly instalments commencing from 1 July 1971, i.e. there is a moratorium of two-and-a-half years.

Interest at the rate of 3% on the outstanding deferred debts will be raised. It will be recalled that at the London meeting, it was agreed, after very hard bargaining, that interest would be charged at rates of Government borrowing and this has turned out to be more than 6% for the United Kingdom. This therefore makes the Yugoslav Agreement on debt deferment more favourable than what the creditor countries of the West offered at the London meeting.

These terms were embodied in an agreement which was signed on 15 March 1967.

Tractor Assembly Plants

The United Ghana Farmers' Cooperatives Council had contracted with firms in Yugoslavia for the supply of tractors and the construction of two tractor assembly plants in Kumasi.

After the Revolution, the Government rightly decided not to proceed with further deliveries of tractors and the construction of the tractor assembly factories. The Yugoslav companies involved are:

Messrs Agrovojvodina
Messrs Bratstvo
Messrs Rudnap (Import and Export)
Messrs 14 Oktober.

Messrs Rudnap and 14 Oktober had raised a claim for compensation amounting to ₵650,000 payable in two instalments of 50% (₵325,000) not later than 30 June 1967 and 50% (₵325,000) not later than 30 November 1967, providing also for payment of an interest of 9% in case of delay of payment. These claims had been considered in Accra by the representatives of the Ministry of Agriculture and the Attorney-General's Office. According to our legal experts, there is a basis for these claims, since in some cases the Yugoslav firms had gone to great expense to meet the terms of the contract.

The Yugoslav side explained that they had incurred expenditure in the stocking of certain specific items for the Ghana orders like Perkins Engines, Clutches, etc., which could not be used other than for the production of tractors in fulfilment of the Ghana order which had been cancelled. There was therefore the need to reimburse them for the losses.

The Ghana delegation however, maintained that there was over-supply of tractors which were not in service and the first thing to do was to put these into service and to provide essential facilities for their effective use. It was only when this had been done that the needs of the country for more tractors could be more correctly assessed.

The Ghana delegation therefore put forward a proposal for the establishment of a Joint Venture between the Ghana Government and all the various Yugoslav companies.

    (a)   to provide for the servicing of the tractors in Ghana
    (b)   later, for the assembly of tractors in Ghana
and
    (c)   for the manufacture of miscellaneous agricultural tools and implements.

If this were done, the size of the compensation now being asked for would have to be reviewed.

This proposal was agreed in principle by all parties and it was decided that a joint meeting be held in Accra during the second part of April to work out the details of the Joint Venture and to consider the claim for damages, if any...

B. USSR

Trade Matters

In the *aide-mémoire* which was sent to the Soviet Government before the departure of the delegation, it was intimated that the Ghana delegation would discuss, *inter alia*, the negotiation of a new Trade and Payments Agreement and the Protocol for the exchange of goods and services for the current year. In sending this *aide-mémoire*, the delegation was aware of the rigid stand taken by the Soviet Government to the effect that because the Ghana Government was late by about three weeks in giving the 90 days' notice stipulated in the Trade Agreement of 1961, that Agreement was automatically renewed for a further period of five years. The Soviet delegation maintained this stand at the negotiations and insisted on concluding only a Trade Protocol for the exchange of goods for 1967, based on the 1961 Trade Agreement.

The Ghana delegation was therefore obliged to accept this course, more especially as the basic difference between the 1961 and the revised draft was in respect of a 'non-resale' clause which had been adequately provided for in the 1967 Protocol.

A Trade Protocol was therefore prepared and signed on 24 March 1967 providing for the exchange of Soviet goods worth ₡14½ million and Ghanaian goods worth about ₡28 million, 20% of the latter to be paid for in convertible currency.

An interesting issue arose during discussions on List 'B', i.e. goods to be exported from the Republic of Ghana to the USSR. In this, the Soviet Union were asking for 80,000 tons of Cocoa beans and 1,000 tons of Cocoa butter. In this connection, it will be recalled that when a Ghana delegation led by Mr Kwesi Amoako-Atta, ex-Minister of Finance visited the Soviet Union in November 1965, they contracted to sell 150,000 tons of cocoa to the Soviet Government at a fixed price of £172 per ton that was at the time when cocoa prices were rather low. They further contracted to deliver 70,000 tons from the 1965/66 main crop and 80,000 tons from the 1966/67 main crop. Deliveries of the first 70,000 tons were completed only last February.

As 1967 happens to be the 50th Anniversary of the Russian Revolution and, as promises appeared to have been given to Soviet children for the supply of chocolates during the celebrations, the Soviet delegation insisted on a schedule of deliveries of 50,000 tons by 1 September 1967 and the balance of 30,000 tons between October and December 1967.

The Ghana delegation were hard put to it to explain that this could only be supplied from stocks which were very low and the mid crop, the size of which was between 15,000 tons to 20,000 tons only, and the whole of the 80,000 tons could be supplied by 31 December 1967, since the main crop for which we hoped to get sufficient supplies started from the middle of October. Eventually, the delegation had to give a guarantee by way of exchange of letters that the Ghana Government would inform the Soviet Government through their Trade Representative in Accra of the quantity that could be delivered before 1 September 1967.

Although the Ghana delegation fully appreciated the circumstances in which the Amoako-Atta delegation entered into the contract on behalf of the Ghana Government and also the subsequent circumstance of short supply of cocoa, which made it impossible to supply the full quantity of 150,000 tons before the close of the second main crop, the delegation was seriously embarrassed by the force of argument of the Russian delegation.

Settlement of Overdue Debts

The Ghana delegation was presented with a bill for £983,000 sterling representing overdue debts in respect of fishing vessels and expert services supplied to Mankoadze Fisheries, Solis Fisheries, the State Fishing Corporation and passenger cars, trucks spares, tractors and other agricultural machinery supplied to the GNCC, the Accra-Tema City Council and the Ministry of Agriculture, instalment payments on which were overdue as at 1 January 1967.

The delegation argued, in respect of the fishing vessels, that as these were immobilized because of the departure of the Russian expert crew soon after the Revolution, the debtors could not operate the vessels to enable them to pay the instalments, when due. Furthermore, the suspension of foreign exchange transfers by the Ghana Government might have affected currency transfers from Ghana to the USSR.

The delegation therefore requested the Soviet Government to regard these debts as part of the overall debt to the USSR, the re-scheduling of which was being negotiated with the Soviet Government.

The Soviet Trade delegation gave a categorical negative answer to this request. The Ghana delegation could therefore only give the undertaking to contact the debtors, on return, to see how best they could be made to honour their obligations.

Indemnity for Losses

The Ghana delegation was also presented with a claim for compensation amounting to 1,171,8000 Roubles (£465,00) for losses sustained by various Soviet foreign trade organizations as a result of the Revolution. This was in four parts as follows:

(a) Losses caused by forced urgent departure of personnel of the Soviet Trade Representation and Soviet experts on training and consulting engaged for the State Fishing Corporation and Mankoadze Fisheries.

(b) Losses caused by the return of the Illyshin 18 planes to the USSR.

(c) Losses caused by the breakage and theft of samples from the Soviet Showrooms in Cocoa House.

(d) Losses caused by long storage of sugar, at Soviet ports and, in some cases, the non-acceptance of goods ordered.

This matter had been raised by the Soviet Government in a note which was presented to the Ministry of External Affairs in Accra.

The Ghana delegation was at a loss to understand the basis of these claims. It could, however, be argued that some losses had been sustained by the Soviet side under the circumstances. The Ghana delegation did not go into the legalities of the matter or the details of individual claims to avoid committing the Ghana Government one way or the other. The delegation, however, undertook to bring this matter to the attention of the Ghana Government.

This matter is likely to crop up in all future dealings with the Soviet Government, and it is necessary that a thorough examination is carried out to enable the Government to have a ready answer to future Soviet claims.

Other Economic Matters

The delegation met a delegation of the Soviet Government at the Ministry of Foreign Economic Relations on 20 March 1967. The matters discussed fall into two parts:

(a) the re-scheduling of debts, and
(b) other outstanding economic matters.

Re-scheduling of Debts

The Ghana delegation explained to the Soviet delegation the present economic difficulties of Ghana and requested that the debts owed by Ghana to the Soviet Union might be stretched out over a longer period to enable Ghana to put her house in order. It was explained to the Soviet side that what the Ghana Government wanted was a settlement similar to, or more favourable than, the treatment accorded by the Western creditors at the London meeting which carried out a similar exercise, when the Soviet Government agreed to a stretch out at $2\frac{1}{2}\%$ interest as against the 6% granted by the Western countries. The Soviet side undertook to convey the request to the authorities and to convey the decision later to the Ghana Government.

Future of Soviet Projects in Ghana

The *aide-mémoire* sent to the Soviet Government mentioned that the delegation would wish to discuss the problems connected with the following uncompleted projects as a result of the change in Government in Ghana:

  (a) The Fish Processing Plant;
  (b) The Gold Refinery;
  (c) The Atomic Reactor;
  (d) The Reinforced Concrete Panel Factory; and
  (e) The Training Centre.

The Soviet side was rather disturbed because all these projects were stopped through no fault of theirs and personnel engaged on these projects had to be urgently repatriated through no fault of theirs. They, however, very much appreciated the gesture of Ghana in seeking solutions to the problems created but they were of the opinion that the stay of the Ghana delegation in Moscow was too short to settle all the problems.

They were also concerned that some of these projects which had been stopped were nearing completion. The stoppage had occurred over one year ago and they felt that it was not just a matter of discussing problems, but an effort should be made to obtain an understanding of the relative positions correctly, e.g. will the Soviet side be required in case a general agreement is reached (a) to deliver additional equipment? or (b) to supply additional experts? Nevertheless, if it is decided to go ahead with some of the projects, it will be necessary to depute specialists to go to Ghana to examine the state of the projects abandoned 13 months ago. The Soviet Government would require a general undertaking that their experts would not be mishandled before agreeing that the personnel should go to Ghana.

It was explained by the Ghana delegation that the Government would be prepared to consider all these matters and arrange a satisfactory settlement.

It was emphasized that Ghana would like to make a selection of the useful projects, agree firmly upon them and negotiate for their completion.

Atmosphere of the Talks
The discussions in Moscow were held in an atmosphere of utmost cordiality. The Ghana delegation was very much impressed by the sense of reasonableness and maturity displayed by the Soviet Government during the talks....

Miscellaneous Matters
(a) *Ghana International Trade Fair*
It was brought to the notice of the delegation whilst in Moscow that the Soviet trade delegation was refused visas to attend the First Ghana International Trade Fair, even though they were very enthusiastic to do so. The delegation considers this action most unfortunate as the Soviet Government were at that time finding ways and means of normalizing relations with Ghana.

Moreover, since it had been decided at that time to continue bilateral trading with the Soviet Union, Russian participation in the Fair would have afforded them the opportunity to display their wares as Ghana is anxious to diversify her sources of supply and buy in the most advantageous markets....

Ghanaian Students in Russia and the East European Countries
Whilst in Moscow, the delegation had occasion to meet a delegation of Ghanaian students now studying in the Soviet Union. The students were worried about their future so far as recognition at home of their qualifications was concerned. The delegation feels that this problem is common to all students studying in Russian and the other Eastern European countries. The delegation also feels that if the problem is not solved early, it will constitute a serious social problem in the near future. We therefore recommend that immediate steps be taken to send a team from the Scholarship Secretariat and the University of Ghana to assess correctly the contents of the courses the students are taking to enable the Ghana Government and/or future employers to decide on suitable employment prospects.

The National Liberation Council is invited...

7. To note the reported change in atmosphere in the Socialist countries as far as relationship with Ghana is concerned, and to consider whether in the light of this, current Ghana thinking may not be modified should the change be proved to be a real one....

Part IV: State Enterprises for Sale

Introductory Note

The documents in this chapter deal with one of the most controversial aspects of the economic policies of the Military Government, those concerning the state enterprises. Document 28, a report commissioned by the NLC after the coup, analyses the background and performance of the state enterprises under the Nkrumah Government. Written by H. P. Nelson, the Executive Secretary of the State Enterprises Secretariat, it is a classic statement of the problems of import-substitution 'industrialization' in African countries. The enterprises were the subject of sometimes contradictory advice from many international and local agencies, but possibly the most influential was the World Bank. Document 29 contains the recommendations of the World Bank mission that advised on the first development budget of the NLC. The Bank generally favoured private participation in the state enterprises, but urged care in disposing of enterprises and in negotiating joint ventures with private capital. In this report, as in others, the proclivity of the World Bank for foreign 'experts' is clearly demonstrated. Its recommendation that foreign specialists, rather than Ghanaian officials, be brought in to appraise the state enterprises prior to disposal led to the recruitment of a team of USAID officials for that purpose.

Documents 30 to 33 are records of the negotiations undertaken with various multinational corporations for participation in the state enterprises. Apart from the Ambassador and Continental Hotels, the enterprises were financed and constructed under Eastern credits and had yet to commence operations at the time of the coup. With the exception of those relating to the Hotels, the documents are copied from the records of the 'Negotiating Committee for the Sale of and Participation in Selected State Enterprises', which was appointed by the NLC in April 1967 to carry out these negotiations. They expose the myth of foreign 'investment' and offer an unusual insight into the negotiating strategy of the MNCS and their real interests with regard to Third World economies. On a different plane, Documents 34 and 35 catalogue the events leading to Lonrho's acquisition of the Obuasi mines, an event hailed in the British press as a 'commercial coup' but followed in Ghana by a miners' strike which was brutally suppressed by the police with the loss of four lives and several injured.*

The original memorandum from the Ministry of Lands and Mineral Resources recommending support for the Lonrho takeover (Document 34) was conspicuously silent on the issue of Lonrho's South African and Rhodesian connection. Obuasi was the main but by no means the exclusive Lonrho interest in Ghana; as the next documents (36 and 37) demonstrate, the company also attempted to secure a foothold in the brewing and sugar industries (unsuccessfully in the latter case). Lonrho's *pito* brewery at Tamale, which the company had confidently anticipated would dispossess the peasant brewers and turn them into hired hands, in fact failed to compete and was closed down in the early 1970s after only a brief period of operation.

The state banking sector did not escape the denationalization of the economy. The two British colonial commercial banks, Barclays and Bank of West Africa (now Standard Bank of Ghana), were able to recover much of the ground lost before the coup to the state-owned banks, Ghana Commercial Bank and the Bank of Ghana. So good was business that Standard was able to expand its loan portfolio by 700% within four years after the coup. A large part of the increase in business came from the diversion of 50% of the banking business of the Cocoa Marketing Board from the Bank of Ghana to the two banks (Document 39).

A particularly good example of the use of 'conditionality' in Western loans to enlarge the area of private capital in Ghana appears in the attempt to divest the Ghana Government of controlling shares in the National Investment Bank (NIB) in order to qualify it for IFC financing (Document 38). This failed partly because of the insistence of the IFC on an overhaul in the management of NIB as a further condition for the loan and secondly because refinancing loans from the West German KFW in 1968 and 1970 made unnecessary the deal with the IFC.

Not surprisingly the agreements with foreign capital attracted considerable public criticism.† Document 40 was circulated by R. S. Amegashie, the Chairman of the Committee that negotiated the participation agreements and also the joint venture with Lonrho, in answer to criticisms of the agreements. The reasoning advanced in this paper – that successful industrialization and transformation of Ghana's economy could only be effected on the basis of multinational penetration – is only too typical of many Third World 'planners'. The controversy generated by

---

*See Document 46 and Ghana, *Report of the Commission of Enquiry into the Obuasi Disturbances, 1969*. Accra-Tema: State Publishing Corporation (n.d.).

†See the public debate on the Abbott agreement reproduced in the *Legon Observer*, 8 December 1967. In early 1968 Abbott Ltd withdrew from the joint venture in response to the volley of criticisms.

these agreements and more generally by the influence of foreign capital in the regime, reached into the highest levels of the NLC Government itself. While the Economic Committee was deeply involved in negotiating these agreements, the Political Committee tended to oppose them – sometimes vehemently – and to adopt a more nationalist position. The Political Committee was particularly critical of the Inter-Continental Hotels agreement (Document 41). By the end of 1966, partly because of these disagreements over policy, relations between the two highest civilian committees had degenerated into bitter squabbling (see Documents 42 and 43).

Document 28: Performance of State Enterprises
H. P. Nelson, A Report on the Administration and Operation of State Enterprises under the Work Schedule of the State Enterprises Secretariat for the Period 1964–65, Accra: State Enterprises Secretariat, 1 September 1966.

Introduction

...3. The experience in Ghana in industrialization as in other developing countries has often raised the question as to the extent to which the state should participate in economic activity in a developing country, instead of providing a well-planned infrastructure which forms the spring-board for economic activity. While capital and skilled manpower are scarce in developing countries, it becomes inevitable that private foreign capital should play an important role in economic development, but it is equally important that the state must participate in economic activity, at least for strategic reasons. Nevertheless, often the state is forced to enter into economic activity just because foreign capital is not forthcoming, either in the quantities in which they are required or in those fields in which they are urgently required, or both. Private capital naturally seeks for [sic] the highest return and has several alternative opportunities throughout the developing world from which the safest choice could reasonably be made.

4. But in view of the many social and economic problems facing a developing country including those enumerated in paragraph one above, it is important that a reasonable balance should be established for contributions towards development by both of [sic] state and the private sector, in order to avoid any undue strains on the national economy. In fact every encouragement should be given to both local and foreign private capital to play a useful and important role in economic development.

5. In this report an attempt has been made to review the operations of

state enterprises. The report is naturally limited in scope, since it has not been easy to collect enough data and statistics on each of the enterprises. Facts and figures have been produced to cover those which are at present available, but it is hoped that this will form the basis for a much more detailed research by the Secretariat in future and for the production of Annual Reports. The report is restricted to those manufacturing enterprises which are directly owned and controlled by the state as well as Joint–Private enterprises...

Organization and Administration of State Corporations

State participation in business enterprises in Ghana began in 1951 with the establishment of the Ghana Industrial Development Corporation, a holding company now in liquidation, with the object of promoting industrial expansion by providing financial, advisory and technical assistance in the establishment and development of new and existing industries both within the public and private sectors, and to train local personnel for management positions. The operations of the Industrial Development Corporation (IDC) was therefore not confined to the public sector. In fact in addition to establishing its own enterprises, the Industrial Development Corporation advanced considerable sums of money in long-term loans to private entrepreneurs. Similarly, the Agricultural Development Corporation (ADC) which was established in 1954, had more or less similar objectives in promoting expansion in agriculture, animal husbandry and deep sea fishing.

2. With the achievement of Independence in March 1957, the first national government declared its support for increased public ownership of the means of production and distribution. Consequently the Industrial Development Corporation proceeded to establish a number of new industries within the public sector and also acquired a few from private entrepreneurs. State participation in economic activity began to expand and a number of new projects were initiated, especially after 1960.

3. In 1962, the Industrial Development Corporation was sent into liquidation and its functions transferred to the Ministry of Industries. The Agricultural Development Corporation, was similarly dissolved and its functions transferred to the Ministry of Agriculture and the Department of Fisheries. Since then a number of state corporations have been established and at present about 54 of these operate within the state sector including industrial, commercial, agricultural, trading, transport, construction and service enterprises. In addition to these, there are 12 Joint State–Private or 'Mixed' enterprises in which Government participates with private enterprise in doing business, with Government's participation ranging from 10% to 94%.

4. Each state enterprise is established by a Legislative Instrument of Incorporation which, in addition to the objects and other matters, provides

for a Board of Directors as the governing body to direct its policy. The Instrument also assigns certain responsibilities to the State Enterprises Secretariat and others to Ministries and the Head of State. The question of responsibility for state corporations is therefore diffused, sometimes uncertain, and occasionally resulting in confusion. A general review of these instruments is to be carried out shortly with the view to establishing a clear-cut line of authority and responsibility for the corporations.

5. If the enterprises are to operate efficiently and profitably, it is essential that their operation should be based on sound commercial principles and should be independent in their day-to-day commercial operations. However, since there are a number of important matters which will require policy decision and control in accordance with Government policies, there should be but one central body responsible for all state corporations which operate as commercial organizations.

6. The State Enterprises Secretariat was established in April 1964 to exercise general supervision over state corporations and to ensure their efficient and profitable operation, and to look after Government's interest in joint or mixed enterprises. This was in fact the first attempt to lay down a clear line of responsibility. The Secretariat does not interfere in the day-to-day decisions and operations of the enterprises. Each enterprise is autonomous in the sense that responsibility for operations is left in the hands of the Managing Director and the Board of Directors. Decisions relating to current operational problems are all within the competence of management.

7. But although there is evidence that some order has been injected into the operations of state corporations and that in general the enterprises have shown improvement in their operations, responsibility continues to remain diffused and uncertain. It is therefore considered desirable to examine the advisability of reconstituting the State Enterprises Secretariat into some kind of a Holding Company responsible for the control of all state corporations operating as commercial ventures. All such corporations shall be subsidiaries of the Holding Company except where it is clear that they could otherwise be more profitably and efficiently operated, or for some other compelling reasons.

8. Such a holding company will interpret, communicate and control the implementation of Government policies in respect of statutory corporations; advise government on these policies and within the framework of these policies, given decisions, instructions and guidance on, and exercise control over such matters as the formulation of long-term objectives, appointment of Board of Directors, appropriation of profits, commencement or acquisition of new business, closure, sale, splitting up or amalgamation of existing business; major capital and development projects; broad aspects of labour and staff policy; receive from corporations long-term and annual budgets and production plans, periodic checks of actual results compared with the budgets and plans; quarterly, half yearly and annual financial and production reports. Such a Holding

Company, directly responsible to the Government will afford the enterprises sufficient degree of freedom and their efficient operation as commercial enterprises.

9. In the past, state enterprises were directed, operated and managed as if they were public utility services established to produce and sell goods and services without having to show profit. They became the dumping ground of unskilled and unqualified men and women. For these and other reasons which I shall discuss later, state corporations as a rule operated at very heavy losses. Up to a point, it became quite clear that the corporations were not set up to lose money at the expense of the tax payer, and that like all other business undertakings, they were expected to operate efficiently and show profits. The State Enterprises Secretariat was established as a corporate body to give realization to this objective.

10. Recently, great interest has been expressed by the public in the operation of state enterprises, especially with regard to efficiency in their administration and management. It is difficult to generalize in this matter in view of the immense variety of the calibre of managers within state enterprises. In the past appointments to top managerial posts and other positions in state enterprises were not necessarily based on qualifications and experience, consequently a number of incompetent persons were appointed as Managers. Nevertheless, the fact remains that Ghana, as a developing country, lacks the men with the requisite knowledge and experience in industry and therefore the level of management is generally relatively very low. Not only is the efficiency of top management relatively low, but the efficiency of supporting supervisory and technical staff is also very low. The State Enterprises Secretariat, realizing the seriousness of the problem of management, has in collaboration with the National Productivity Centre and the Ghana Association for the Advancement of Management (GAAM) organized series of courses and seminars for management and supervisory staff. The result during the past two years has been quite encouraging.

11. Management have shown some awareness of their responsibilities, and even those enterprises which had hitherto shown heavy losses have either reduced the level of losses considerably or else have touched break-even point. Others are now showing profits. But there are, however, a few managers who continue to show indifference towards new ideas and systems. Such managers are being given every opportunity to show improvement or else face inevitable replacement by men who are more competent and willing to learn. During the past three years attempts have been made to overcome managerial, as well as technical problems by employing Management Agents to run state enterprises. Although, in general, the use of management agents has resulted in profitable operation of the enterprises, in a few cases, owing to certain inherent difficulties, the enterprises continue to show losses.

12. Apart from the problem of lack of competent management, there is acute shortage of qualified and skilled manpower, especially in the

supervisory grades, as well as skilled technicians who are urgently required in our enterprises, including qualified and experienced accountants. The result is that there has been haphazard planning and budgeting. In many cases lack of planning and adequate financial controls have contributed to heavy losses, where there should have been profits.

13. There are a number of other problems which have militated against the efficient operation of state enterprises. Some of these are difficulties arising out of inadequate or bad feasibility studies prior to the implementation of the project. For example, there have been instances where after completion of factory projects essential raw materials which were expected to be produced locally were either not available in adequate quantities to feed the factory at full capacity or not available at all. In some cases training of technical personnel has lagged far behind the completion of a project. Usually contracts for the sale of machines provide for training of Ghanaian technicians overseas. Unfortunately the majority of trainees have returned from overseas with very little knowledge and skills which makes them unable to perform the functions required of them efficiently. It appears that either the training programmes are not well planned and supervised, or that the period of training is inadequate to enable the trainees to acquire the necessary knowledge and skills, or else that the background knowledge and experience of the candidates for training are such that they are incapable of taking advantage of the training programme, or a combination of these and perhaps other reasons.

14. Overstaffing is one of the major problems of state enterprises. There is hardly any state enterprise which is not overloaded with redundant staff. Although every effort is being made to transfer redundant staff from established industries to new enterprises, the problem is not easy to solve, since most of the redundant staff are either semi-skilled or unskilled. The solution to the problem is to lay off redundant staff, but there is also the social aspect of the problem which has to be considered. Since the February 24 Revolution, barely eight months ago, there has been a vigorous review of state enterprises with a view to eliminating waste of all kinds and to ensure their efficient operation. This has inevitably resulted in laying off redundant labour. A special Commission has, however, been set up to deal with the redeployment of such labour.

15. Financial problems have in large measure affected the efficient operation of state enterprises. Almost all our enterprises have had to begin operation without any provision for working capital, thus these enterprises have had to depend on huge overdraft facilities provided by the commercial banks at an interest rate of 8% recently increased to 11%. The total overdraft accommodation of all state enterprises is estimated at over £25 million sterling. Sometimes difficulties in securing adequate facilities have made it impossible for orders to be placed for the importation of essential raw materials and spare parts, well in advance, to avoid possible temporary stoppage of production, resulting from shortages. The fact that huge sums of money secured as overdraft facilities have to be tied down in stocks of

raw materials and spare parts for periods ranging from three to six months, as well as in stocks of finished goods long before these are sold for cash, does create financial problems for the enterprises and has a direct increasing effect on price. As a result of the present financial difficulties facing the country, it is not possible to provide working capital for such enterprises now, but as soon as the financial position improves the question will be reviewed.

16. The imposition of customs duties on raw materials, excise duties which vary from commodity to commodity, and sales tax of $11\frac{1}{2}\%$ on all finished goods also have considerable effect on the price of finished goods and also militate against the profitability of the enterprise. Although the Capital Investment Act originally passed in 1963 makes provision for exemption from these taxes, especially in the case of newly established enterprises, it is surprising to note that in the past whereas private industrial enterprises have been freely accorded tax relief and other pioneer privileges under the provisions of the Capital Investment Act, state enterprises have until recently been subjected to all payments of taxes. It was not until after the establishment of the State Enterprises Secretariat that some state enterprises have been accorded these privileges.

17. Since 1960 Ghana has been experiencing balance of payments difficulties, resulting from the depression in the world price of cocoa. Shortage in foreign exchange has had effect on the operation of state as well as private industrial enterprise with regard to the establishment of letters of credit for the importation of raw materials and spare parts. In the case of private enterprises owned by foreign firms, the overseas parent companies have, however, often provided foreign exchange cover for such imports on favourable terms, whereas in the case of state enterprises such facilities as, for example, one hundred and eighty days credit have not been readily forthcoming.

18. One practicable step of [sic] solving the numerous problems facing state enterprises has been taken since the February 24 Revolution by a Government decision to turn over a number of state enterprises to private sector and to invite private participation in eleven others. In deciding which enterprises are to be sold to private enterprises and those in which private participation was to be invited, the following factors were taken into consideration:

(a) the strategic nature of the enterprise;
(b) the suitability or otherwise of the enterprise for private operation as against state operation;
(c) the ability of the enterprise to earn revenue to support itself or otherwise;
(d) the need for additional capital;
(e) the need for efficient management and technical know-how.

19. It is important to mention that some of our state enterprises are so small in size and of no strategic importance and so simple to operate, that

they are considered more suitable for small private entrepreneurs, as for example the Bakery. Furthermore, a number of enterprises have failed to operate efficiently within the state sector and have therefore been incurring losses. The state cannot afford to subsidize such enterprises indefinitely, and the transfer of some of these enterprises to the private sector will not only relieve the state of undue financial burden but will also, it is hoped, result in the efficient utilization of capital and thus contribute towards the national economic growth. The need for additional capital and technical know-how for the efficient operation of state enterprises, has made it necessary to invite private participation in eleven others as this will ensure a reasonable hope of recovery.

20. Another important step which has been taken since the February 24th Revolution to assist state enterprises to operate efficiently, was to invite the United Nations Centre for Industrial Development to send a team of experts to assist in reviewing the operations of state enterprises. The team of four experts which stayed in the country for a period of three weeks during the month of April made positive recommendations in connection with the reorganization of certain enterprises. Furthermore, following their recommendation, the Centre for Industrial Development is expected to send to Ghana, four top level Directors with considerable experience in various fields of industrial operations to be attached to the State Enterprises Secretariat for a period of two years initially as operational heads of four important divisions within the Secretariat. In addition, the Centre is to provide experts in specific fields to be employed in a number of state enterprises. It is expected that this assistance from the Centre will contribute in no small measure to improving the standard of efficiency of state enterprises.

21. A decision on state enterprises in our economic development will not be complete without emphasizing the need to patronize our locally manufactured goods. The enterprises were not set up merely to produce goods for show, but to produce and sell. The enterprises cannot sell if local demand is diverted to imported goods, although the latter may be said to be of slightly superior quality. Our local industries need the encouragement of all our people as consumers to patronize their products. This will enable the enterprises to operate profitably and thereby carry out research and adopt advanced technology to improve the standard and quality of their products.

22. I am not advocating for undue protection for inefficient enterprises which produce inferior goods at high cost. I accept the challenge that our enterprises must be exposed to some degree of competition if they are to make any effort to operate efficiently. But competition must be fair and this requires a full appreciation of the initial problems of an infant industry in a developing country, in relation to the very many years of experienced and technical know-how in industrial countries.

23. As a rule, however, we cannot afford to subsidize enterprises which continue to incur losses without any hope of recovery. Such enterprises

must be handed over to the private sector with reasonable hope of recovery or else they must be closed down. Our enterprises must either show *profits* or *perish*....

III

Performance of Manufacturing Enterprises for Year 1965

32. The performances of 15 State and 6 Joint Enterprises, directly supervised by the (State Enterprise) Secretariat are described below for the period January to December 1965. The activities of the enterprises are presented in tables indicating *gross output, total costs of production* and *sales*. Statistics from other Enterprises were not available to the Secretariat. See Appendix I, Tables 1 and 2.

1. Gross Output
33. The gross output in value of manufacturing enterprises amounted to approximately ₵20,000,000 in 1965 compared with ₵12,000,000 in 1964 for the same number of Corporations, an increase of 40%. The increase in output which took place in the following corporations needs special mention:

>Distilleries Corporation
>Paints Corporation
>Metal Industries Corporation.

2. Cost of Production
34. There was an increase in cost of production in 1965 compared with 1964 by about 12%, partly due to the difficulties experienced in obtaining import licences for the importation of raw materials and spare parts. The shortage of raw materials resulted in under-utilization of plant capacities and low labour productivity. In addition the increase in cost of production may also be attributed to new indirect taxes, imposed on certain raw materials.

3. Sales
35. Total sales [rose] in 1965 to ₵18,000,000 as compared with ₵12,000,000 in 1964, an increase of about 33% ... Where competition between imported and locally manufactured goods is intense, our local industries have failed in their efforts of organization and salesmanship to take a reasonably good share of the market. This has often resulted in some state and joint enterprises seeking for [sic] administrative protection through the issue of import licensing. In a fire and competitive economy

state corporations must intensify their sales promotional activities by using all available media of advertising and publicity in promoting the sale of their products. Corporations must as a matter of policy aim at a continuous improvement in their marketing and distribution methods. Above all Corporations must ensure that the quality and price of their products are competitive.

4. Pricing
36. The price structure of most state enterprises does not seem to encourage the level of patronage and support which will induce a healthy expansion of the home market. Since the use of administrative measures as a means of protecting local enterprises does not provide a lasting solution to the problem, it is important that in the long run the price of locally manufactured products should be competitive to [*sic*] imported commodities.

5. Export Opportunities
37. A number of enterprises, as for example the Metal Works Corporation and Paints Corporation, received enquiries for exporting paints to neighbouring countries, but due to shortage of raw materials the order could not be confirmed. The Ghana Pioneer Aluminium Factory also received orders from Mali for various household utensils to the tune of about £114,400 for delivery in 1966. In order to promote the export of goods it is necessary to review taxes imposed on raw materials and locally manufactured products as for example sales and excise taxes. This will enable the enterprises to produce goods at reasonable prices not only to meet existing home demand but also offer possibilities for export.

APPENDIX I

Table 1

State Enterprises	Gross Output	Cost of Production	Sales
	₡	₡	₡
1. (a) Boatyards Corporation, Tema	518,403	350,383	236,297
(b) Boatyards Corporation, Sekondi	224,669	259,948	191,520
2. Brick and Tile Corporation	109,270	108,962	91,134
3. Cannery Corporation	442,605	359,529	335,425
4. Cocoa Products Corporation	5,008,713	6,195,169	4,051,237
5. Distilleries Corporation	4,669,041	1,946,194	4,918,130
6. Fibre Bag Manufacturing Corp.	814,423	1,259,260	750,011
7. (a) Furniture & Joinery, Accra	479,683	419,299	440,144
(b) Furniture & Joinery, Kumasi	222,261	188,904	193,156
8. Match Corporation	436,953	373,018	471,292
9. Metal Industries Corporation	496,112	330,884	503,998
10. Paints Corporation	600,052	430,773	634,480
11. Paper Conversion Corporation	1,164,310	751,583	1,169,028
12. Sheet Metal Works Corporation	299,303	231,655	262,183
13. Steel Works Corporation	1,012,847	1,871,637	951,120
14. Vegetable Oil Mills Corporation	549,630	411,328	530,267
15. GNTC (Bottling Department)	2,719,700	1,960,396	2,549,348
Total	19,767,975	17,448,922	18,278,770

Table 2

Joint State/Private Enterprises	Gross Output	Cost of Production	Sales
	₡	₡	₡
1. Crystal Oil Mills Limited	273,729	245,928	194,083
2. Dorman Long (Ghana) Limited	403,461	430,959	375,840
3. Ghana Aluminium Products	2,770,224	2,424,860	2,734,985
4. Ghana Bottling Company Limited	603,418	329,007	595,152
5. Ghana Pioneer Aluminium Factory	1,565,063	1,171,874	1,564,631
6. Kumasi Brewery	5,333,984	1,557,477	6,366,820
Total	10,948,879	6,160,105	11,831,511

Brief Review of Manufacturing Enterprises*

...3. Brick and Tile Corporation
The main machine is very obsolete and breaks down very often. There is therefore the need to overhaul the entire plant. A second line has recently been installed to supplement the production of the first line, and there is some indication that the enterprise will increase its productivity in the future. Although the enterprise does not at present face any sales problems, because the demand for its products is not high, expansion in production must be backed by a vigorous sales promotion both to encourage people to use bricks in building construction and also teach masons the art of brick laying. The new Manager, Mr Ahia-Lamptey, seems to be more on top of his job and shows prospect of achieving better results. Under an agreement entered into between the Ghana Government (Ministry of Communications and Works) and Messrs NIKEX of Hungary, 15 transportable brick making factories have been arranged to be supplied to the Corporation to enable them to expand their activities into the regions. Eleven of these factories have been delivered but the Corporation has no need for them. As a matter of fact no further expansion must be undertaken without careful feasibility studies. But the eleven mobile units may be sold to private entrepreneurs before the machines get rusty and unserviceable, and also in order to realize funds to pay NIKEX as the Corporation has no funds to pay the instalments when they become due.

4. Cannery Corporation
The Cannery at Nsawam is relatively unhygienic and in addition the Corporation has had to suffer frequent shortages of raw materials. The management has tried to overcome this difficulty by producing a large variety of products. In spite of repeated advice to the Manager to limit the variety of products, he has paid no heed and instead continues to increase production. The Corporation has accumulated losses of ₵228,000 by December 1965. This has resulted in high wastage of imported raw materials. The Ministry of Industries are constructing a number of food processing industries in addition to the Nsawam Cannery at the following places:

      Nsawam   —pineapple etc.
      Wenchi   —mango
      Pwalugu —tomatoes.

It appears that enough consideration has not been given to the supply of raw materials, and it is evident that the same problem of raw material

---

*Excerpts on selected enterprises.

shortages at present facing the Nsawam Cannery may face the others. The Ministry of Agriculture must be brought into the picture as early as possible to commence operations for the supply of raw materials, either through the efforts of individual farmers or through the State Farms Organization and the Workers Brigade. Furthermore, although it is intended that all these enterprises should be grouped under one State Cannery Corporation and under the direction of one Managing Director, the present Managing Director of Nsawam Cannery has not proved himself capable of managing the Nsawam factory efficiently. Therefore in the event of appointing a Managing Director to look after the operations of all the canneries, someone else with good business experience who can effect proper planning and marketing should be appointed to the post of Managing Director.

The National Liberation Council has decided that this Corporation should be sold to private enterprise. It is recommended that each factory should be sold as one unit and not all the factories sold together as a unit.

5. Cocoa Products Corporation

(1) *Takoradi Factory:* The operations of the Takoradi plant for a period of 16 months commencing from 15 April 1963 to 31 December 1964 ended up with a loss of ₵298,215, i.e. £124,256. This amount includes the sum of about £60,000 which was spent on initial expenditure in connection with the establishment and opening of the factory, which normally should have been capitalized. It appears also that fees were paid to Paterson Simons, the Management Agents by the Ministry of Industries even before the factory was completed, and these fees are included in the total loss. The unit cost of production of the Takoradi factory is relatively very high, and is about double the cost of the West African Mills, a joint enterprise. The Management Agency Agreement and the general efficiency of the machines and operation of the factory need to be examined. There has been a major breakdown in Press No. 3, which took over four months to replace but it has again been reported that a crack has developed in Press No. 2. The Ministry of Industries who at present hold the relevant information on the Takoradi factory should be brought into these investigations which should be undertaken as soon as possible. There is also the need to call on Messrs Stahl Union, the suppliers of the machines, to submit an inventory of the machines and equipment, etc., supplied to the factory under contract and the cost of each item. This will facilitate the preparation of future estimates for the replacement of plant.

(c) *Tema Factory:* The Tema Factory is partially in operation with the opening of the chocolate manufacturing plant. The Management of the factory is under an Agency Agreement with Reiss and Richman. The future of the entire complex is now being considered by the Economic Committee and recommendations will be made to the National Liberation Council in due course....

7. Electronic Products Corporation

This is a new Corporation which has been in operation for over a year and during this period made a profit of over £44,000. The Corporation is at present engaged in assembling transistor radio sets called 'Akasanoma' from component parts supplied by Messrs Philips. It is not quite clear why the name Akasanoma was adopted, but one would have thought that in view of the fact that Philips radio is very popular all over the world this brand name would have been adopted to give these transistor sets the best chance of entering overseas markets. Furthermore, since it is envisaged that the Corporation will engage in the production of a large variety of electrical equipment and appliances it might be advisable to enter into partnership with either Messrs Philips or some other well-known electronic firm, to take advantage of their technical know-how and branded names. The National Liberation Council has accordingly decided that private participation in this business should be sought. The Management of this enterprise is competent....

13. Match Corporation

The State Match Corporation which was formerly the Ghana Match Company was established as a subsidiary in March 1956 by the erstwhile Industrial Development Corporation at Kade at a cost of £150,000 to produce 1,400 gross boxes per day. From the outset the Corporation encountered stiff competition from imported matches and it was not until the middle of 1962 that its products began to find ready market. Since then additional machines have been installed at a cost of £79,000 which has made the corporation potentially able to satisfy the country's demand.

Operations: About forty-five per cent of its raw materials in the form of chemicals is imported but the wood is obtained locally. Potentially the factory can produce all Ghana's needs but because of frequent breakdown and inefficient operation of the machinery resulting in considerable wastage, sometimes as high as 45%, it has found it difficult to keep up with demand and the factory's profitability has been adversely affected. Apart from the fact that the original machines are now about 8 years old, their inefficiency and frequent breakdown have been greatly contributed to by inefficient and inexperienced operation and maintenance and lack of proper supervision. This is borne out by the fact that even the new machines installed only a year ago are showing inordinately high rate of wastage. The profitability of the corporation has also been affected by overstaffing due to a disorganized shift system and lack of versatile trained operatives.

Solutions:
  (i) To arrest this decline in efficiency the United Nations Centre for Industrial Development has agreed to arrange for a firm of consultants to run the factory under a management contract

agreement for a period of two years with Ghanaian counterparts as understudies.
(ii) In the meantime additional machines which will streamline production have been ordered.
(iii) A cost accountant has been provided by National Investment Bank to prepare costing schedules to be applied in reviewing the cost of production as well as the selling price of machines ex factory....

16. Paper Conversion Corporation

The Corporation was established by the erstwhile Industrial Development Corporation in 1961 to produce toilet rolls at an original cost of £30,000. This is one factory which presents a clear case of bad feasibility studies and planning. The original factory was an unbalanced unit and presented excessive wastage in the utilization of machinery. Consequently since the factory was commissioned, additional machines have had to be installed in the factory to give it more or less operational equilibrium. In 1962 when the Cocoa Products Corporation at Takoradi was being planned it was decided to expand the Corporation to produce packing materials in the form of cardboard boxes and cellophane bags for cocoa butter. But when these extensions were completed, it was realized that further expansion was necessary. The factory now has an investment of £1,800,000. During the first two years of the factory's operation it made a loss of £69,000 approximately. With the installation of additional machines and necessary adjustments to the factory layout it is expected that the third year's operation 1964/65 will show better results but the balance sheet for this period is still in preparation. The prices of the products of the Corporation are relatively high and a special investigation into its cost of production is to be carried out jointly by the Secretariat, the National Investment Bank and the National Productivity Centre, with a view to cutting down costs. Arrangements are also being made through the United Nations Centre for Industrial Development to employ a full-time Cost Accountant to keep a close watch on the cost of production. The accounts of the Corporation have been in a complete mess and meanwhile the Secretariat has sent a qualified accountant to take over the operations of the accounts. This will be followed by a thorough review of the operations of the Corporation by experts from the United Nations Centre for Industrial Development and assistance to be given to the enterprise to enable it to operate efficiently....

19. Vegetable Oil Mills Corporation

The Corporation was established in 1963 and has six branches namely Essiama Oil Mills which produces copra oil, Denu mills (copra oil), Atebubu, Tamale and Bawku oil mills (groundnut oil), the original total cost being £18,522. Whereas the last four oil mills are all small size mills, the Essiama Oil Mills is about four times the size of any of the others, and is at present being expanded. The Essiama Oil Mills is by far the most important. The factory, in addition to producing edible oils for home consumption produces crude oil for the use of the Tema Soap factory. For some time now considerable difficulties have been experienced in securing copra to feed the mills, with the result that the factory has been operating below capacity. Recently the Nzima Copra Farmers' Co-operatives was re-organized to take on the functions of purchasing copra for the mills, and the price of 1 cwt. of copra was also increased as an incentive to the farmers to sell to the mills instead of selling to private dealers. Reports indicate that the situation has improved. Denu Oil Mills which is about a quarter the size of Essiama Mills has also been experiencing difficulties with the supply of copra and has been producing below capacity. Somtimes copra has had to be sent all the way from Essiama to Denu for crushing at the mill, but this is a most uneconomic operation. With the opening of the border between Ghana and Togo it is expected that copra may be obtained from Togo and Dahomey. The other three small groundnut oil mills have also been experiencing difficulties with the supply of groundnuts in spite of several attempts which have been made to get the erstwhile United Ghana Farmers Co-operative Council, the Workers Brigade and the State Farms to produce adequate groundnuts to feed the mills at Atebubu, Temale and Bawku. Since these three mills are situated in areas suitable for the cultivation of groundnuts the Ministry of Agriculture must now assist local farmers to intensify the cultivation of groundnuts in these areas to feed the three mills as well as the Crystal Oil Mills, a joint State/Private enterprise, located in Accra which also consumes large quantities of raw groundnuts imported from Nigeria. The Head office of the Vegetable Oil Mills is located in Accra and is mainly responsible for the marketing operations of the mills. Unfortunately the Corporation's overall financial position is not yet known as it has not yet been able to produce a balance sheet. The Corporation's accounts have been in an awful mess and a firm of Chartered Accountants have had to be employed to bring the accounts up to date and to have to prepare an audited balance sheet. The Secretariat after an investigation into the operations of the Corporation has had to dismiss the Accountant for inefficiency. The operations of the Corporation are to be reviewed by a team of experts as soon as the balance sheet is produced. Meanwhile it has been decided that the enterprises of the Corporation should be transferred to the private sector.

Document 29:
Recommendations of World Bank Mission on 1966/67 Development Budget, excerpts from section on 'Industries'.

1. Government has made a considerable effort to reduce capital expenditure in industry. Planned capital expenditure for industrial projects has been decreased by one-third since the period 1964–1965. The capital budget for 1966 amounted to ₵17 million, while the new budget for 1966/67 is about at [sic] the same level. This compares with actual expenditure for 1965 of ₵26.5 million and budgeted expenditure for the 12 month periods 1964 and 1965 of ₵22.7 million and ₵26.1 million.

2. Reductions have come almost entirely from the elimination of new projects, i.e., uncommitted projects or projects which had been under frame agreement but upon which work had not yet started. There are some exceptions (Incandescent Lamp, Ghana-Sanyo Television, Solo Motors, Asbestos Cement) but in general Government has retained projects upon which work has started in the budget.

3. Firm policy on individual projects (and operating enterprises) has still not been formulated. Faced with contractual commitments, half finished works, and enterprises operating under potentially heavy fixed charges (high cost buildings, office space, housing, machinery and civil engineering) development estimates are per force only tentative.

4. In screening the weakest projects initial Government procedure was sound. Essentially this procedure was:

   (a) To obtain progress reports on the implementation of each project.
   (b) To eliminate those in which commitments could be terminated at little cost.
   (c) To request studies of committed projects about which there was most doubt as to continued viability.
   (d) To seek participation in certain enterprises from private firms having experience and knowledge in the matter.
   (e) To continue the execution of work at the sites, but in some cases on a slow down basis.

5. Two observations are to be made about this procedure:

   (a) It should not be a once-and-for-all effort. In state-owned industries, development programmes should be subjected to continuous scrutiny and control.
   (b) The decisions as they stand have not been based on a thorough execution of the procedure. It has not been followed through. In part this has been because of insufficient time, in part because of an understandable but dangerous tendency to dispose of difficult issues quickly....

7. Government appears to have adopted the policy that an economic use

can be more easily found for completed than incomplete [*sic*] projects, Among the economic uses envisaged are sales to private enterprise or participation with private enterprise on a mutually acceptable basis. Alternatively Government might continue to operate the enterprise itself.

8. The Mission is of the opinion that the policy of completing projects is not necessarily applicable in specific instances. In some cases the original plan of construction is too elaborate and capital costs could be reduced (for example office blocks at Nsawam, housing estates at Komenda). In other cases alternative uses should be found for facilities other than those for which they were intended (for example machinery at Wenchi or the rural industries programme). In certain instances private enterprise might be interested in participating in a portion of the facilities if alternative uses could be found for the remainder (shoe factory, pharmaceuticals). Finally when Government believes that even though economic returns are low social benefits will be sufficient to justify operating the enterprise, the cost of retaining the enterprise should be fully appreciated.

9. Decisions on these matters cannot be made on the basis of status reports and 'one time' surveys. The proper allocation of these capital resources will occupy Government over the coming year. This fact is reflected in the reserve provisions of the Mission estimates, which in turn are based on the following general considerations:

10. *Increased participation of private sector:* The Mission supports wholeheartedly Government's efforts to increase the participation of private enterprise in its industrial development programme. On the one hand it will lower the capital contribution required of Government to the extent that private enterprises purchase assets outright, lease them, or take equity in the businesses. The burden of providing working capital may in particular be lifted from Government and be made a condition of entry on the part of private firms. On the other hand private enterprise can help to provide scarce managerial and technical resources. As is true of existing state enterprises, management is *the* critical factor in obtaining maximum returns from existing facilities.

11. *Conditions [for] successful implementation:* To increase private participation in state-owned facilities is, however, a delicate problem. Government must maintain a firm bargaining position, while knowing on what points to give ground. The objective is to get the plants into operation on the basis of a mutually acceptable *continuing* relationship. If either party gains much at the expense of the other, difficulties will be created in the future. To make successful deals Government will have to undertake serious and difficult groundwork. Its purpose should be to have as many rational alternatives as possible and to know their various costs and benefits. Among others:

  (a) Government must know the investment cost of the project;
  (b) Government must consider alternative uses for the facility;

(c) Government must have some idea of the present value of future returns from the completed project, at least within ranges;
(d) Government should know who potential partners, buyers or agents are and have room for choice among them.

12. *To continue or not:* Much the same reasoning applied to private sale, agency, or partnership applies equally to the decision whether or not to abandon a project. The Economic Committee has singled out some projects for special review (fruit canning plants, cement clinker, leather tannery, food complex, cocoa processing facilities). In no cases were independent feasibility studies made, and in some work has gone forward virtually unknown to responsible authorities. The result is that information must be developed from scratch. The problem is similar to that of a man who suddenly finds that he has inherited a portfolio of securities, some bad, some good. The difference is that in most cases he will have an assured market and a known price.

13. *Alternative procedures:* In view of these uncertainties the Mission has reserved working capital expenditure and some capital expenditure until information to support the required decisions can be developed. To do so Ghana essentially has two broad categories of alternatives. One is to undertake to do the studies with available Government personnel. The other is to seek the services of a qualified group of international industries specialists. In weeding out the marginal incompleted [*sic*] and uncommitted projects and as an expedient prior to completing the 1966/67 budget estimates, Ghana has per force followed the first path. The Mission recommends that for the remaining thirteen projects,* Ghana elect to follow the second.

14. The following considerations underline the Mission's recommendation:

(a) The number of qualified personnel in the Ministries who can undertake this work on a serious basis is limited.
(b) Those few who are available could be used to better purpose in reformulating industries policy, planning for the future, and overseeing the implementation of the consultants' work.
(c) Properly undertaken the execution of this work would provide training in techniques, methods and procedures of project appraisal.
(d) Although concentrating on specific projects, a by-product of the analysis would in all probability be the identification of future

---

*The projects are pharmaceuticals, three fruit and vegetable canning factories, two sugar projects, cocoa products and food complex [Tema], leather, shoe, tyre, gold refinery and cement clinker [Takoradi].

investment opportunities. In fact it is likely that a focus on the specific economics of these enterprises would produce more tangible opportunities than a general survey.
(e) Ghana lacks knowledge of the suppliers of foreign investment capital and their interests. A requisite of the proposed team is that it have the best available knowledge of the world-wide structure of investors having potential interest in these projects.
(f) Among the members of the team should be a man experienced in negotiating strategy.

Table 29.1: Ministry of Industries Projects to be Discontinued

> Metchet and Black Tool
> Central Machine Tool
> Asbestos Cement (invite fresh tenders)
> Toy Factory
> Akosombo Textile Mill (until submission of project report)
> Veneer and Plywood Factory (to private buyer)
> Metal Fabrication
> Incandescent Lamp
> Vehicle Assembly
> Pulp and Paper (cancel GDR contract)
> Textile, Tamale
> Gammalin
> Textile, Juapong (private enterprise)
> Pencil
> Axim Textile
> Rubber (Try to sell to private)
> Tannery (Try to sell to private)

Table 29.2: State Corporations. Recommendations of the Economic Committee

I. Corporations recommended to be kept and operated by State Sector:
1. Brick and Tile
2. Cocoa Marketing Board
3. Cocoa Products Corporation
4. Diamond Marketing Corporation
5. Diamond Mining Corporation
6. Distilleries Corporation
7. Electricity Corporation
8. Electronic Products Corporation

continued

continued

9. Fibre Bag Manufacturing Corporation *Tech. Assistance*
10. Fishing Corporation
11. Food Marketing Corporation
12. Ghana Airways Corporation
13. Ghana National Trading Corporation
14. Ghana National Construction Corporation
15. Glass Manufacturing Corporation
16. Gold Mining Corporation
17. Gold Refinery Corporation
18. Housing Corporation
19. National Insurance Corporation
20. Steel Works
21. Match Corporation *Tech. assistance*
22. Metal Industries
23. Paper Conversion *Tech. assistance*
24. Sheet Metal Works Corporation
25. Shipping Corporation
26. State Enterprises Audit Corporation
27. State Industries
28. Tema Development Corporation
29. Textile Manufacturing Corporation
30. Tobacco Products Corporation
31. Transport Corporation
32. State Cement Works Corporation.

II. Corporations for which the participation of the Private Sector is to be invited:

1. Boatyards Corporation
2. Bonsaso Rubber Tyre Factory
3. Film Industry Corporation
4. Footwear Corporation
5. Furniture and Joinery Corporation
6. Hotel Corporation
7. Meat Products Corporation
8. Paints Corporation
9. Pharmaceutical Corporation
10. Publishing Corporation
11. Sugar Products Corporation

III. Corporations which are recommended *for sale* to the Private Sector:

1. Bakery Corporation
2. The Nsawam Cannery
3. Laundries Corporation

4. Marble Works Corporation
5. Timber Products Corporation
6. Tyre Service Corporation
7. Vegetable Oil Mills

Corporations which are still being studied, and therefore no recommendation can be made:

1. State Farms Corporation
2. Tannery Corporation

Document 30: Terms of Lease of State Hotels

Proposals contained in letter from Robert E. Smith, (Inter-Continental Hotels Corporation) Vice-President of Pan-American World Airways (parent company of IHC) to Michael D. Quist, Chairman of State Hotels Corporation (SHC) on 23 June 1966, and accepted by the SHC:

This is a letter of understanding between the State Hotels Corporation of Ghana and Inter-Continental Hotels Corporation (IHC), subject to ratification by the Board of Directors of each company and incorporation in an agreement between the two parties.

1. IHC, or a wholly-owned subsidiary of IHC, will lease the Ambassador and Continental Hotels in Accra, Ghana from the State Hotels Corporation in accordance with IHC's standard lease, except that the rent payable by IHC under the Lease Agreement will be 80% of adjusted gross operating profit (after deduction of 3% of total sales paid to IHC as reimbursement of System costs). You have a copy of our standard Lease and attached hereto is a new Article III describing the rental formula in more detail.

2. The effective date of the Lease with respect to the Ambassador Hotel will be 15 August 1966 or such earlier date as IHC may be able to make available a General Manager, a Chief Accountant, an Engineer and a Housekeeper. These employees will be the personnel required initially to be followed by other expatriates as may be required in the opinion of IHC. The effective date of the Lease on the Continental Hotel will be as now described in the standard lease. The Continental Hotel will be opened as soon as possible after the commencement of the IHC operation of the Ambassador Hotel. These hotels may be renamed by IHC subject to approval of the State Hotels Corporation, which approval will not be

unreasonably withheld. The hotels will not be designated as Inter-Continental Hotels until IHC is satisfied that the hotels meet the minimum standards of IHC for its operations. It is believed that these hotels will reach these minimum standards when the IHC recommended rehabilitation programme on the Ambassador is completed and the Continental Hotel is opened and any equipment changes recommended by IHC for the Continental are incorporated. The Standard Lease Agreement will be modified to include such limitations on the naming of these hotels as Inter-Continental Hotels and a provision will be added permitting the cancellation of the Lease Agreement by IHC with respect to either or both of these hotels if they do not reach this minimum standard within one year after the effective date of the Lease of the Hotel Ambassador. It is contemplated that one Lease Agreement will cover both hotels.

3. At the same time that IHC takes over the operation of the Ambassador Hotel it will send a team of technical services experts to Accra with the operating personnel assigned to this hotel for the purposes of evaluating a rehabilitation programme for the Ambassador Hotel. Our general estimate at this time is that the cost of this rehabilitation programme of the Ambassador Hotel and training of personnel for both hotels and the addition of kitchen equipment for the Continental Hotel will be approximately $800,000. IHC will prepare a report which will serve as a basis for the rehabilitation programme and its financing by either the Government of Ghana or AID.* The cost of preparation of this report, exclusive of the IHC costs of negotiating any loan agreements, will be approximately $22,500, which includes payroll costs plus 75% overhead and all out-of-pocket expenses including travel costs. If the State Hotels Corporation provides transportation on Ghana Airways London–Accra–London, the cost of preparation of the report will be approximately $17,000. The State Hotels Corporation will advance the $17,000 or $22,500 as the case may be prior to 15 August 1966 to IHC which payment will be adjusted to the exact amount upon completion of the survey and presentation of invoices and supporting documents.

4. The State Hotels Corporation will provide all of the funds for the rehabilitation programme, training programme, purchase of kitchen equipment for the Continental and technical services costs of IHC. IHC will exercise its best efforts on behalf of the State Hotels Corporation to obtain a capital loan from AID to finance the foregoing. IHC services in this connection will be charged on a payroll cost plus overhead basis. AID has informed IHC that under its procedures the Government of Ghana should advise the AID Mission in Ghana that the Government considers this project of a high priority and request the necessary loan as part of the United States AID programme for Ghana. If for any reason such a loan is not available from AID, or is not available in time to bring the hotels up to

---

*(United States) Agency for International Development—*Editor.*

IHC standards by 15 August 1967, the State Hotels Corporation agrees to supply the funds from sources within or without Ghana upon notification from IHC of the need to provide such funds.

5. Initially, and in order to undertake the minimum essentials of the rehabilitation programme on the Ambassador at the time the IHC management and technical services group arrives in Accra, the State Hotels Corporation will provide by 15 August 1966 up to the equivalent of $60,000 in local and foreign currency to cover the purchases and work to be accomplished under such initial programme. This amount is part of the estimated $800,000 for the entire programme.

6. IHC will provide working capital, but it will not purchase the receivables of the Hotel Ambassador. IHC will, however, exercise its best efforts to collect such receivables and remit same to the State Hotels Corporation as collected. IHC will purchase reasonable quantities of usable operating supplies from the State Hotels Corporation, but any operating supplies returned to the State Hotels Corporation warehouse will be available for future purchase by IHC at cost.

7. The State Hotels Corporation will obtain all assurances to the satisfaction of IHC from the Government of Ghana that:

   (a) IHC will be granted the full privileges and benefits of the Capital Investments Act of Ghana granted to foreign companies including property and income tax exemption for a minimum five years with every possible consideration being given to an extension for another five years;
   (b) IHC will receive convertibility and transfer of all of its earnings under the Hotel Lease and fifty per cent (50%) of the gross salaries of the expatriate personnel engaged by IHC and such other convertibility and transfer of the expatriate salaries as may be permitted by the Exchange Control Act;
   (c) IHC will obtain full convertibility and licences for the purchase of and/or importation of goods, supplies and services as requested by IHC for the operations of the Hotel;
   (d) IHC and the hotels operated by IHC will not be subject to any control on hotel rates and prices;
   (e) IHC will be granted all immigration and work permits for expatriate personnel engaged by IHC for the operation of the hotels.

8. IHC will be given full latitude of action and Government support on any reorganization of the expatriate or national personnel of the Ambassador Hotel. After IHC has evaluated the qualifications of all such personnel, it may exercise its independent judgment on dismissal or reassignment of this personnel in the Ambassador or Continental Hotels. All separation costs will be borne by the State Hotels Corporation.

9. Promptly after the commencement of the Lease Agreement on the

Ambassador Hotel, IHC will review the Meridian Hotel in Tema with a view to operating this hotel when it opens in 1967 if this can be done, in IHC's opinion, on an economic and profitable basis. It is understood that IHC will not be expected to incur any operating losses on the Meridian Hotel and that IHC will be assured of a reasonable compensation for its management on a basis to be mutually established.

10. You will notify IHC of your Board's approval of the foregoing during the week of 4 July 1966. IHC will notify you of its corresponding approval within one week thereafter. Upon approval by both parties, IHC will prepare and execute a Hotel Lease Agreement and any other agreement considered necessary by IHC and send such agreements to you for execution. Any delay in execution of the agreements beyond 15 July 1966 will delay the commencement of the Hotel Lease on the Ambassador Hotel. This letter of understanding will terminate on 31 August 1966 if all action contemplated herein is not taken by that date or if the parties hereto do not otherwise agree in writing on an extension of this letter.

ATTACHMENT

ARTICLE III

Section 1. *Rent*. The Lessee will pay to the Lessor, in such coin or currency as is legal tender for the payment of public or private debts in Ghana, at the latter's principal office in Accra, or such other place as the Lessor shall designate in writing, a sum of money equal to eighty per cent (80%) of the Hotel's Gross Operating Profit (as hereinafter defined for each calendar year during the term of this lease). Such rent for each calendar year shall be paid by the Lessee to the Lessor as follows:

(a) Within sixty (60) days after the end of the first six months' period of each calendar year, a preliminary instalment shall be paid equivalent to eighty per cent (80%) of the hotel's Gross Operating Profit for such six months' period as set forth in the hotel's income statement certified by the Lessee's auditor.

(b) Within sixty (60) days after the end of each calendar year, a final instalment shall be paid based upon the hotel's Gross Operating Profit for the entire calendar year, as set forth in the hotel's income statement as certified by an independent public accountant, after deducting therefrom the amount of the preliminary instalment paid, if any.

In the event that the preliminary instalment in any calendar year exceeds the rent due for the entire calendar year, the Lessor shall refund the amount of such excess to the Lessee within sixty (60) days after the close of the calendar year.

Section 2. *Calendar Years.* The first calendar year shall be the period between the commencement date of the term and December 31st of the same year. If the term of this lease commences prior to June 30th the first preliminary instalment of rent shall be calculated and paid for the period from the commencement of the term to June 30th; if the term commences after June 30th, no semi-annual preliminary instalment of rent shall be calculated and paid during the first calendar year, but the entire rent for the first calendar year shall be paid in one final instalment at the end of the year in the manner provided in Section 1(b) above.

Section 3. *Hotel's Gross Operating Profit – Books and Records.* The term 'Gross Operating Profit' shall mean the gross operating profit for each calendar year as determined by the books of account of the hotel, which shall be kept in accordance with the Uniform System of Accounts for Hotels adopted by the American Hotel Association of the United States and Canada as set forth in the book entitled *Uniform System of Accounts for Hotels* as revised from time to time, with the exceptions provided for in this lease.

'Gross Operating Profit' of the hotel shall mean the excess of the 'Gross Income' from the operations of the hotel over 'Deductions' as herein defined.

'Gross Income' shall mean all income resulting from the operation of the hotel, including rental or other payments from sub-lessees and concessionaires, but not including the gross receipts of such sub-lessees or concessionaires.

'Deductions' shall consist of only the following and only insofar as the same relate to the operation of the hotel:

1. Cost of sales; salaries and wages; departmental expenses; administrative and general expenses; payroll taxes; cost of training employees and employee relations expenses; advertising and business promotion; heat, light and power; and repairs and maintenance.
2. All other expenses necessary for the operation of the hotel, including, without limitation, the cost of replacements to (a) the inventories referred to in Section 1 of Article IV hereof, and (b) china, glassware, silverware, utensils, linen and similar equipment necessary for the proper operation of the hotel.
3. A reserve for uncollectable accounts receivable equal to one per cent (1%) of the total accounts receivable outstanding at the end of the calendar year, or such other amount as the Lessee shall determine on the basis of experience.
4. Insurance expenses on all policies maintained by the Lessee pursuant to Section 2 of Article IX.
5. Taxes, if any, payable by or assessed against the Lessee, excluding taxes based on net income.

6. Amortization of Pre-Opening Expenses, pursuant to Section 4 of Article IV.
7. All costs and fees of any independent public accountants who perform services required or permitted pursuant to any Article of this Lease.
8. The costs of technical consultants, supervisors and other specialized personnel, while such consultants, supervisors and specialized personnel so employed are in the hotel in connection with the operation of the hotel, and their travel expenses to and from the hotel.
9. Amortization charges for capitalized alterations, additions or improvements, pursuant to Section 1 of Article VII hereof.
10. Any operating loss incurred during prior years as a result of any cause referred to in Section 3 of Article IV hereof.
11. The amount to be credited to the reserve for capital expenditures provided for in Article V.
12. An amount equal to three per cent (3%) of the annual Gross Income as reimbursement to the Lessee for the hotel's share of the Lessee's annual costs and expenses incurred in group advertising and sales promotion on behalf of the hotel and in maintaining for the benefit of the hotel as a part of the Intercontinental Group:

    (i) its system staff of executives and operational experts;
    (ii) its worldwide sales offices and facilities;
    (iii) its communications and reservations system; and
    (iv) the services of its operational experts on routine and periodic inspection and consultation visits to the hotel.

13. Such other deductions as are specifically provided for in this lease.

Section 4. *Reports.* The Lessee will deliver to the Lessor, within each calendar month, monthly reports of the operations of the hotel for the immediately preceding calendar month. Such reports shall include a summary of Profit and Loss (short form) for each such month, in substantially the form in the Uniform System of Accounts for Hotels.

Section 5. *Transfer of funds by Lessee.* Since it is essential to make expenditure in US Dollars and other foreign currency in order to operate the hotel in a manner which will successfully cater to the international tourist and business trade, the Lessee will make expenditures in such dollars and currency to the extent necessary in its judgment to operate the hotel in such manner. Without limiting the generality of the foregoing, the Lessee will make such expenditures for the importation of food, beverages, household and consumable stores and similar inventory items for the hotel, for reimbursement to the central organization of the Inter-Continental

Group for the cost of maintaining a staff and facilities to assure modern and efficient hotel management and operating methods for the members of the Group, and for selling the services of and advertising the hotel; provided, however, that the Lessee shall only be obligated to make such expenditures to the extent such currency control authorities or other governmental authorities as may have jurisdiction make US dollars or other convertible foreign currency available therefore pursuant to applications referred to below. The Lessor agrees to join with the Lessee in all applications to such authorities to make such dollars and other currency available to the Lessee at non-discriminatory rates of exchange, in amounts not in excess of those received by the Lessee in the Operation of the Hotel, with permission to remit the same to such place or places as the Lessees may designate, to the extent necessary to make the foregoing expenditures and to pay the Lessee its share, if any, of earnings under this lease.

[Note: Section 6 of Article IV of the standard hotel lease form is deleted.]

Document 31: Private Participation in State Rubber Project: Goodyear, Firestone, etc.

Memorandum from R.S. Amegashie, Chairman, Negotiating Committee for the Sale of and Participation in Selected State Enterprises, to the National Economic Committee, 4 May 1967.

1. The Ghana Rubber Project consists of three sections:

   (a) The Rubber Plantations,
   (b) A Latex Processing Plant, and
   (c) The Rubber Tyre Factory at Bonsasu.

2. *The Rubber Plantations* are now in the ownership of the State Farms Corporation. The Corporation has about 75,000 acres of land, about 22,000 acres of which are under rubber although less than half the trees planted have been bud-grafted. About 400 acres of plantation in the Dixcove area are now mature and ready for tapping.

There is, however, no latex processing plant available anywhere in the whole rubber area. Thus, until a latex processing plant is built, there cannot be derived any revenue from the rubber plantations.

3. Available statistics show that up to 1965 December ending, total expenditure incurred on the Rubber Plantations by the State Farms Corporation, including acquisition costs, was about £$1^{3}/_{4}$ million. It is estimated that some £$10^{3}/_{4}$ million more will have to be spent between now and 1979 when the area now planted would have come into full production.

This extra expenditure includes provision for a latex processing plant valued at around £300,000.

This processing plant, if built early enough, would enable revenue to be earned, during the period up to 1979, of about £$11\frac{1}{4}$ million. Thus, given the necessary finances required between now and 1979, total projected expenditure over the period would be £$12\frac{1}{2}$ million as against total projected revenue of £$11\frac{1}{4}$ million. This would leave a deficit of £$1\frac{1}{4}$ million which would be amortized over the two subsequent years by the end of 1981. It is absolutely necessary to bear in mind that these projections depend on the prompt availability at the right time of the financial investments required to be injected into the operations every now and again. If the necessary finances are not forthcoming at the correct times, the break-even year will be postponed indefinitely. On the other hand, if investment is speeded up, the break-even year will be hastened and may be reached within 7 to 8 years from now. Experienced rubber plantation management is vital for success.

4. *The Latex Processing Plant* is a *sine qua non* of the economic and financial success of the plantations. The Plant necessary for operations of the size of the State Farms Corporation's plantations will cost around £300,000. It needs to be built now, for some of the plantings are now mature and are ready for tapping. They, however, cannot be tapped unless there are available facilities for processing the latex into raw rubber.

5. As long as there is no processing plant, the rubber trees are yielding no revenue; and there is a notional loss of a minimum of £500,000 foreign exchange per annum now – this figure of loss rising yearly until 1979 when it settles down to £2 million per annum. Here also good and interested management is vital.

6. *The Rubber Tyre Factory* is situated at Bonsasu. The Civil Engineering work for this factory is in progress and the factory is scheduled to be completed before the end of this year. The Land and the Factory together with ancillary buildings are estimated to cost £1.2 million. The Machinery and Equipment supplied under credit by Messrs Technoexport of Czechoslovakia, cost £295,300 f.o.b. Total cost of the factory completed would be about £$2\frac{1}{4}$ million.

7. *General*: Ghana's total investment in the Ghana Rubber Project by the time they Tyre Factory is completed at the end of this year will be, at cost, about £5 million, made up as follows:

	£ million
Expenditure on Plantations up to Dec. 1965	$1\frac{3}{4}$
Total Cost of Rubber Tyre Factory	$2\frac{1}{4}$
Plantation Expenditures 1966 and 1967 and factory extras say	1
	£5 million

8. Among the various considerations that will determine the selection of a partner to enter into joint venture with the Ghana Government on this project will be the consideration of how much of this investment is likely to be recouped from the new venture, i.e. the valuation by the partner of Ghana's assets purchased by the new venture.

9. Originally it was intended to invite participation only into the Rubber Tyre Factory Project, the Plantations being intended to remain in the full ownership of the Government of Ghana. As the study and analysis of the Ghana Rubber Project progressed, however, it became clear from the capital requirements manifested by the projections that it would be in the best interests of Ghana to seek both technical know-how and financial participation into all three sections of the Rubber Project.

10. The Negotiating Committee is convinced that financial participation ensures the interest of the partner-manager in the proper economic management of the project, bearing in mind the absolute necessity for aiming at and achieving profitability. For this reason, financial participation is to be preferred to management contracts in which the manager-firm is guaranteed his fees irrespective of the financial results of his management operations.

11. Furthermore, according to the projections for the Ghana Rubber Project, heavy capital investments are going to be necessary for the meaningful operation of the project. All these considerations have been fully taken into account by the Negotiating Committee in the study of the proposals submitted by three world-famous rubber companies:

    (a)   Promoci France
    (b)   Goodyear Tire & Rubber Company of Akron, Ohio, USA.
and
    (c)   Firestone Tire & Rubber Company of Akron, Ohio, USA.

12. The proposals of the above-mentioned companies have been thoroughly thrashed out with high ranking executives of each of the companies and the following are summaries of the final proposals submitted by the Companies:

Promoci propose that a 10-year Co-operation Agreement be entered into by the Ghana Government with Promoci (France) on the following terms:

    A. (i)   A joint limited liability company be established to build, equip and run a latex processing plant in Ghana.
        (ii) The share capital of the company shall be US $200,000 to be subscribed as to 51% by Ghana and 49% by Promoci (France).
        (iii) Promoci (France)'s 49% which is US $98,000 shall be brought by way of imported equipment for the latex processing plant, while Ghana's 51% which is equal to US $102,000 shall be contributed as to two-thirds in cedis and one-third in convertible currency to provide the buildings, stores, civil engineering works, water supply, accommodations and all

other local items required to provide material accommodation for the imported equipment and machinery.

B. Promoci (France) will provide the experts needed for setting up the appropriate organization, and advising locally-based personnel on cultivation methods and will ensure overall management and supervision of both the plantations (only the acreage already planted and no more) and the processing plant.

C. Promoci (France) shall be guaranteed the following fees free of tax in foreign exchange by the Ghana Government whether or not the proceeds of sale are capable of accommodating such fees:

	US $
1967:	30,000
1968:	50,000
1969:	80,000
1970:	90,000
1971:	100,000
1972:	110,000
1973:	120,000
1974:	130,000
1975:	140,000
1976:	150,000

D. The new company will raise a five-year loan from a local bank, under the guarantee of the Ghana Government, for its first year's expenses. Expenses of years subsequent to the first shall be financed from long-term loans which, it is hoped, can be raised from an international organization.

E. At the expiration of the 10-year Agreement, the parties shall have the following options:

(i) continuation of the existing arrangement
(ii) buying out in convertible currency, of Promoci (France)'s participation in the new company by the Ghana Government, the rate of exchange applicable being the rate prevailing at the time of purchase,
(iii) any other solution acceptable by the parties.

14. *GOODYEAR* propose the establishment of two new companies: one for the Plantations and the other for the Tyre Factory on the following terms:

(A) Goodyear will negotiate for the purchase of 80% ownership of the Bonsasu Tyre Project and 20% of ownership of the Plantations.
(B) Goodyear has tentatively appraised the value of the proposed ownership shares at one million pounds (£1 million). This

tentative appraisal is based among other considerations upon the valuation of completed buildings and land appurtenances.
(C) The value of the assets of the Tyre Project and the Rubber Project will be determined by negotiation.
(D) Goodyear will exercise full management and control of the Tyre Project and the Plantations by ownership or assignment of voting shares and by management contracts.
(E) Goodyear will build at its own expenses latex processing plant of sufficient size to process all rubber produced by the Plantations and by small farmers in the area.
(F) Goodyear will buy all raw rubber produced by the Plantations and by small farmers in the area.
(G) Goodyear will agree to offer equity participation to the public in graduating amounts provided the total portion of shares held outside Goodyear does not exceed 30% of the total.
(H) Capital Investment privileges shall be a condition of their participation.

15. *FIRESTONE* proposes that a new company be established to mount an economically viable project for (a) the production, consumption and export of processed rubber and (b) the manufacture and sale of vehicle tyres, tubes and retread materials on the following terms:

(A) The new company shall have equity capital of US $10 million subscribed as to 55% by Firestone and as to 45% by the Ghana Government.
(B) Firestone would acquire its 55% interest by payment to the new Company in Ghana of US $4,700,000 and provide services to the value of US$800,000.
(C) The new company would lease from the Ghana Government its rubber plantations but purchase the tyre plant interests at a valuation to be agreed between the parties. The Ghana Government would then acquire its 45% interest for local currency.
(D) The US $4,700,000 payment by Firestone would result in an immediate contribution to Ghana's foreign exchange position as the funds would not be required for external expenditures by the new company.
(E) Additional capital required for the projects would be raised by the new company from a combination of loans (Exim Bank $2.5 million in year I repayable over 7 years.
   Foreign loans—$1.5 million in Year II repayable over 7 years and the Cedi counterpart of some of the dollars paid to the Government and perhaps from the banking system).
(F) The new company will operate the useable acres of the plantations of which about 20,000 acres have already been

planted, and planting of the second 20,000 acres would begin during the second year of operation at the rate of 2,000 acres per year.

Within approximately eight months following its incorporation the new company would have completed the erection of a modern latex processing plant adjacent to the existing tyre plant site at Bonsasu.

(G) The new company would immediately proceed with finalizing the construction of the Bonsasu Tyre Factory, based upon the work completed and the tyre plant equipment located there as well as in accordance with the technical and engineering recommendations of Firestone.

(H) Firestone estimates that the tyre plant could come into production within 12 to 18 months following incorporation of the new company.

(I) The tyre plant would be designed to supply about 90% of the Ghana market.

(J) Firestone would undertake that, while selling prices of tyres, tubes and retread materials would be permitted to find their own levels, unless there were increases in wage levels or power, fuel or raw material costs, such prices would not exceed those prevailing at 1 February 1967.

(K) Free housing would be provided to personnel of the new company employed to work on the plantations.

(L) Recreational and clinical services would be provided free of charge to all employees.

(M) The new company will employ at the outset about 3,780 Ghanaians as against 29 foreign personnel. Of the 29 foreigners, 1 shall serve among the Management staff of the Plantations, 1 among the Management staff of the Latex Processing Plant and 27 in the Tyre Factory. (Ten (10) of the 27 foreigners shall be considered as temporary and these and more shall be repatriated at later dates, as Ghanaians become qualified for more responsible factory and administrative positions).

The number of Ghanaian employees will rise to 6,400 when the first 40,000 acres come into full production.

(N) The new company will undertake an extensive programme to supply, at a nominal charge, bud-grafted planting material and also free advisory services to Ghanaian citizens wishing to embark upon rubber farming.

(O) The grant of Capital Investment privileges shall be a condition of their participation.

(P) In addition to the initial foreign investment the operations of the company would affect the foreign exchange position of Ghana as follows:

Import and Export Scheme
Foreign Exchange Results

1. Firestone estimates that the overall foreign exchange results of the Rubber and Tire Project would be as below:
Table 31.1

Year From Date Operations Begin	Savings of Foreign Exchange	Raw Material Imports	Processed Rubber Exports	Net of Foreign Exchange
1	$1,441,800	$ 821,500		$620,300
2	2,296,800	1,189,200		1,107,600
3	2,883,300	1,385,700		1,497,600
4	2,883,300	1,253,700		1,629,600
5	2,883,300	1,067,500	$157,800	1,973,600
6	2,883,300	1,067,500	503,800	2,325,600
7	2,883,300	1,067,500	909,800	2,725,600
8	2,883,300	1,067,500	2,361,800	4,177,600
9	2,883,300	1,067,500	3,397,800	5,213,600
10	2,883,300	1,067,500	4,433,800	6,249,600
15	2,883,300	1,067,500	6,433,800	8,249,600
18	2,883,300	1,067,500	7,633,800	9,449,600

2. The above figures are based upon Firestone's best estimates of the current value of tyres imported into Ghana, and assume that Firestone Ghana produces and sells 90 per cent of the total tyre, tube and retread materials market in Ghana. Calculations are based on sales of 120,000 tyre units annually: as sales increase from that figure the savings of foreign exchange would accordingly increase from the figures shown.

Material Imports

The figures shown are based upon production of 120,000 tyre units during and following the third year after the tyre plant starts operations, and take into account crude rubber imports for the first four years during which production from the rubber farms of Firestone Ghana would not meet the requirements of the tyre plant. Firestone Ghana would make every effort to develop sources of supply in Ghana for such items as bead wire, tyre cord, etc., which could reduce the figures shown above.

4. The figures shown are based upon production from the 20,000 acres presently planted and from the additional 20,000 acres developed and planted at the rate of 2,000 acres annually. To these figures would be added the foreign exchange proceeds from exports of processed rubber from the private farms in Ghana developed as a consequence of Firestone Ghana's programme.

Comment and Recommendations

16. From the foregoing, it is evident that the Promoci proposals are unquestionably the least attractive for the following reasons:

   (a) There is not enough financial provision contemplated to carry out the size of operations necessary.
   (b) They propose to establish a company with $200,000 for Latex Plant when the right size plant will cost about $1 million.
   (c) They do not wish to consider participation on the Plantations. All they want is a Management Contract without financial commitment.
   (d) They do not wish to consider anything about [sic] the Tyre Factory.

17. Since the Ghana Government has not the resources to finance the projects by itself, Promoci's proposals do not provide answers to our problems. That leaves a choice to be made between Goodyear and Firestone.

18. Goodyear in fact prefers to buy the Rubber Tyre Factory outright. They would prefer not to meddle with ownership problems regarding the Plantations while they will want to own the Tyre Factory a hundred per cent. They appear to be afraid of prospects of the growth of Communism on Plantations and they would not like to be involved with part-ownership. Their last-moment agreement to buy 20% of the Equity of the Plantations seems to be dictated by their eagerness to enter into this deal at all costs.

19. Goodyear is well aware of the fact that the Tyre Factory is the section of the Project that will yield returns fastest and they want to keep this all to themselves to the exclusion of the Ghana side. They know that the Plantations will need a lot of capital investment and will yield returns slowly, hence this must be wholly or substantially borne by Ghana, even when it was made known to them that resources were scarce for the Ghana side.

20. The Negotiating Committee formed the impression that Goodyear really had no interest in entering into partnership operations with us.

21. Goodyear's insistence on at least 70% in the Tyre Factory is not acceptable.

22. Goodyear's indication that the valuation of 80% of the Tyre Factory and 20% of the Plantations is likely to be around £1 million is unrealistic. They insist on owning the Latex Processing Factory to the exclusion of the Ghana Government.

23. On the whole the Goodyear representatives did not impress us as serious outside Management Contract Arrangements.

24. Firestone's proposals are the most reasonable of all. In their projections, indications are given of the right valuation of the Ghana assets. The large amount of foreign exchange to be infused is attractive. We tried to get them to accept a minority holding but they refused on the grounds that if they did Firestone's Consolidated Financial Statements

would not show their Investments; besides, then, the arrangement would not be Firestone. They however moved from 60% to 55% which is an improvement.

25. Insistence by the Ghana side on a majority holding would reduce the foreign capital to be infused; besides it would increase the future commitment of the Ghana side for any additional capital that may be required for expansion.

26. It seems to us that Firestone will be quickest off the mark if an agreement was entered into with them. They have put a lot of work into the study of the Project and the Negotiating Committee thinks that they deserve to win the bid for participation in the Ghana Rubber Project.

27. The Negotiating Committee, therefore, invites the Economic Committee to pass on its recommendation to the NLC that approval be given for Firestone to be selected for participation with the Ghana Government in the Rubber Project on the terms of their proposals submitted to the Negotiating Committee.

4 May, 1967

Document 32: Private Participation in State Cement Factories
Memorandum from the Chairman of the Negotiating Committee to the National Liberation Council, 4 May 1967.[1]

1. Consequent upon the directions of the National Liberation Council, the Negotiating Committee recalled A/S Norway Cement Export Limited[2] and requested them to:

   (a) consider reducing their quotation for the price of clinker deliveries geared to two years' supply.

   (b) give a firm undertaking for the exploration of the Nauli limestone deposits,

   (c) consider infusing a substantial amount of foreign exchange into the proposed new company by way of equity contribution and for Working Capital and

   (d) consider abandoning the provisos included in their Original proposals concerning fluctuations in the price of oil.

2. The Negotiating Committee has held several meetings with Mr Backe the chairman and sole-owner of A/S Norway Cement Works Ltd together with his colleagues and advisors. The following is a summary of the new proposals put forward by A/S Norway Cement Export Limited:

   (i) A new company will be formed to be known as "Ghana Cement Works Limited".

(ii) Ghana Cement Works Limited shall purchase all the assets which now constitute the Tema Clinker Grinding Mill and which shall constitute the Takoradi Clinker Grinding Mill when the latter shall have been completed.

(iii) Ghana Cement Works Limited shall have Equity Share Capital of £400,000, of which the Government of Ghana will subscribe 75% and A/S Norway will subscribe 25%.

(iv) A/S Norway Cement Export Limited will supply the Ghana company's total requirement of clinker for a period of two years at 79/- per metric ton, c.i.f.

(v) The new Ghana Company under the management of A/S Norway shall, at the Ghana Company's expense, explore the possibility of exploiting the Nauli Limestone deposits. This exploration shall be completed within 18 months.

(vi) The grant of Capital Investment privileges shall be a condition of their participation.

3. The Negotiating Committee considers the above terms satisfactory all except those relating to

(a) the price of clinker
(b) the exploration of the Nauli deposits at the expense of the new Ghana Company and
(c) the total capitalization of the new Company.

4. The Negotiating Committee considers the clinker price of 79/- per ton too high. The Negotiating Committee feels certain that had the price negotiation been left to the Committee, it would have been possible to attract a more favourable quotation for clinker price from A/S Norway. It is considered that A/S Norway would have been prepared to come down lower than 79/- per ton for two years but for the fact that they had formed the impression that the NLC itself wished them to have it for 79/- per ton.

5. The Negotiating Committee considers further that the exploration of the Nauli deposits should *not* be at the expense of the Ghana Company in which A/S Norway has only 25% investment. A/S Norway is bringing in only £100,000 which is barely enough for the working capital of the new company. This amount is certainly not going to be sufficient for both working capital and exploration expenses. Consequently the exploration expenses must be provided by A/S Norway in foreign exchange. Alternatively, the capital of the new company should be increased so that A/S Norway's contribution should provide enough funds, *ab initio*, for working capital as well as for exploration expenses.

6. Attached Marked 1 and 2 respectively are a draft Master Agreement and a draft Clinker Supply Agreement[3] stating the terms of partnership between A/S Norway and the Ghana Government in the proposed new Company as well as the terms governing the supply of Clinker.

7. In the Clinker Supply Agreement, under 'Payments' in paragraph 6

A/S Norway insist on payments for clinker being effected in pounds sterling against Irrevocable Letters of Credit confirmed by Den Norske Creditbank, Oslo. The Negotiating Committee *cannot* agree to the provision for confirmation, since this might compel a deposit to have to be placed with the Den Norsk Creditbank, thus nullifying the credit and turning it into a sight payment.

8. Attached Marked 3 is a letter received from APCM* improving on their previous offer for the price of clinker deliveries.[4]

9. The Negotiating Committee wishes to draw the attention of the NLC to the fact that the acceptance of the Norwegian proposals would give rise to the need for abrogating the existing clinker contract with APCM, the term of which does not come to an end until 1972.

10. The National Liberation Council's direction is sought as to the following:

(i) To accept the Draft Master Agreement, submitted by A/S Norway, for execution, subject to the Attorney-General's vetting, in its entirety or subject to a reduction in the price of clinker deliveries as well as to an improvement in the capitalization and provisions relating to exploration expenses.

(ii) To accept the Draft Clinker Supply Agreement, subject to the vetting of the Attorney-General and of the Ports Authority, in its entirety or subject to a reduction in the price of clinker deliveries as well as to the deletion of the provision relating to the confirmation of the Letters of Credit by a foreign bank.

(iii) The abrogation of the existing clinker supply agreement with APCM and consequent payment of compensation.

(Draft) **Master Agreement**[5] '*1*'

The Government of Ghana, represented by... hereinafter called the Government, and A/S Norway Cement Export Limited, hereinafter called Norcement, have agreed to develop jointly the cement industry of Ghana on conditions hereinafter set out.

The Parties will cause to be formed a Ghanaian limited company, Ghana Cement Works Limited, hereinafter referred to as the Company, to have as its object the manufacture and sale of Portland Cement. The equity share capital of the Company shall be equal to £400,000 of which the Government will subscribe to 75% and Norcement and its associates will subscribe to 25%.

2. The Government will sell and transfer to the Company its cement works at Tema and Takoradi on conditions to be set out in a Purchase Agreement, the basic provisions of which shall be:

*Associated Portland Cement Manufacturers' Limited—*Editor*

(a) The works shall be transferred free of encumbrances and with all existing installations, equipment, inventories, and spare parts.
(b) The Tema Works shall be transferred as soon as possible, but not earlier than two months after the signing of this Agreement and not later than 1 September 1967. The Takoradi Works shall be transferred at the time of its completion and delivery by the Contractor to the Government, and when found by the Company to be in full working condition with adequate supplies of water and electricity available. The Company shall undertake no financial obligation for any maintenance or administration of the works prior to that time.
(c) The purchase price for the two works shall be equal to £1,900,000 payable by the Company to the Government as follows:

- (i) £300,000 to be paid at the time of transfer of the Tema Works through issue to the Government of shares in the Company.
- (ii) The balance to be paid in cash in equal instalments annually for six years, it being understood, however, that, depending on its financial position, the Company may repay the loan sooner or apply to the Government for an extension. The first instalment shall be paid one year after the transfer of the Takoradi Works to the Company.
- (iii) The unpaid balance of the loan shall carry interest at 5% per annum payable in arrears annually together with the capital instalments.

3. Norcement undertake to supply the Company's total requirement of cement clinker for a period of two years commencing at such time as the Takoradi works will start its operation. Norcement furthermore undertake to supply the cement clinker requirements of the Tema works prior to that date. The price shall be 79/- per metric ton c.i.f. and shall be payable 180 days after the date of shipment from Norway. The price shall remain firm for the delivery period. The Government undertake to make currency available for the payment for clinker whenever it falls due. All terms for the supply of clinker shall be set out in a Clinker Supply Agreement.

4. Norcement undertake to explore, at the Company's expense, the possibility of utilizing the limestone deposits at Nauli for the production of cement clinker. Norcement will endeavour to complete such exploration within 18 months after the Takoradi works has commenced its operation. The exploration shall include the evaluation of existing data and obtaining further data through a diamond drilling programme, chemical and physical analysis of the cores, calculations of the necessary admixture of clay, shale, iron ore or silicon sand for making a correct raw meal composition shipping of samples to Norway for testing, including test turns

in laboratory scale, and making cost and profit studies relating to the utilization of the deposits.

5. Norcement's part of the Company's share capital in the amount of £100,000 shall be paid in cash in foreign currency of pounds sterling when the Company has acquired title to the Tema Works. The said amount shall be used to meet the Company's requirement of working capital during the initial period of operation. If the Company should prove unable to meet any added requirement of working capital through income from the sale of cement, including the capital requirements for the exploration of the Nauli deposits, Norcement undertake to adjust the credit terms for the supply of clinker to the extent that local credit cannot be obtained.

It is understood and agreed that the Government shall not be called upon to make cash contributions to the Company. The share capital to be contributed by the Government in the amount equal to £300,000 shall be set off against an equal amount of the purchase price for the Tema and Takoradi Works and shall be considered paid in at the time of transfer of title of the Tema Works from the Government to the Company.

6. In order to facilitate a sound development of the Company the Government undertake, during such period as any part of the purchase price for the cement works shall remain unpaid, to grant to the Company as a pioneer enterprise all privileges under the Capital Investments Act, 1963. The Government furthermore undertake, for the same period, to exempt the Company from paying customs duties and other levies on the import of cement clinker, gypsum, grinding media, paper bags, machinery, internal transport equipment including barges and spare parts. No licence should be granted to other companies for the import of cement so long as the Company is able to supply the total required quantities and qualities from its works.

7. The Parties agree that it is of the utmost importance to provide for a sound and efficient management and operation of the Company and its works. It is therefore agreed that the Company's Managing Director shall be chosen among such candidates as Norcement shall recommend.

The Managing Director shall have exclusive power to manage the Company in accordance with sound business principles. More specifically, but not limited to, he shall have the power to hire and dismiss all staff members and employees, including such expatriates as he deems necessary, and decide their employment terms, to place, on a competitive basis, all orders necessary to meet the Company's requirements, to set the Company's prices for cement, and to decide its sales policy.

It is understood and agreed that the number of expatriates to be employed should be limited and kept as low as possible.

8. Having regard to the partner relationship to be established between them the Parties agree that the Company should be organized so as to give both of them a deciding influence in the Board of Directors and otherwise. To that end the following provisions should be included in the Company's Regulations:

(a) The object of the Company shall be the manufacture and sale of Portland Cement.
(b) The object of the Company may not be altered unless all Directors of the Board unanimously agree.
(c) The Board of Directors shall have all Company powers which have not been conferred upon the Managing Director. More specifically the Board shall have the power, upon the recommendation of Norcement, to appoint and dismiss the Managing Director, to declare dividends or otherwise decide on the disposition of the Company's net profits upon the recommendation of the Managing Director, to sell the Company's property or acquire additional property and to apply for loans and mortgage Company property as security.
(d) The Board of Directors shall consist of six members of whom the Government shall nominate three and Norcement shall nominate the other three, one of whom shall be the Managing Director. He shall also be the Chairman of the Board. In case of a deadlock in matters where unanimity is not required the Chairman shall cast the deciding vote.
(e) The Board members nominated by Norcement shall be highly experienced in the operation and management of industrial or commercial enterprises. The Board members nominated by the Government shall equally be of high standing and shall, in case of a civil servant, hold a position not inferior to that of Principal Secretary, and, if otherwise employed, hold a similar high position.
(f) If either Party wishes to sell shares of the Company he shall obtain the consent of the other Party, such consent shall not be unreasonably withheld.

9. This Agreement shall be governed by the laws of Ghana. Should any dispute arise between the Parties in respect of the implementation or interpretation of this Agreement such dispute shall be referred to arbitration in The Hague, each Party appointing one arbitrator and the two so chosen appointing an umpire.

All procedural matters relating to the arbitration shall be governed by Dutch law.

Accra,
April 1967

Document 33: Private Participation in State Pharmaceutical Corporation

Memorandum from the Chairman, Negotiating Committee, to the National Economic Committee, 15 May 1967.

1. The book values of the assets of the State Pharmaceutical Corporation are as follows:

	£
Buildings	820,000
Machinery	172,000
	£992,000

2. Enquiries were received from several overseas firms about this enterprise. However, serious proposals were submitted by only two organizations:

   (a) *Major & Company (Ghana) Limited* in conjunction with and on behalf of *Farbwerke Hoechst Ag* Frankfurt/Main, Western Germany
   (b) *Abbott Laboratories* of North Chicago, Illinois.

3. The following are summaries of their proposals:

(A) *Hoechst/Major:*

   (i) A new Company should be formed to operate the project and that its full management should be vested in Hoechst.
   (ii) The shareholding of the new Company to be in the following proportions:

Ghana Government	40%
Hoechst/Major	60%

   (iii) The Authorized Capital of the New Company should be £500,000 (N₵1,000,000.00) but the initial call-up to be £250,000 (N₵500,000.00) and subscribed in the following manner:

   £100,000 (N₵200,000.00) by Ghana Government—by making available existing machinery
   £150,000 (N₵300,000.00) by Hoechst/Major—by cash payment.

   The balance of the Authorized Capital is to be called up as necessary if required.
   (iv) The new Company should purchase from the Government the whole of the land, buildings and machinery as it now stands, subject to their condition being normally acceptable, (e.g. the machinery not having deteriorated in storage), and to be

responsible for any vital additions or variations to be made to bring the factory into production.

(v) The new Company will undertake to pay to the Government for all the above the sum of £500,000 (N₡1,000,000.00) as set out below:

			£
(a)	*Immediate payment*		
	Machinery		100,000
	Initial payment for bldgs.		50,000
			£150,000
(b)	*Balance*		
	£23,333.6.8 per annum over 15 years		350,000
			£500,000

(vi) The grant of the following facilities shall be a condition of this offer:

(a) Obligation of the Ghana Government to purchase the pharmaceuticals which are locally processed exclusively from the company if the price does not exceed the lowest import price from a renowned manufacturer by more than 25%.

(b) In case the company should take up the processing of antibiotics for parenteral use – penicillin/streptomycin preparations etc. – a price difference of 35% should be accorded to these items.

Obligation of the Ghana Government to use the pharmaceuticals purchased from the company only for the Government sector and not to sell them to the private sector.

(c) Obligation of the Government not to permit the establishment of another pharmaceutical factory for a period of ten years.

(d) Permission to process all pharmaceuticals including the full range of Hoechst, Behringwerke and Chemiche Werke Albert.

(e) Permission to enter into technical assistance agreements with other pharmaceutical manufacturers to process their pharmaceutical specialities.

(f) Permission to manufacture cosmetics, baby foods, insecticides and similar products.

(g) Royalties of 10% on the net sales value of all medical specialities processed by the Company.

(h) Sufficient import licences for machinery, spare parts, raw materials, packing materials and auxiliaries.

(i) Import stop for all identical and similar pharmaceuticals processed by the new Company for the Government Sector and the Private Sector.
(j) Free choice of the source of supply of machinery, spare parts, raw materials, packing materials and auxiliaries.
(k) Realistic freedom to fix the prices for the locally processed pharmaceuticals in the private sector, whilst complying with local price control.
(l) Duty/Sales Tax exemption for the import of machinery, spare parts, raw materials, packing materials and auxiliaries.
(m) The Company should be free to arrange Loans from the Bank of Ghana to the extent of the investment of Hoechst, i.e. £150,000; such loans to be accorded a preferential interest rate.
(n) Tax free transfer of Royalties.
(o) Exemption from Income Tax for a period of ten years.
(p) Expatriate Quotas for Managerial and Technical Staff.
(q) Guarantee that the Company will not be nationalized.

(B) *Abbott Laboratories:*

(i) A new Company to be called Abbott Laboratories (Ghana) Limited (Abbott Ghana – for short) shall be formed.
The Authorized and Issued Capital of the Company shall be £500,000 (N₡1,000,000.00).

(iii) There shall be two classes of shares:

(1) those with voting rights.
(2) those without voting rights.

(iv) The Share Capital of the new Company shall be held as follows:

(1) *Ghana Government*
Shares with Voting Rights   40%
Shares without Voting Rights   15%   55%

(2) *Abbott Laboratories*
Shares with voting Rights   45%
                                       100%

(v) Abbott's 45% shareholding which is equal to £225,000 (N₡450,000.00) shall be paid in dollars in one sum upon the formation of the Company.

(vi) The new Company shall purchase from the Ghana Government the buildings, equipment, supplies and land of the Pharmaceutical factory at £500,000 (N₡1,000,000.00) on the following terms:

(a) *Immediate:* by issue of shares in £275,000 new Company to Ghana Government
(b) *Balance:*
by issue of Debentures to Ghana Government at Interest Rate of 6% per annum; the first payment of principal to be made upon the expiration of the tax exemption period

£225,000
───────
£500,000

(vii) The grant of the following facilities shall be a condition of this offer:

  (a) The buildings, equipment and supplies contributed by Ghana will be provided free and clear of any liens or claims whatsoever.
  (b) The land on which the factory is established shall be leased to the new Company for ninety-nine years, subject to renewal; at a fixed rental.
  (c) Abbott shall have complete responsibility and control of the operation of the new company including a majority on the Board of Directors.
  (d) Exemption from taxation for a period of ten years from the date of commencement of operation.
  (e) Ghana will facilitate the issue of all necessary construction permits and import licences required for the commencement of production by the new Company.
  (f) Ghana will approve and facilitate the issuance of all guarantees available under the Investment Guarantee Programme of the US Agency for International Development.
  (g) Ghana shall appoint the new Company the exclusive supplier of all its products to Government hospitals and other agencies of the Ghana Government.
  (h) Ghana will limit the number of import licences granted for the import of completely manufactured products competitive with those produced by the new Company during the 'pioneer' period of the new Company.
  (i) During the 'pioneer period' there shall be no duties levied on the importation of raw materials for use in the production of pharmaceutical products.
  (j) There shall be no restriction after three years on sale or transfer, inside or outside Ghana, of shares held by Abbott in the new Company to other qualified manufacturer.
  (k) The new Company may manufacture hospital solutions and devices, baby foods and agro-vet products.

4. *Comment and Recommendations:*
   (i) The two proposals are not very dissimilar in many respects. The differences that stand out are as follows:

      (a) Hoechst/Major insist unbendingly on holding a majority in the new Company, whilst Abbott, although they also originally wanted to hold a majority, will accept a minority holding if Ghana so desires (hence Abbott's acceptance of Negotiating Committee's suggestions involving 2 classes of shares – with voting rights, and without voting rights).

      (b) Hoechst/Major is prepared now to contribute only £150,000 for as much as 60% of the ownership of the new Company. Abbott, on the other hand, is prepared to put up £225,000 for 45% of the ownership of the Company; besides they will contribute more in foreign exchange if we are agreeable to push up their portion of the ownership above 45%.

      (c) Hoechst/Major insist on charging Royalties of 10% on the net sales value of all the new Company's products. The Negotiating Committee regards with disfavour this charge when the relationship that subsists is one of *partnership* as distinct from a management agency. Abbott backed down on this charge, on the insistence of the Negotiating Committee; but Hoechst/Major would not abandon their stand on this matter.

      (d) While Hoechst and Abbott are two internationally famous pharmaceutical companies, it is noteworthy that Abbotts sent a team of 10 experts including chemists, technicians, lawyers and a Vice-President (finance) to these negotiations. Hoechst, on the other hand, have not as yet put in a direct appearance. They have been represented all along by Major and Company (Ghana) Limited. Hoechst have not shown the same depth of interest as have Abbotts.

      (e) Abbotts appear very genuine about their undertaking to seriously explore the possibilities of using locally produced raw materials and packaging supplies as well as to produce basic and intermediate pharmaceutical materials in Ghana. The Negotiating Committee did not form the same impression talking to the representatives of the Hoechst/Major group.

      The Negotiating Committee, after due deliberation, supported by the counsel of Mr Nielson, who has had many years of experience in the pharmaceutical industry and who is now one of the Opex experts from the United Nations attached to the State Enterprises Secretariat, recommends that the Economic Committee obtain the approval of the National Liberation Council that Abbott Laboratories be invited to send a delegation to Ghana to finalize negotiations leading to the drawing up and execution of a definitive

and comprehensive Investment Agreement providing for the formation of a Company for the purpose of purchasing and operating the Pharmaceutical factory at Accra.

Document 34: Acquisition of Ashanti Goldfields by Lonrho

Memorandum from the Commissioner, Ministry of Lands and Mineral Resources, to the National Executive Council, 5 October 1968.

My colleagues will recall that in March 1968 Council approved that I should lead a delegation to London to meet representatives of the Board of Ashanti Goldfields Corporation, Limited, and negotiate with them the terms of a joint venture proposed to be formed by the Ghana Government, Ashanti Goldfields Corporation Limited, and the International Finance Corporation for the purpose of owning and operating gold mines over the area of some 100 square miles now the exclusive leasehold property of the Ashanti Goldfields Corporation, Limited. The lease which was originally granted for a period of 90 years will come to an end in 1986, i.e. 18 years hence.

2. The mandate of the Ghana delegation was to negotiate for the Government to take a reasonable share in the equity of a new company to be formed to take over the operation of the mine in lieu of the present 5% royalty payments which amount to about £300,000 yearly.

3. In the detailed negotiations which followed, the Ghana side was asked by Ashanti Goldfields Corporation, Limited to abandon all its rights to royalties in consideration of a grant to this Government of 10% of the equity of the new company. This in effect meant hardly any change in the returns at present received by Ghana under the existing concession. The negotiations therefore fell through.

4. My Ministry has since then given serious consideration to the matter and over the recent weeks discussions have been held with representatives of Lonrho Limited.

5. Lonrho Limited is a company registered in London and has substantial world-wide interests in mining and other industries. It has currently industrial undertakings in fifteen countries in Europe, Africa and Asia. Its present annual turnover is approximately £100 million and it employs over 70,000 people in Africa alone. During the seven-year period, 1961 to 1968, its financial record has been as follows:

Table 34.1   Consolidated Figures in £000's

30th September	Net Equity Assets	Profit Before Tax	Net Earnings	Dividends Distributed
	£	£	£	£
1961	2,155	158	114	77
1962	2,602	469	193	126
1963	3,002	502	239	161
1964	3,657	1,033	256	161
1965	4,830	1,823	602	189
1966	5,737	3,056	1,220	384
1967	6,487	3,598	1,446	812
1968 (estd.)	14,000	5,000	2,300	1,367 (estd.)

6. Initially, I was arranging that Lonrho Limited should only undertake an economic feasibility survey of our State gold mines and provide, in addition to technical advice, essential personnel as well as taking a direct interest in the operation of the mines. Two officials of the Company, the Chief Geologist and the Chief Mining Engineer recently visited our State gold mines and were quite impressed about [sic] possibilities for their development.

7. However, in subsequent discussions with the Managing Director of Lonrho Limited who was in Accra last week, it was disclosed, in strict confidence, that his Company intends in the immediate future to make a bid for the entire share capital of Ashanti Goldfields Corporation, Limited. After lengthy negotiations, the following offer is submitted to the Ghana Government for its urgent consideration in return for a new lease for 50 years:

(a) Lonrho Limited will make an allotment of a 40 per cent shareholding in the new company to the Ghana Government. Of this,

  (i) 20 per cent of the equity of the company will be assigned to the Ghana Government at once for no consideration;

  (ii) the remaining 20 per cent will be available for the Government to acquire by purchase at par out of profits earned;

(b) the new company will guarantee that the return on the Ghana Government's holding will at no time fall below the amount of royalty currently in payment;

(c) the new company will undertake the immediate development of the mine by increasing its monthly milling capacity from 45,000 tons to about 80,000 tons. This will involve the development of new areas as well as mining of lower-grade ores;

(d) free technical guidance and assistance will be offered to the State gold mines subject, of course, to reimbursement in respect of expenses for services.

8. I consider that the offer arrived at is fair and is in line with the mandate given by Council earlier this year in connection with the negotiations with Ashanti Goldfields Corporation, Limited.

9. The proposed takeover will not affect the present employees of Ashanti Goldfields Corporation, Limited, as they will continue to serve under their existing terms.

10. In view of the confidential nature and urgency with which takeover bids are effected, I invite my colleagues to approve:

(a) that Lonrho's proposals as specified in paragraph 7 be accepted in principle subject to the details being worked out;
(b) that my Ministry should communicate Government's agreement to the Company by Wednesday 9 October 1968 in order to facilitate its takeover arrangements.

Document 35: Acquisition of Ashanti Goldfields by Lonrho
Memorandum from Secretary to the National Liberation Council, 7 November, 1968.

At its meeting held on 8 October 1968, the Executive Council had before it a memorandum by the Commissioner for Lands and Mineral Resources on the above-mentioned subject and *approved:*

(a) that in the event of its bid for the entire share capital of Ashanti Goldfields Corporation Limited succeeding, the proposals by Lonrho Limited as set out below be accepted in principle, subject to the details being worked out:

(*a*) Lonrho Limited will make an allotment of a 40 per cent shareholding in the new company to the Ghana Government. Of this:

(i) 20 per cent of the equity of the company will be assigned to the Ghana Government at once for no consideration;
(ii) the remaining 20 per cent will be available for the Government to acquire by purchase at par out of profits earned;

(*b*) the new company will guarantee that the return on the Ghana Government's holding will at no time fall below the amount of royalty currently in payment;
(*c*) the new company will undertake the immediate development of the mine by increasing its monthly milling capacity

from 45,000 tons to about 80,000 tons. This will involve the development of new areas as well as mining of lower-grade ores;

(d) free technical guidance and assistance will be offered to the State gold mines subject, of course, to reimbursement in respect of expenses for services.

(b) that the Ministry of Lands and Mineral Resources should communicate Government's agreement to the Company by Wednesday 9 October 1968 in order to facilitate its takeover arrangements.

2. It was urged that the matter should be treated in strict confidence. It was also urged that confidential rating of either Seyd's or Dunn and Bradstreet on Messrs Lonrho's should be obtained through the Bank of Ghana to determine whether the Government should accept their offer which was otherwise attractive.

3. During the discussions the Council *directed* that the Lonrho Company should also be requested to look into the viability of the projected gold refinery. In addition after the takeover of Ashanti Goldfields Corporation Limited by Lonrho Limited had been finalized, the future of C.A.S.T.* should be examined by the Ministry of Lands and Mineral Resources.

Document 36: Lonrho: Proposals for Participation in Sugar Industry

1. These notes are compiled on the understanding that the Ghana Government would welcome private enterprise participation in the sugar industry, subject to the requirement that Government would almost certainly wish to retain final control in its own hands. The following suggestions are put forward as a possible basis for such participation. They are, however, tentative at this stage and, if acceptable in principle, would require further investigation before final commitment on either side. The purpose of this memorandum is therefore to submit guidelines and seek to establish whether these would meet with Government's approval as a foundation for further negotiations.

2. The present investment in Komenda and Asutsuare exceeds £9 million (on basis £1 = N₡2.45). The true value of the assets concerned is probably around £6 million. It is suggested that all the present industry's

*Consolidated Amalgamated Selection Trust, a diamond mining company – *Editor*

assets, including land holdings and both fixed and movable property, should be transferred for the latter figure into a new company, Ghana Sugar Corporation Limited.

3. The share capital of GSC would be £3 million, divided into £2 million ordinary shares and £1 million 'B' non-voting shares. The price of the existing assets would be satisfied by the issue to Government or its nominee of £1.2 million ordinary shares and a loan of £4.8 million. This loan would be interest free and would be redeemable after a 5-year moratorium by the application of all GSC annual profits over £1 million (i.e. after sufficient profits to pay a 20% dividend on the shares covered $1\frac{3}{4}$ times) or over 15 years, whichever redemption payment was the less.

4. Lonrho Limited would procure the injection of the capital required to establish the industry as a viable entity over the next 3 years. This is estimated at £1.8 million including a cubing plant, and would be satisfied by the issue of £800,000 ordinary shares and the £1 million 'B' non-voting shares in GSC.

Government would thus hold 60% of the voting shares to ensure final control.

5. The presently proposed sugar marketing board would be converted into a public company which would be wholly owned by GSC and which would be the sole licensee for sugar imports.

6. Lonrho could discuss the supply over the next 3 to 5 years of, say, 40–50,000 tons of sugar for which GSC would pay in Ghana, thus saving foreign exchange, and the resulting funds would be used by Lonrho to establish its participation in the industry.

7. GSC would be exempt from tax until the loan of £4.8 million had been repaid.

8. Controlled retail prices would be established at, say, 15 NP per lb. for granulated and 20 NP per lb. for cube sugar. These prices are higher than those now officially in force, but lower than the prices the consumer in fact pays. Allowing a 25% mark-up to the retailer, GSC would receive 12 NP and 16 NP per lb. respectively at distribution depots which it would establish in Accra, Kumasi and Tamale as well as effecting deliveries direct from Asutsuare.

9. The sugar to be supplied as per 5. above could be either refined, or raw for further processing at Asutsuare in the off-season if this was found to be economic.

10. The future of Komenda must be discussed. If this scheme is to continue, it will have to be subsidized by higher prices to the consumer.

11. GSC would undertake to increase local production to the design capacity of the factories within 3 or 4 years at the most. Thereafter, decisions must be taken whether to expand the local industry to produce the whole of Ghana's internal consumption, in which case GSC's profits from sugar imports would supply part of the funds required.

12. Lonrho would provide the management of GSC, both as to local production and the administration of imports, under the control of the

GSC Board which would be constituted in proportion to shareholdings.

13. Government would undertake to make available whatever additional land might be required by GSC to reach its production targets.

14. If the above proposals are acceptable in principle to Government, Lonrho is prepared to enter into detailed negotiations immediately.

Document 37: Lonrho: Proposal to Establish Beer Industry

1. This application is made for the purpose of establishing a traditional beer brewing industry in Ghana, initially in Tamale, and is submitted by Lonrho Limited, a public company incorporated in England.

2. Through various subsidiary and associate companies, the Lonrho Group operates over 25 breweries, including companies in Tanzania, Zambia, Malawi, Botswana and Swaziland. Negotiations are also currently under way in Kenya, Uganda and Lesotho.

3. From experience in other countries, Lonrho are convinced that the establishment of breweries along the lines proposed below is economically and socially beneficial to the community concerned for the following reasons:

(a) It replaces the brewing of pito* under unhealthy and unhygienic conditions with the controlled and scientific production of a clean and nutritional product. Health conditions connected with the present production of pito are of a very poor standard and in few cases is there any regular inspection of the process and premises, and in virtually none has any analysis of the product taken place to check on what ingredients are being used and what the final product contains. Spot analyses have indicated that there is a potential menace to public health involved in this system. Also, to provide the authorities with qualified staff and facilities over the whole of the country to make thorough inspections and analyses would constitute an impracticable burden.

(b) It guarantees that no harmful ingredients are used in traditional beer, and affords a permanent and reliable method of controlling the alcoholic content to a reasonable level.

(c) It gives the community a traditional type beverage brewed to the highest standards, providing both food and drink with valuable dietary properties.

*local beer, brewed from millet and other grains.

- (d) Properly managed, it eliminates illegal pito brewing and also puts a virtual stop to the illicit distillation of harmful spirituous liquors.
- (e) It enables proper control to be exercised over the places and hours in which traditional beer is consumed.
- (f) It provides congenial social meeting places which are an asset instead of a disgrace to the areas concerned.
- (g) Through the consumption of large quantities of cereal crops, it gives a boost to agricultural production, providing increased cash income to the farming community.
- (h) It leads to the manufacture of other products such as carbon dioxide, dry ice, yeast and animal foodstuffs.
- (i) It is appreciated that in any given area there are a number of persons engaged in the brewing and selling of traditional type beer for their livelihood. In this connection, Lonrho's intentions are that such persons be given the opportunity of selling the new product or will be employed in the new breweries.

4. It is now proposed that the following steps should be taken:

- (a) The formation of a public company with sufficient resources to build and operate breweries in the main centres of Ghana.
- (b) The erection by this company of a brewery for Tamale with an initial production capacity of 100,000 gallons a month but designed for considerable expansion if necessary, and the erection of further breweries to serve the needs of other centres such as Kumasi, Accra and Takoradi in due course.
- (c) The cost of the Tamale brewery is estimated at not more than N₵250,000 for the initial stage.
- (d) The grant to the company of licences to manufacture and sell a traditional type of beer known in many other African countries as 'Chibuku' within the areas concerned.
- (e) The estimated selling price of traditional beer from the breweries will be approximately 30 NP per gallon, this figure to be varied where necessary to take account of transport and other factors. The current retail price of pito, which must allow very large profit margins, is in the region of 5 to 10 NP per large size beer bottle, or around 5 NP for a small calabash, equivalent to 40 to 80 NP per gallon. If produced with industrial plant and sold as proposed above, Chibuku could be retailed at 40 NP per gallon, giving a $33\frac{1}{3}\%$ mark-up to the retailer.
- (f) The company will operate a contract ploughing organization designed to assist farmers in the cultivation of their land in order to expand the production of cereal crops to the necessary level.

5. Lonrho is prepared to proceed with this project immediately after receipt of Government consent.

Document 38: Proposals for Privatization of National Investment Bank
E.P.L. Gyampoh, Managing Director of NIB, to E.N. Omaboe, Chairman of NEC, 15 November, 1966.

I wish to bring formally to your attention a subject which has been discussed informally with you and other members of the Government during the past six months. This concerns the refinancing and recapitalization of the National Investment Bank (NIB) with possible additional financing and participation of the International Finance Corporation (IFC) an affiliate of the International Bank for Reconstruction and Development (IBRD).

The need for additional financing for the NIB arises from several causes:

The NIB's authorized share capital, at its organization in 1963, was £10m. Of this, Government was to take up £2.5m at its inception and an additional £5m when NIB's lending activities had committed this amount. Private investors were permitted to take up one-third as much equity capital as the Government, and this has been done.

Thus, total present paid-up equity capital of NIB is £3.25m. including Government's £2.5m. and private investors £0.75m.

Lending activities of NIB have proceeded according to its original schedule, so that the remaining £6.76m capital is now required to continue its financial support to viable projects of benefit to the economy. With the average NIB loan term being approximately six years, the annual average expected commitment of its £10m total capital is slightly over £1.5m.

In the three years since its organization the NIB has financed, or assisted in the financing of, projects totalling in excess of £10m. It now has new projects totalling over £2m ready to be financed, for which its resources, after reserves for previous commitments and guarantees, are insufficient.

The procedure now required, if the original NIB capitalization plans were followed, would be to call on Government for its further commitment of £5m, and private investors for their corresponding maximum permitted contribution of £1.75m. However, several events since 1963 have occurred which open up a considerably greater latitude for inducing financing support of the NIB without requiring a 3 to 1 Government contribution.

First, Government policy on private investors' contributions has changed, making it possible to invite and obtain more private capital in foreign exchange.

Second, the Government's financial position, especially in foreign exchange, makes it desirable to obtain the maximum amount of new NIB capital from private rather than Ghana Government sources.

Third, the desire and willingness of private investors to commit their funds to projects in Ghana has increased significantly under the present Government, so that the NIB now has a considerable backlog of potentially viable projects to implement in concert with private investors, but now has insufficient free resources for supporting this encouraging trend.

Fourth, the NIB's participation in these new private investments is highly important, since NIB's contribution will generally include a share of the equity capital of these new enterprises, which it subsequently will distribute to private Ghanaian investors, under its policy of thus maintaining an indigenous participation in these new private investments.

Fifth, without IFC participation in a development bank, the World Bank Group normally is reluctant to support financially the projects promoted by a development bank. Also, with such IFC participation, it is easier to get support from other financial institutions, both Government and private, especially in foreign exchange.

In pursuit of new investment capital for the above purpose of NIB, informal and preliminary discussions have been held with a number of overseas sources of investment capital, to assess the amount of capital which might be obtained, and the refinancing and recapitalization principles under which adequate additional investment capital could be acquired. These general principles now are sufficiently crystallized to bring to Government's attention, and to seek its permission now to engage in formal discussions leading to the NIB's actual recapitalization.

Several basic principles are involved, on which Government consideration is desired, as follows:

1. IFC participation needs to be obtained on the basis of an NIB which is 'privately controlled', as this is a basic IFC principle. However, since Ghana is a contributing member of IFC and is represented on its Board of Governors, IFC's financial contribution to NIB can be considered as for and on behalf of the Government. IFC indicates that its requirement of private control of development banks in which it participates is based on its experience with development banks over the past fifteen years, and its objective of assuring that development bank investments are made on the basis of sound economic, financial and management principles rather than on political considerations.
2. With IFC participation in NIB recapitalization it will be more easily possible to obtain comparable financial contributions from private investors, both here and abroad, especially from banks and corporations that are in a position to consider and support continued private investment in Ghana.
3. The NIB's recapitalization would necessarily involve a revision of the National Investment Act, 1963, to give effect to the principle enunciated by IFC.

Other development banks already have profited from IFC and private investor participation under the above described pattern. The Nigerian Industrial Development Bank has obtained £500,000 in capital from IFC alone. The Liberian Bank for Industrial Development and Investment has obtained £250,000 similarly. Both banks also have access to IFC for possible loans in the future, in addition to equity capital. The extent of possible future IFC and IBRD contribution to such development banks is illustrated by the experience of those banks established earlier on the IFC pattern. The Pakistan Industrial Credit and Investment Corporation has received loans and capital in excess of $80m; the Industrial Credit and Investment Corporation of India has received some $90m. Total support in both equity and loans to development banks from the World Bank Group (IFC, IBRD and IDA) has exceeded $300m over the past fifteen years.

It thus appears highly desirable for the NIB to reconstitute itself so that it may share in this large and continuing source of investment capital, not only to meet the exigencies of the present but also to provide a source of continuing development loan funds in the future. This background leads to the following specific proposals and request by NIB to Government:

(a) The Economic Committee appoint a committee to consider the pattern and alternative plans by which the National Investment Bank can avail itself of IFC participation with particular reference to the extent of Ghana Government participation in a reconstituted NIB.
(b) The Committee be composed of the Chairman of the Economic Committee, the Principal Secretary of the Ministry of Finance, the Governor of the Bank of Ghana and the Managing Director of the National Investment Bank.
(c) The Committee meet at an early date to consider proposals to be submitted by the NIB on matters referred to in paragraph (a) above.

Negotiations with IFC of the nature here proposed are necessarily deliberate and time consuming, normally requiring up to a year or more to arrive at the point at which new capital is available for commitment. Accordingly, it is desirable to initiate the above proposed action as early as possible.

Document 39: Liberalization of Bank Financing of Cocoa Sector

Memorandum from R.S. Amegashie to the Economic Committee, 12 April 1966 (Approved by the Economic Committee).

My colleagues would recall that permission was sought by the Managing Director of the State Cocoa Marketing Board to share the Board's banking business among the three Commercial Banks. I was then asked to take the matter up with the Ghana Commercial Bank with a view to ascertaining what portions of the Board's business the Commercial Bank would wish to retain. My enquiries disclose the following:

(a) The Banking business of the Board amounts to between £40 and £50 million per annum.
(b) The financing of the Board's business at the present is shared between the Ghana Commercial Bank and the Bank of Ghana roughly in a 50:50 ratio.
(c) The Ghana Commercial Bank wishes to retain its portion of this business amounting to between £20 and £25 million per annum.
(d) It is considered that the Bank of Ghana might wish to relinquish its portion of the Board's business to the two Commercial Banks namely Barclays and B.W.A.
(e) I have discussed the matter with the Governor of the Bank of Ghana and he sees no objections to the Bank of Ghana's portion of the Board's business passing on to the two expatriate Commercial Banks.

Approval of the Economic Committee is now sought for the following to be communicated to the Managing Director of the State Cocoa Marketing Board:

> That the Board's Banking business be shared among the three Commercial Banks in such a manner that the Ghana Commercial Bank retains its existing portion of the business; the remaining portion hitherto undertaken by the Bank of Ghana be shared among Barclays Bank and the Bank of West Africa.

Document 40: Government Response to Criticisms of Participation Agreements

'R.S. Amegashie, Commissioner for Industries, Replies the Critics.'

Hardly a day has passed, within the last fortnight, without some critical comment appearing in one or the other of Ghana's newspapers regarding the Agreement signed recently between the Ghana Government and Abbott Laboratories of Illinois, USA for the establishment of a joint venture company to acquire and operate the pharmaceutical factory built by the Ghana Government at Kwabenya . . .

Here are the facts about the various agreements and the principles underlying their execution:

Soon after the coup of 24 February 1966 the new Government of Ghana set out, among other things, to identify the economic problems prevalent within the country and to find solutions for them. A report* commissioned on the status of the State Enterprises disclosed that very few of the existing fifty-five State Corporations were operating satisfactorily. Most of them had been making losses consistently. There was a remarkable lack of managerial leadership in all but a few of them. These persistent losses meant a steady diminution in the capital employed in these enterprises.

Failure to arrest the trend of these losses must soon enough result in the complete devastation of what net assets were left in the enterprises at the time of takeover by the new Government. The Government, in keeping with its duty to the people of Ghana as well as in keeping with its responsibility as a Government which has forcibly removed the one before it on the ground of its conviction and knowledge that there was need to reverse the trend of misdeeds and negligences of the previous regime, *had to take a well considered and firm decision on these enterprises so as to stop once and for all the losses of assets, and to put the enterprises on a footing which will ensure successful operations leading to the recovery of some of the losses and to a quick step forward into useful production and profitability.*

It was clear to the Government that adequate working capital, both in foreign and local currencies, had to be found for those enterprises which were in difficulty on account of lack of operational funds; efficient managements had to be found; and managements with vested interest in profitable operations had to be sought and found; the labour force employed in some enterprises had to be trimmed down to sizes compatible with efficiency; and in some cases, where specialized and highly skilled operations were involved, it was considered a *sine qua non* to seek and find association with organizations with world-renowned expertise and undoubted standards of quality such as were necessary to ensure success and acceptability of the products of those enterprises.

The financial situation in which the Government was at the time when the decision as to what to do with the State Enterprises had to be taken, is no secret to anyone in this country nor to many outside it. Ghana's creditworthiness was at the lowest ebb imaginable. None of the banking institutions even in Ghana could be expected to lend money to the Government to infuse into state corporations. The national debt, owed to sources both within and outside Ghana, was at such a level that nobody except charitable institutions and Benevolent Aid organizations, would listen to any mention of further advances. Yet these enterprises stood in need of cure; some already in a state of crippled operations, others at various stages of completion waiting to be commissioned.

The decision of the Government of Ghana in these circumstances was, as, in my earnest submission, it ought to be that

---

*H. P. Nelson, 'A Report on the Administration and Operation of State Enterprises under the Work Schedule of the State Enterprises Secretariat for the period 1964–65', September 1966. See Document 29—*Editor.*

(1) a selected number of the state enterprises should be sold outright to private enterprise, which had better chances of finding the money very much needed to keep their operations going; and
(2) participation by private entrepreneurs should be invited into a second lot of selected enterprises.

The outstanding merits of this decision are as follows:

(1) There would immediately, on the completion of a sale or on the establishment of a joint venture, be a stop put to further requests to Government for money for running the enterprises; money which, in any event, Government did not have.
(2) There was a chance of these enterprises remaining in operation producing the products they were established to produce. There was equally a chance of those remaining in the employment of these enterprises continuing to receive remuneration from the resources of the buyer or participant.
(3) The enterprises stood a much better chance of operating successfully and profitably in the hands of private entrepreneurs who were, undoubtedly, in business to make profits both for themselves and for their partner (Government).
(4) The scope of operations of the enterprises stood a much better chance of being expanded in the hands of private entrepreneurs and competent profit-motivated partners with prospect of offering increased employent to Ghanaian labour.
(5) Proceeds of sale of enterprises would yield funds to the Government for support to the national budget.
(6) Foreign exchange contributions from overseas participants would provide foreign exchange support for the country's balance of payments.

In arriving at the decision to invite participation the Government had held the view that a joint venture with private enterprise – the partner being one who has proven know-how and who will be entrusted with full management powers and responsibilities, is preferable to hiring management with no financial stake in the enterprise – management hired merely for a fee which accrues irrespective of profit or losses.

It is thus clear that Government in a move to find solutions to problems facing it has taken a decision in absolute good faith to sell some enterprises and to invite private participation into others. There can be no doubt that the Government has every right to take a decision it deems fit regarding the finding of solutions to its problems. *Any criticism of such a decision can only be valid if it shows clearly that the Government had not exercised sufficient care nor applied sufficient thought in arriving at the particular decision; and that had enough care been taken an alternative solution would have been readily found.*

I should like the critics in this case to tell us what alternatives were open to the Government, in the circumstances, as possible solutions to the problems of the state enterprises. I pose this question because I believe that some of the critics question the wisdom of even the decision to invite participation into some of our state enterprises. What are the alternatives to participation? Some will immediately answer as follows:

(1) Engage more efficient personnel both indigenous and foreign – perhaps this is possible, but I cannot see that it has merit over participation which involves the participant staking his own money in the venture and his return measured by the success of his efforts. Besides, where are the liquid resources to pay this hired labour as well as to furnish the operational funds required?
(2) Borrow. Ghana could not and I doubt that it can even now find sources to supply all the money required as working capital for the State Enterprises.

These problems are still with us regarding some of the State Enterprises. For example, the Sugar Products Corporation – there is no money for developing the plantations in Asutsuare and in Komenda. There is no money with which to buy equipment vital to the development of the farms and for transporting cane from the fields to the mills. The current sugar and alcohol production is insufficient to yield funds, through sales, enough to pay wages, salaries, debts and other disbursements. In short money is needed badly to keep the place going. Furthermore, experienced sugar plantation management and efficient mill management must be found if we are to expect Ghana's sugar projects to head towards breaking even and eventually yielding good results. We do not have the money or enough men with the requisite experience and expertise. What do we do? Dilly-dallying only results in a steady diminution and deterioration of the farms and the factory assets; and a steady loss of the funds already infused and still being infused. What should a responsible Government do in these circumstances? Remember it is no longer possible to merely draw money from the Central Bank. I submit seriously that if firms like Tate and Lyle of the United Kingdom, or Bouchon of France or Saint Louis Sugar would submit participation proposals to us regarding the Sugar projects we should be extremely interested in considering them in a genuine effort to conclude a reasonable joint venture agreement with the proposer.

It is my very serious view that participation agreements are the only answer to most of our state enterprises' problems at present. We have tried Management Agencies and quite frankly they have failed miserably. They may produce managements but most of our state enterprises need money, and management without working capital merely results in losses. In many cases it is the Management fee that aggravates the losses. Moreover I do *not* believe that an arrangement which guarantees to the manager a fee irrespective of the gains or losses of his operations is preferable to one in which the manager's remuneration is linked directly with the results of his efforts.

There can be no question, therefore, about the wisdom of the decision to invite participation into some of the enterprises in our present circumstances.

The procedures in arriving at the terms of the Agreements and the Agreements themselves have also been so bitterly criticized that some explanation and clarification would doubtless help to enable the public to decide whether or not the Government and its advisers have committed all the 'dreadful sins' with which they have been charged by the critics.

First of all, I should like to say categorically that there is only one Abbott Agreement. The Indenture dated *22 August 1967* merely corrects and amends and deletes certain provisions of the Indenture dated 3 June 1967 and these corrections, amendments and deletions are to be read into the Indenture of 3 June 1967 of which they form part. The 3 June 1967 Indenture as amended by the Indenture of 22 August 1967 is therefore the one and only Abbott Agreement. The Indenture of 22 August was made and executed long before the criticisms of the Agreement had begun and was not occasioned by these criticisms. There is therefore only one Abbott Agreement.

Under this Agreement the Ghana Government and Abbott Laboratories of Illinois, USA have incorporated a limited liability Company, registered under the Ghana Companies Code 1963 (Act 179), called Abbott Laboratories (Ghana) Limited. The Share capital of this new company is one million new cedis subscribed as to 55% by the Ghana Government and 45% by Abbott Laboratories of USA. The American partner's shares are payable in one lump sum in United States dollars amounting to N₵450,000.

Ghana Government's shares are payable by the transfer to the new Company of five hundred and fifty thousand new cedis worth of Ghana's assets comprising the assets constituting the pharmaceutical factory at Kwabenya together with the grant of a lease on the real property on which these assets are located. All these assets including the land are valued by mutual agreement at *one million new cedis*. Since the assets, including the land, which belonged to the Ghana Government cannot be split into bits, according to value, for transfer to the new company formed purposely to acquire and operate the pharmaceutical factory, and since the new company requires to have the entire factory to enable it to commence operations, the whole factory has been made over to the new company. The result of this transaction is that the excess of the total value of Ghana's assets transferred to the new company over the value of shares allotted to Ghana remains a debt against the new company in favour of Ghana. Ghana's total assets transferred having been valued at one million new cedis, and shares allotted to Ghana being N₵550,000, an amount of N₵450,000 is owed to Ghana by the new Company on the coming into being of the new company. If Ghana insists on being paid this amount at once, the N₵450,000 subscribed by the American partner could be paid over to the Ghana Government. But this would result in the need for the new company, the majority of whose shares are held by Ghana, to find liquid resources with which to start up and carry on its operations. The American partner is unwilling or unable to infuse more money by way of equity contribution into the new company which itself, by reason of the fact that it is new, is not likely to be capable of raising a substantial working capital through borrowing except possibly against the guarantee of the American partner alone. And if so, at what cost? In these circumstances, what could the Ghana side do other than to allow its entitlement of N₵450,000 in the new company to provide funds for start-up and initial operational expenses? Ghana consequently agreed to retain the N₵450,000 in the new company as a *debenture* at an interest rate of 6% per annum. Had there been other possible partners able and willing to put more money than Abbott was prepared to into the venture, Ghana would have turned to them. There were no such others.

The negotiations for the joint venture in the pharmaceutical factory were by no means easy. There were originally eight drug manufacturing companies in the running for consideration for participation in the Kwabenya factory. Five of these companies dropped out before we got to serious bargaining, leaving three for the final negotiations. Of the three, UTC's terms were the least attractive. UTC* proposed a consortium of the following overseas firms to join up with the Ghana Government in the ventures: Ciba, Sandoz, Geigy, Hoffman, Laroche, an American enterprise and UTC itself. UTC's proposals went on:

(i) We consider N₵900,000 to be the value of the buildings, machinery and equipment which are necessary to make full use of the market potential.

(ii) The Consortium is willing to invest foreign exchange up to N₵50,000, this being needed for the purchase of additional machinery for the production of ointments, etc., not yet provided for.

(iii) All expenditure in excess of these sums must be considered as interest-free loans by the Ghana Government to the Pharmaceutical Factory for at least the first five years, repayment conditions to be negotiated at a later date.

(iv) UTC is willing to purchase shares from the Ghana Government up to the amount of N₵200,000 with the proviso that this is by re-investment of profits.

The two remaining companies out of which a choice had to be made were:

> [Mr Amegashie then goes into a detailed description of the negotiations with Major and Co. (Ghana) Limited and Abbott Laboratories of Illinois.]

*Union Trading Company of Basel, Switzerland – *Editor*.

The Negotiating Committee therefore recommended that negotiations be finalized with Abbott Laboratories leading to the drawing up and execution of a definitive and comprehensive Investment Agreement providing for the formation of a Company for the purpose of purchasing and operating the pharmaceutical factory at Kwabenya.

When the Abbott representatives came to Accra finally to sign the Agreement, our fundamental objection to the monopoly and restrictive clauses in their proposals was made very firm to them. They agreed to refer the matter back to their Board of Directors in the United States. It was when their Board agreed to our request that the corrections, amendments and deletions embodied in the Indenture of 22 August 1967 became necessary.

On the question of Management Control, it must be pointed out that with the numerous instances of interference by the old regime in the running of the State Enterprises fresh in everybody's mind, it is very unlikely that any investor is going to be willing to put his money in a State venture the operations of which are within his field of expertise without demanding full management control. Besides, if the investor is invited on account of his proven know-how and expertise in the particular function of the enterprise, then I see no reason for our concern over this matter of management control. The investor is in the business to make money; and given average honesty, he will only make money when he makes money for us well. For sure, management control does not mean that the foreign investor will only engage foreigners. This will be too expensive for profitability. In the Abbott case, the controversy over management control would not have arisen if Ghana had not insisted on and obtained a majority of the shareholding in the new Company. For, in that case, there would not have been any ostensible incongruity. It would have been as normal as, say, Ghana's position at the present time as shareholder in Lever Brothers (Ghana) Limited at Tema. In the Abbott case, Ghana insisted on and obtained a majority holding in the shareholding so as to earn a larger share of the distributable profits which will now surely be forthcoming because of the efficient management which will be brought to bear on the factory operations. I think this is an arrangement for which we should be congratulated, and certainly not insulted. Several Ghanaians have already been appointed to key positions in the new company including the position of Statutory Secretary.

Some say that an American Company has been given some unhealthy monopoly in Ghana. Where is the monopoly in the Abbott Agreement? This country is acutely short of foreign exchange. Is it a sin, in these circumstances, to restrict the importation of drugs which can be made in this country by a Company in which the Ghana Government holds the majority of the shareholding? It is better for us to spend a few more cedis than to disburse a little less of our very insufficient pool of foreign exchange. There is no monopoly in the Agreement, but even if there was this monopoly with regard to the importation of drugs, which there is not, any profits made by Abbott-Ghana would benefit Ghana, whereas all the Commission earned by a private company would only benefit that company.

The grant of Capital Investment privileges to the new Company has been criticized by some of the critics. The Capital Investments Act has been on the statute book since 1963 and benefits have been given and are being given regularly to firms deemed to be in need of such benefits. The purpose of the Act is to attract investors who will cause healthy capital inflow into this country. To attract capital from elsewhere, it must be made distinctly manifest to the Investor that the return on his capital here is superior to the return he may expect elsewhere. This means positively throwing benefits at him to make him move his resources from somewhere else to here. Why shouldn't a State enterprise in need of help be aided with Capital Investment privileges? . . .

It has been said that assets 'worth' N₡2.0 million have been transferred to the new Company at N₡1.0 million and that this is a grievous offence. The truth of the matter is that the assets *cost* N₡2.0 million, i.e. they are on the books at that amount, but they are certainly *not worth* N₡2.0 million. What is more, as assets built for the manufacture of the factory's capacity of drugs as a business venture, they are worth even less. The old regime built grandiose structures for factories – structures the cost of which could never be economically amortized over a reasonable period of time in a venture projected to make profits. There are many examples of this disparity between 'cost' and 'worth' in the Ghana system . . .

It has also been alleged that we are handing over the control of Ghana's economy to foreigners. How ridiculous. If indeed we were doing this, it would be a grievous sin indeed. To date six (6) participation contracts have been signed relating to enterprises, which, in our judgement, will only succeed with foreign participation. They are as follows:

1. Kade Match Factory – Ghana/French SIFA.
2. Tema and Takoradi Cement Works – Ghana/Norway Cement.
3. Pharmaceutical Factory – Ghana/Abbott, USA.
4. Bonsaso Rubber Tyre Factory – Ghana/Firestone.
5. State Farms Rubber Plantations – Ghana/Firestone.
6. State Furniture and Joinery – Ghana/CFC.

In all the above joint ventures but one – the Bonsaso Rubber Tyre Factory – the Ghana Government has the majority of the shareholding in the new companies established. Hence Ghana will be entitled to a greater share of the profits which must now be made in these new ventures. Does the formation of these joint ventures in Enterprises which would otherwise have been dying, constitute a handing over of Ghana's economy to foreigners?

These new ventures have all been established under the Ghana Companies Code. This Code gives adequate protection to any member or debenture holder of any Company registered under the Code. Thus there really is nothing to be afraid of by the grant to our partners of management control through their majority of numbers on the Board of Directors as well as voting control of the new Companies . . .

Document 41: Objections to Management Agreement with Inter-Continental Hotels

Political Committee Memorandum PC/M.6: 'Second Memorandum to the National Liberation Council on the Management Agreement with Inter-Continental Hotels Corporation of America for the Operation of Ghana State Hotels', 23 July 1966.

In the first memorandum on the above subject (Management Agreement with Inter-Continental Hotels of America) sent to the National Liberation Council (PC/M.1 dated 18.7.66) the Political Committee of the National Liberation Council promised to send a fuller memorandum to the Council after meeting with Mr R. S. Amegashie, the member of the Economic Committee directly responsible for the negotiations with the Inter-Continental Hotels Corporation, and Mr M. D. Quist, Acting Chairman of the State Hotels Corporation.

2. At the Political Committee's meeting of Friday, 22 July 1966, both Mr Amegashie and Mr Quist were present for part of the discussion of the proposed Management Agreement. We subsequently called in the Manager of the Ambassador and asked him a few questions about the running of the Hotel without disclosing to him our reasons for doing so. They all provided the Committee with information that was of considerable help to it in coming to its decision.

3. It appeared to the Committee that the reason why it was decided to negotiate the Management Agreement was that the Ambassador has not been making enough profits that would normally be expected from such a hotel and that, by inferring from experience, the [new] Continental [Hotel] will not make enough profit. The reason apparently was not difficult to come by: over-staffing and lack of both working and development capital. The occupancy rate in the Ambassador, the Committee was informed, is 79.8 per cent, whilst the normal rate to enable a hotel make satisfactory profit is between 40 and 50 per cent. On the other hand, the number of workers per each room is 3.95 at the Ambassador, 5 at the Airport Hotel and 3.5 for all the State Hotels. The normal number should be between 0.5 and 1; where there is very heavy ground service (e.g. five or four banquets per day) the number should be 2. Over-staffing has meant that 85 per cent of the gross turnover at the Ambassador has gone into wages and salaries; the normal percentage should be about 22 per cent.

4. According to the Memorandum from the Economic Committee to the National Liberation Council recommending approval of the Agreement ₡700,000 would be needed to put the Hotel in a position to make profit. The Manager of Ambassador informed the Committee that about ₡500,000 would be enough to achieve this aim and that with this a gross profit of 12 to 15 per cent could be realized. The Economic Committee is of the view that the money needed to renovate the Ambassador cannot be raised in the country.

5. It was also maintained that the Ambassador smelt of general shabbiness and that 'seasoned expertise' was needed to lift it out of this shabbiness. It was further maintained that the great name and experience of Inter-Continental Hotels Corporation was just what was needed to raise the efficiency of the Hotel and lend respectability to it. On the other hand, the Star Hotel was so far beyond the pale and the Meridian so costly as not to be of interest to the hard-headed businessmen of the Inter-Continental Hotels Corporation.

6. It was maintained by Mr Amegashie that the lease was the only way of getting the Hotels run efficiently and profitably, and further that there was no difference between a management agreement and a lease. Besides, he admitted that the Agreement would result in a joint venture although the country would have no share in the management.

7. The Committee considered these points carefully. *It is of the firm and considered view that the National Liberation Council should not approve the Agreement.* It was not convinced that a lease is the only way of putting the Ambassador on its feet.

8. The Committee is of the opinion that the basic trouble with the Ambassador – overstaffing – can easily be cured by the present management. It is also of the opinion that the present management, in the changed circumstances, ought to be given the opportunity to manage the hotel on a proper basis before contemplating the idea of calling in outside aid. The Manager informed the Committee that overstaff [*sic*] there was due to two factors: (i) political appointees forced on it by members of the last regime, true to the character of that corrupt and inefficient regime; and (ii) training of the staffs of other State Hotels at the Ambassador Hotel at the expense of the latter. He gave the specific example of the Manager-designate of the Continental who has been paid for months by the Ambassador because of repeated postponement of the opening of the Continental. He also stressed that the Ambassador has been subsidizing some of the other State Hotels in other ways. Thus, the Star Hotel owes the Ambassador about £70,000. Besides, the Ambassador had to pay staff salaries for the City Hotel for the month of May to the tune of £3,500. In addition, the Ministry of Foreign Affairs owes the Ambassador a lot of money for entertainment, apart from debts owed it by individual ex-Ministers and politicians. The Committee feels that this is a problem the solution to which does not need foreign expertise, especially as a list of redundant hands has already been prepared.

9. The Committee is not convinced that the possibilities of finding

money locally to develop the Ambassador and to use as working capital have been exhausted. *It decided to recommend that the Investment Bank be approached.* It was assured on very good authority that this is the type of business venture in which the Investment Bank would be particularly interested.

10. The Committee decided that if, in spite of its considered advice to the contrary, the National Liberation Council should wish to approve the Agreement the following points should be taken into very serious consideration:

(i) The option given to the Inter-Continental Hotels Corporation to renew the lease for another twenty years should be struck out altogether.
(ii) The twenty years' duration for the lease is too long and should be cut down to about fifteen years.
(iii) The power to terminate the Agreement within the first year should be accorded not only to the Inter-Continental Hotels Corporation, as at present proposed in the draft agreement, but to the Ghana Government as well.
(iv) The hotels should not be operated in such a way as to prejudice airlines other than Pan-Am. In this connection the interest of Ghana Airways should be particularly safeguarded.
(v) The training programme for Ghanaians should be such as to enable the management of the hotels to be transferred into Ghanaian hands with the least possible delay.

It is considered important that the training scheme should be embodied not only in the letter of understanding, as at present, but also in the lease itself.

11. The Committee was highly disturbed by certain features of the negotiations that emerged out of its discussion and examination of the memorandum sent to it by the National Liberation Council and documents relevant to it. It decided to invite the National Liberation Council to note these carefully.

12. It will be recalled that in the memorandum to the National Liberation Council on the Management Agreement the Economic Committee claimed that a letter of understanding had been drawn up 'after detailed and lengthy negotiations both here and in the United States' (paragraph 2 of the Memorandum), that the Board of Directors of the State Hotels Corporation had 'discussed and approved the terms of the management lease agreement' (paragraph 3), and, consequently, the Economic Committee 'recommended that the National Liberation Council should authorize the State Hotels Corporation to sign the lease Agreement with the Inter-Continental Hotels Corporation' (paragraph 6).

13. In spite of these claims it became clear to the Committee during its discussion that the principal negotiators on our side were unaware of some very vital provisions in the lease and the letter of understanding which they

were asking the National Liberation Council to approve. Thus, although the memorandum to the National Liberation Council claimed that the lease 'will last for a period not exceeding 20 years' (paragraph 4), *the true position is that the lease is effective for 40 years* unless the Inter-Continental Hotels Corporation chose not to renew it after the first twenty years, and that this option is not open to us, too. Again, the Memorandum claimed that the Agreement 'can be terminated during the first year of the agreement' (paragraph 4). *The correct position, however, is that only the Inter-Continental Hotels Corporation can terminate the Agreement during the first year.* In other words, although we will be advancing the capital we cannot terminate the Agreement during the first year. The impression the Memorandum gives that the option to terminate the Agreement in the first year is available to both sides of the contract is thus misleading. This the Committee considers rather serious since the country may have sunk thousands of cedis into the venture by the end of the first year. It is to be noted that these anomalies would not have come to light if the Chairman of the Committee had not, on his own initiative, called for the letter of understanding and the lease.

14. The political implications of a simple handover of such an important Ghanaian State enterprise to a foreign concern are so serious that it should only be contemplated as a last resort after all other avenues have been explored and it is found that there is no other means of remedying its defects.

15. The Committee is very surprised that our principal negotiators should have recommended to the National Liberation Council for approval a document the vital clauses of which they themselves had failed to understand. It notes that this is the result of the fact that up to this last stage our principal negotiators had not seen fit to call in any legal expert to help negotiate. This, when they must have known that they were dealing with complicated legal documents and it is common knowledge that such big corporations as the Inter-Continental Hotels Corporation command some of the best legal brains of their country. The Committee is completely at a loss to understand how this could have happened.

16. *In view of this grossly unsatisfactory behaviour of the official advisors of the National Liberation Council* the Committee considers it necessary to advise the National Liberation Council to submit proposals for agreements between the country and foreign bodies recommended to it by its official advisers for approval to its Political Committee for scrutiny and advice before they are approved, as in the present case.

Document 42: Economic Committee Response
Economic Committee Memorandum: 'Pre-financed Enterprises (Drevici Group of Companies)' (n.d.).

At its meeting held on 15 November 1966, the National Liberation Council directed that the attached memorandum from the Political Committee concerning pre-financed enterprises[6] should be referred to the Economic Committee for examination and advice.

2. The Economic Committee has studied the various papers sent by the Political Committee to the National Liberation Council and has given due consideration to all the points raised in the paper.

3. The Economic Committee takes strong exception to the various inferences in the paper which tend to cast considerable doubt on the integrity and honesty of the Economic Committee as a body and on its individual members. In this connection the Economic Committee wishes to remind the NLC that this is not the first time that the Political Committee has sent papers to the National Liberation Council which tend to question the honesty as well as the efficiency of the Economic Committee. We would like in particular to refer to the comments of the Political Committee on the proposed association with the Inter-Continental Hotels of America.

4. It is a matter of deep regret to the Economic Committee that the Political Committee should be adopting this attitude to us, especially as the various inferences are without substance. In the following paragraphs we shall attempt to examine some of the implied allegations in the Political Committee's papers. It is necessary, however, at the outset to state that the Economic Committee feels that in order to clear itself, as well as its members, of all the allegations implied in the Political Committee's memorandum, an independent Commission of Inquiry should be appointed with terms of reference to be worked out by the Political Committee and approved by the NLC. We feel that unless this is done considerable damage may be done to the economic policies of the NLC through stories that may be circulated about some members of the National Liberation Council's only advisory committee on economic matters....

5. Quite apart from the appointment of a Commission of Inquiry to examine the connections between members of the Economic Committee and Mr Drevici, we would like to suggest that the National Liberation Council may wish to authorize the appropriate governmental agency to collect information on the backgrounds of both Mr E. C. O. Adjaye and Mr W. R. P. Ephson,* the two gentlemen whose allegations have been used as an excuse for making these attacks on the integrity of the Economic Committee and its members.

6. The Political Committee has recommended that the International Monetary Fund should be invited to send a team of experts to 'investigate'

---

*Two of the authors of the Drevici report—*Editor*.

the investments of Mr Noe Drevici in the country. This recommendation as made without proper knowledge of the functions of these International Financial Agencies. Neither the International Monetary Fund nor the World Bank would touch an assignment of this nature. We wish they could! This would have saved us from the attacks of the Political Committee.

7. The National Liberation Council will remember that on the recommendations of the Economic Committee, the International Finance Corporation, a member of the World Bank Group has been requested to provide us with a list of companies experienced in this type of job, from which one will be selected to carry out a comprehensive evaluation of not only Mr Drevici's projects but all the other suppliers' credit projects. This is as far as we can go with any of these International Organizations, and this has been done at the initiative of the Economic Committee which is now being maligned for its alleged involvement with Mr Drevici.

8. In the attached table,* the list of all the Drevici projects has been given together with information about the terms of the original contracts with the old regime and the payments that have been made since 24 February 1966. The NLC is invited to decide for itself whether on the basis of the data and the very little payments which have so far been made since 24 February the suspicion that the Economic Committee is involved with Mr and Mrs Drevici can be sustained.

9. In conclusion, we would like to recommend to the National Liberation Council the appointment of a Special Committee, maybe composed of members of the Political Committee to 'handle' the Drevici problem, until such time that the integrity and honesty of the Economic Committee will be cleared.

Document 43: Political Committee Response
Political Committee Memorandum PC/M.67/66: 'Memorandum on Pre-financed Enterprises Drevici Group of Companies: Comments by the Political Committee on the Economic Committee Memorandum', 16 December 1966.

The Political Committee has read and discussed at considerable length the memorandum submitted by the Economic Committee on the memorandum submitted by the Political Committee on the Pre-financed Enterprises (Drevici Group of Companies)... The Political Committee would like to point out at the outset that the Economic Committee has made very serious but false accusations against the Political Committee...

*Omitted—*Editor.*

2. The Political Committee is deeply concerned over the deteriorating relations between itself and the Economic Committee. These two Committees are extremely important and their functions are such that it would do Ghana very little good if they are unable to co-operate and work in amity. The importance of their work at present transcends any personal interests and this should at all times be placed foremost. The tone of the Economic Committee memorandum shows that it has persuaded itself that the Political Committee has somehow an axe to grind with it and has deliberately been acting prejudicially to the interests and functions of the Economic Committee. The Political Committee would like to state that it has no personal grudge against any members of the Economic Committee nor against the Economic Committee as such. Its memoranda have been written in good faith bearing in mind its responsibilities to the National Liberation Council and to the country.

3. Members of the Political Committee realize that because the problems that face both Committees are so important and quite often overlap in many respects, there is likely, since the two Committees operate separately, to be a conflict of interests as a result of different premises assumed by both Committees with respect to certain major issues. It must be remembered that whereas the Economic Committee regularly sees the minutes of the Political Committee, the Political Committee itself never sees the minutes of the Economic Committee. Consequently, it is not in a position to know precisely what the Economic Committee is doing about certain matters. It can therefore only work on certain assumptions based on facts available to it. To obviate such difficulties the Political Committee has often sought to meet either the Economic Committee collectively or members of it in order to bridge any possible gap in information that might lead to divergent advice being given to the National Liberation Council.

4. It would be wrong to assume that economic and political matters can be separated completely in the present situation in Ghana and for that matter in any country. Politics was allowed to infiltrate so much into so many aspects of Ghanaian life that the process of disentangling much of this cannot be done by economic considerations alone. Moreover, the narrow construing of the Political Committee as being simply a political committee does not help matters. The terms of reference of the Political Committee make it much more of a general purposes committee than anything else. At any rate, it is so regarded by the general public who we think have interpreted these terms correctly. The compartmentalization of portfolios and functions in the past led to considerable harm being done to this country since it meant that a great many committees or offices were unable to know what others were doing. Such a situation should not be permitted to arise in which the left hand does not know what the right hand is doing. Moreover, the essence of democracy is that no aspect of public life shall be free from scrutiny.

5. No Committee which has been set up can claim to be so expert in its own field that it cannot have its views examined or considered by others

who may have ancillary or even peripheral interests in them. The imputation of evil motives to the Political Committee's memoranda would have the effect of stifling its attempt to bring free and frank criticism to bear on certain policies that are placed before the National Liberation Council. If this should happen we would be back to the old system whereby views were not examined for fear of treading on other people's toes. In view of what this country has suffered as a result of this sort of policy, it is only fair that in our duty to the country and the National Liberation Council we should always bring our collective wisdom and advice to bear on any matters that come our way. The Political Committee has never claimed infallibility. It has only sought to bring its views to bear on matters of national concern and requests that the same considerations be given to its own views.

6. It is clear from a careful reading of the memorandum from the Political Committee and of the paper from the Economic Committee that the latter has seriously misconstrued the purpose of the memorandum. In the first place, the allegations bitterly complained of by the Economic Committee were not made by the Political Committee. The allegations were made by three persons who submitted these in a memorandum (PC/65/66) to the Political Committee. These same allegations, we were told, had been forwarded in a Report to both the National Liberation Council and the Chairman of the Economic Committee. To forward this report from our office then to the National Liberation Council in no way constitutes an attempt to undermine or question the integrity or efficiency of the Economic Committee.

7. If the Political Committee forwarded these documents to the National Liberation Council it was because it realized that there appeared to be some substance in some of the allegations against Drevici. It must be stressed that these matters which seem to have substance related not to the activities of the Economic Committee but to the activities of the Drevici Group of Companies. This in fact was the substance of what was contained in our memorandum PC/M.61/66.

8. It is not our intention to go into detail about every one of the points made in the Economic Committee memorandum, but we would like to comment briefly on some of the points . . .

17. The Political Committee would like again to state that it is deeply concerned over the deteriorating relations between itself and the Economic Committee. It is aware that such unhappy relations would not be of any help to Ghana and it is anxious and desirous that these should be ended as soon as possible. In an earlier submission to the National Liberation Council the Political Committee proposed regular meetings between Chairmen of some of the National Liberation Council Committees. The idea was to have a free exchange of view and to have these diffused into discussions and policies before they reach the stage where they become crystallized or where entrenched positions are taken and discussion then becomes difficult. In view particularly of the very close relationship

between economic and political matters the Political Committee would like respectfully but in all seriousness to propose that the two Committees should have a slightly overlapping membership; that two members of the Political Committee be appointed to the Economic Committee and two members of the Economic Committee be appointed to the Political Committee. This would ensure that policy attitudes are diffused into both Committees and prevent clashes occurring. The Political Committee itself had on an earlier occasion suggested that the presence of a banker on its Committee might help. It might also help if the Economic Committee had on its membership one or two men with long business experience to help it in perceiving problems that policy makers may not always necessarily appreciate.

18. The problem of the Drevici Enterprises, however, remains. Because of the very extensive operations of the Drevici Group and because of their rather complicated nature, some high-powered committee or commission to look into their affairs might be of help to Ghana. We note that the Economic Committee itself had been thinking along similar lines and we should like strongly to support their proposal for such an investigation.

19. Finally the Political Committee would like to deplore the attitude of the Economic Committee towards the Political Committee and the former's claim to immunity from public scrutiny. The Economic Committee referred, for example, to the Political Committee's intervention on the Inter-Continental Hotels affair. Surely the Political Committee was demonstrably right in calling attention to a serious oversight committed by the Economic Committee? This is not a time for pettiness. All must be big enough to put the national interest foremost. Attempts to discredit committees or persons on personal or sectional grounds are demeaning. In the interest of the nation the Economic Committee and the Political Committee must cooperate and coordinate their activities.[7]

Part V: Labour and the Military

Introductory Note

The period from 1966 to 1969 was one of working-class struggles and frequently brutal official repression of the working-class movement. As may be expected, conditions for the working class as a whole deteriorated still further as a result of the conditions imposed by the IMF and the Military Government. Workers reacted to the growing ranks of unemployed and the rising cost of living (in the face of the wage-freeze) with an unprecedented rash of strikes, slowdowns, and lock-out of managements. Between the coup and May 1968 there were 71 reported industrial strikes (compared to a total of 51 for the previous 5 years). But this was an understatement, as the number of strikes averted by the TUC 'far outnumber(ed)' those that actually occurred. The NLC responded with considerable force: striking workers were repeatedly fired on or attacked by police with many casualties (Document 46). In February 1967 'incitement to a general strike' was decreed a capital offence. The military also contemplated extensive 'reforms' in the Industrial Relations Act that would have emasculated the trade union movement by repealing the giving check-off system, decentralizing the national union structure, and modifying the collective bargaining process (Document 45). Although union resistance to these 'reforms' led to them being dropped by the NLC, the repressive provisions were revived and incorporated into the labour legislation passed by the Busia Government in September 1971. The new privileges extended to the security forces (Document 47) formed an appropriate counterpoint to the sufferings and deprivations of the working class.

Document 44: The Condition of the Ghanaian Working Class
Letter from B.A. Bentum, Secretary-General of the TUC, to Lt. General Ankrah, Chairman of the National Liberation Council, 8 May 1968.

Sir,

I have the honour most respectfully to bring to the notice of the National Liberation Council the following matter that has come to the knowledge of the Trades Union Congress.

1. The cost of living in the country has risen so high that the average worker can no more provide himself and his family with the basic needs of life. This was a long-standing situation before the 24 February 1966 revolution.
2. The old regime completely neglected the working man, ignored his needs and left him at the mercy of money lenders. There was a long and gruesome struggle for existence by all the workers especially those in the low income group. After the change of Government a great ray of hope was anticipated to relieve the workers from this long state of slavery . . .
3. For two years the workers have waited patiently as to [*sic*] what changes could be effected in their wages and salaries. It had not been easy at all, as to the role the TUC has played to quickly organize and educate the workers to understand and cooperate in the bitter and yet healthy exercise the National Liberation Council is embarking upon to resuscitate the economy. This exercise (has) involved over 60,000 workers to be declared redundant and a continued stagnation of wages and salaries . . .
4. I am now constrained to inform you that I consider you may not have been given the correct information as to the magnitude of the workers' problems. The number [*sic*] of an average Ghanaian family is estimated to be four and the daily basic needs are as follows:

Food	N₵2.04
Housing	0.66
Clothing	0.27
Transportation	0.10
Sundries	0.60

    This figure does not include the education of the children, hospitalization, etc., etc.
5. I wish to throw some light on the *real* income of the workers. During the nine-month period from April 1963 to December 1963 the consumer price index rose by 10.12%. In 1964, it went up by 11.3%. In 1965 it still showed an upward trend of 33.5%. By October 1966, it further rose by 21.8%. This shows that the

cost of living went up by 76.7% between March 1963 and October 1966.

In effect therefore, an artisan Gr. I receiving (£265) N₵530.00 per annum was taking [home] a real income of £60.19/- or N₵120.38. A labourer receiving (£9) N₵8.00 per month was collecting a real wage of (£2) or N₵4.00. This is the true picture.

6. How the workers existed and how they continue to do so now is a miracle. They live on recurring loans and/or on alms. Those who cannot have the loans are at the mercy of their wives for one meal a day (evening meals only.) In the morning, they deny themselves of breakfast and attend work on an empty stomach. In the afternoon they either continue the compulsory fasting or take the conventional dry plantain and groundnuts. In short, they just exist but not live. Living rooms are overcrowded and clothing is most difficult to get. That is why the TUC demanded N₵2.00 as a minimum wage, sacrificing N₵1.67. We consider that the least possible consideration should not fall below N₵1.00 minimum wage per day.

Even this will need drastic measures to reduce and control prices before one could live within this wage rate.

7. Some intellectuals and top officials (who themselves have taken high pay increases recently) argue that in view of the already existing large number of unemployed persons and the great economic disaster in which we are, it may be prudent for the Government in deciding what minimum and general rates of wages to fix, to decide on a very low rate and gradually raise it by stages so as to allow some time to increase productivity and *capacity to pay.*

Their argument continues that by such methods drastic dislocation to the economy would be avoided, national income would be gradually increased and capacity to pay would be progressively achieved.

8. Our answer to such theories is that: (1) this is true up to a point whereby the worker should be paid just enough to make it possible for him to provide himself with (a) the minimum food requirements, for enough physical energy and mental alertness, (b) adequate housing for the basic comfort and hygienic needs which are so vital for his general health, and (c) enough money to care for his family to give him that peace of mind and happiness at home which are so important an asset and thus contribute in no small measure to increased productivity. (2) The thousands of unemployed are depending on the workers for their living and this places the worker in a worse situation. (3) The little that the nation can set aside for salary increases should be judiciously distributed to remove the acute pay disparity. We are not asking for a total increase of the overall national sum ear-

marked for the salary increases to be increased beyond what the nation can afford. We are asking that the same amount should be used but be redistributed to the advantage of the low income group.

9. The TUC is sympathetic of [sic] this situation, where thousands of Ghanaians are forced by want to live a life below that of a normal one, and we are convinced that the Government shares with us in this sympathy . . .

    Our suggestion and conviction is that the pay disparity between the low income group and high income group which is on a ratio of 1.22 must be narrowed to about 1.10. The only practical way to achieve this objective is to exercise restraint at the top wage group and release the stagnation at the lower income group . . .

    Unfortunately, before the report (of the Salary Review Committee) was completed some lawyers, university senior staff and doctors had been given fantastic salary increases. This angered the workers . . .

10. They contend that if these people who understand the economy of the nation better than the labourer or carpenter, could not show a spirit of sacrifice and leadership but rather take a bigger share of the national cake the people who profess to be helping the National Liberation Council are not sincere.

11. As you walk through the market, in the public places and in fact in every public gathering you hear 'ebi te yie, ebi nte yie, ebi so nte yie koraa'.*

    The voice of the people is the voice of the nation. The workers support the NLC and if the support is to be continuous then the workers as a whole should be relieved from the present hardship and the only way to do that is for all of us who are in a higher income grade to demonstrate a quality of leadership, sacrifice our gains and allow what should be added to our salaries to be added to those who are at the bottom of the pay ladder . . .

---

*Freely translated, 'The few get wealthier while the majority become poorer and poorer'. This was a popular slogan, used by the urban working classes in this period to describe intensifying class contradictions.—*Editor*.

Document 45: TUC Comments on Proposed Changes to Labour Laws

Excerpts from comments of the Trades Union Congress on proposed amendments to the Industrial Relations Act (Act 299) of 1965.[1]

Industrial Relations Act—299 (Amendment No. 2) Decree 1967

Section 2: **Collective Bargaining**

Repeal of this Section of the Industrial Relations Act is nothing short of a reversal of development in the history of trade unionism in this country. For since the minimum Remuneration Instrument became operative on 1 July 1961 great progress has been made and continues to be made in the determination of wages through the use of Collective Bargaining.

Today, workers in establishments that employ less than five persons are covered by Collective Agreements. This facility that has contributed enormously to industrial peace in the country and which did not exist at the time Wages Boards were in vogue should not be taken away unchallenged.

If Wages Boards (at present designated Labour Boards) are introduced they will be as cumbersome to operate now as in the past.

Section 3: **Another Approach**

Apparently, there is a subtle move to take away from the Trades Union Congress the right to sponsor applications from its affiliated members for Collective Bargaining Certificates.

The imaginable excuses for such a move is that its advocates want 'free play' to prevail in the processes of Collective Bargaining and the signing of Collective Agreements.

Granted that 'free play' is invoked the resulting situation will be that more than the desired and/or reasonable number of Collective Agreements would be signed for the same establishment to cover a small number of workers.

Repeal of this Section of the Industrial Relations Act is a retrogressive move and must be condemned . . .

Section 10: **Effect of Collective Agreements**

1. *Amendment marked (a)*

Apart from containing more words than the text of the Act, it does not improve upon the purpose the subsection is supposed to serve. It should be rejected.

2. *Amendment marked (b)*

This should be rejected. It appears to be bent on weakening the position of the TUC vis-à-vis the affiliated Unions.

Changes in the Unions that could and should negotiate Collective Agreements for specified classes of workers can be negotiated with the TUC as umpire to the mutual benefit of all concerned ...

Section 13: **Power to extend Collective Agreements**

This section should be retained. Repeal should be strongly objected ... [*sic*]

Section 21: **Strikes and Lockouts**

There will be no harm done to organized labour movement if the suggested amendment is accepted.

However it must be noted that it is a bit difficult to reconcile the suggestion made and the stand taken by the advocates of the amendment in relation to this Section of the Act and the attitude exhibited regarding Section 3.

Apparently all they want in the whole exercise is to drive the country's trade union movement to the wall, i.e. to make things difficult for the future development of trade unionism in the country ...

Section 34:

Repeal of Section 34 of the Industrial Relations Act should be considered as a calculated move to disintegrate Congress if not the trade union movement as a whole in this country; for the life blood (live-wire) of any organization is the size of funds available to it and the pattern of dues collection (that is, deduction of union dues at source) is what had made the organization and operation of trade unionism possible in this country up to the present time.

Advocates of the repeal may be haunted by the fact that it is compulsory trade union membership that made deduction of union dues at sources possible in this country. But deduction of union dues at source can continue to be operated even when trade union membership is voluntary, as is the case in USA and some European countries.

Fortunately, efforts are at the moment being made to rid the country's trade union movement of the compulsory trimmings that have been associated with it.

However, if the repeal is effected, National unions would have to have deduction of trade union dues at source entrenched in all Collective Agreements as it is only in this way that organized labour can be kept intact and in which the possibility of future development and growth in strength of the country's labour movement can be contemplated.

Document 46: Threat of General Strike to Protest Shootings of Workers
Executive Board of the Ghana TUC to Brigadier Afrifa, Chairman of the NLC, 6 June 1969 (following incidents of shooting striking workers by the police).

At an emergency Executive Board meeting of the Trades Union Congress held on 4 June 1969 at the Hall of Trade Unions, the Board examined in detail the role the Trades Union Congress and its affiliated national unions have played during the period of the administration of the National Liberation Council in the maintenance of Industrial peace.

The Board noted that the Trades Union Congress and its affiliated national unions have, during this period, done the best they could in the interest of the nation, in the handling of labour and industrial disputes. This has been done in such a manner that even in cases where such disputes have got out of hand and the workers had resorted to strike action the TUC had resolved such problems in an atmosphere of peace and calmness. In many cases issues that would normally have degenerated into violent industrial problems were handled with tact, skill and persuasion thus preventing a more serious situation from arising.

In normal circumstances it is not the function of trade union officials to break strikes or ask striking or demonstrating workers to return to work when the issues that gave rise to the strikes are yet to be satisfactorily resolved.

The Board further noted that this patriotic gesture on the part of the trade unions in Ghana is a clear demonstration of the great concern for the welfare not only of their members but the nation as a whole.

Unfortunately, in many of these cases Government or Government officials who should normally take an impartial position had taken steps by their speeches, actions and behaviour to aggravate the situation instead of bringing it to normal. These actions always tend to pre-judge the issues in dispute against the workers and their trade unions thus prejudicing the issues before final settlement.

The Board decided to draw the attention of Government to the following examples out of many such cases of industrial disputes which justifies its contention that the efforts of the Trades Union Congress and the National Unions have not been reciprocated by Management and Government.

1. Cargo Handling Company:
The workers went on strike on 7 October 1968. The TUC and the Maritime and Dockworkers Union were approached both by the NLC and the Management to intervene, bring the situation back to normal and get the workers back to work. After strenuous efforts the TUC and the national union succeeded in getting the 2,000 workers involved to go back to work the following day (8 October 1968) only to be beaten up, driven away by the police and told that they had been locked-out and subsequently dismissed

to the astonishment and embarrassment of the TUC and the national union. This, the Board considers, constitutes a breach of trust and faith on the part of the Government. What was worse, was that it was later learnt that at the time of requesting the TUC and the national union to intervene new hands had already been engaged on the advice of the Government with the active assistance of the Labour Department.

2. Inter-Continental Hotels:
In the case of the Inter-Continental Hotels, although the demonstration of the workers took place during their break hours, the police forcibly prevented the workers from resuming their normal duties. Here again, several arrests were made which worsened the situation. The TUC arranged for bail for those arrested and the workers unanimously agreed to resume work the following day only to be told that the 500 workers involved had been dismissed. This in the opinion of the Board is not only an irresponsible act on the part of Management for calling in police during a peaceful demonstration but an act of brutality by the police for beating up defenceless workers.

3. Accra/Tema City Council:
In the case of the Accra/Tema City Council, the workers involved sought proper explanation as to a new shift system which was introduced without prior consultations and discussions with the Union. For withholding their labour until they were satisfied with the practicability and justification of the new roster, the workers were summarily dismissed. All appeals by them and their Union to reconsider Management's decision were of [sic] no avail . . .

In spite of the great pressure from the rank and file members of the various national unions for a nation-wide strike in protest against these naked injustices, the Trades Union Congress out of its firm belief in applying peaceful methods of resolving industrial disputes lived up to the challenge and avoided any actions that might lead to serious industrial upheaval. The TUC therefore lodged a formal complaint against the Government of Ghana at the International Labour Office.

4. Railway Permanent Waymen Section:
The Board noted that when the entire Permanent Waymen Section of the Railway and Ports Authority went on a nation-wide strike it was the efforts of the TUC which brought the one week strike to an end. Since the workers returned to work, despite several demands and attempts to get the issues that brought about the strike resolved, no response had been forthcoming from the side of the Government and the Ministry of Communication, and no action has been taken on any of their grievances even though the TUC and the National Union of Railway and Ports Workers were assured by the Government that the grievances would be looked into and solutions found to them as soon as the workers went back to work. The Board considers this

to be ... sheer delaying tactics on the part of the Government. The Board is surprised that up till now the Government has not honoured its promise. This has created a situation in which the workers will not have faith in future promises given by the Government.

5. Obuasi Mines:

In the incident that occurred at Obuasi a few months ago,* instead of the Government applying the normal conventional methods of resolving strikes, it ordered the police to open fire on defenceless workers, killing in cold blood four (4) miners and wounding several others including a schoolboy and railway workers who were in no way connected with the strike.

When the workers were mourning the dead and lamenting for the injured, Government, without any sympathy, gave a 48-hour ultimatum to the 6,500 miners to return to work. As could be expected the workers defied the ultimatum and continued the strike. Conscious of the disastrous effects that such continued strike by the workers and erratic shooting by the police would bring to the nation, the TUC, on its own initiative, promptly intervened through appeal and persuasion and called on the workers to end the strike and return to work. This human approach by the TUC instead of the shooting by the police succeeded in getting the workers back to work. During the strike, while the TUC was making desperate efforts to get the situation back to normal, high ranking officials of the Government were making statements that the workers were not justified in their claims, thus infuriating them. The result of the negotiations that followed a few days after calling off the strike is clear evidence to the nation as to the legitimacy of their claims.

The most disturbing feature is that, immediately the claims were awarded based on Government's own laws, the Government quickly amended that law without any consultations with the Trades Union Congress with the sole aim of preventing other workers from claiming similar benefits as the law provided.

The Board considers the steps taken by the Police in handling the Obuasi strike as crude, cruel and unjustified, especially when it was finally proved that the workers were right in their claims.

The seriousness with which the TUC viewed this matter was conveyed in a resolution to the National Liberation Council on 8 March 1969, in which the TUC condemned shooting as a means of resolving strike action. The text of the relevant sections of the resolution reads as follows:

> That the Extraordinary Executive Board in session having examined the present situation affecting the workers, and considering that a strike action is a human problem that should be handled by persuasion, negotiations and similar acceptable modes of resolving disputes and not by intimidation, mass dismissals

---

*This is a reference to the strike of mineworkers which was precipitated by the takeover of Ashanti Goldfields by Lonrho at the end of 1968.

and shootings, the Executive Board condemns without reservation the shooting of defenceless striking workers of the Ashanti Goldfield Corporation.

Conscious of our obligations as citizens and leaders of the Labour Movement, Congress will continue to employ the methods of persuasion, education and negotiation in resolving all industrial disputes including the present Obuasi crisis.

From the reply of the Government to the resolution, the Board was surprised to note that Government rejected outright the advice of the TUC as to the humane methods to be adopted in handling such matters. This presupposes that Government believes in the use of the gun as a means of resolving strikes.

6. Tarkwa Mines:

The Board finally noted that on 2 June 1969, a few months after the Obuasi incident, when the Tarkwa Miners also went on strike the same crude and cruel methods of intimidation, beating and shooting were adopted. This clearly proves that the Government has in fact no intention to employ a more rational means of resolving [strikes].

The Tarkwa shooting continued the following day and several arrests were made. The Miners were put before a court that very day and remanded in custody for a week. After the Board had examined these matters and Government's methods of handling them, it vehemently deplored the actions of the police who, in the best knowledge of the TUC, are peace officers who are trained and charged with the responsibility of protecting life and property. The Board noted some of the vague arguments put forward to justify the shootings of these workers and came to the conclusion that the modern conventional methods for handling such situations were not applied in any of these incidents. The Board noted also that many of the reports presented to the public in relation to the happenings at Obuasi were inaccurate, hence the demand for a Commission of Enquiry to bring to light the full facts for public judgement. In other cases, including the Tarkwa incident, reports to the public have been couched in a manner to create a false impression that the workers and their trade unions are always wrong.

The Board feels that a strike action, be it legal or illegal, official or unofficial, constitutional or unconstitutional, does not justify arbitrary mass dismissals, shootings and killings of any kind. The Board expects the Government to abide by its own laws enacted to protect the society as a whole.

The Board noted that these strikes have neither been promoted, declared nor encouraged by the TUC. The TUC has always and at all times disapproved openly of the staging of illegal strikes and has opposed the destruction of life and property by striking workers. This is evidenced by our pronouncement during a strike action, the resolution of the Executive Board transmitted to the NLC under the cover of our letter No.

TUC/SG.349(2)/68 of 5 November 1968 and also by our efforts in the education of workers and in getting workers who are on strike back to work at all times.

What has made our efforts difficult is the undue delays on the part of Managements and Government in acceding to the legitimate demands of the workers until they embark on such strikes.

The Board further notes that it has become the habit of certain managements to quickly call in the police, even on issues that can be resolved at the Negotiating Table. It has now become customary for the police to rush to these areas ostensibly to protect life and property, whilst, in fact, they march to these areas with guns fully loaded to take the lives of unarmed and defenceless workers.

The above analysis is an attempt to bring to the notice of Government and the general public the role that the TUC has played in the establishment and maintenance of industrial peace which, in the opinion of the Board, has not been reciprocated by Government and Managements.

As a result of these happenings the patience of the TUC is naturally exhausted and in order to let Government know how seriously it views this state of affairs, the Board has decided *'that in the event of any further shooting of striking workers the TUC will have no alternative but to call a nation-wide strike of all workers in protest against this inhuman treatment.'*

Finally, it is the hope of the Executive Board that the Government will do everything possible to avert the creation of a situation whereby the TUC will be forced to embark upon a nation-wide strike which in our opinion will be one of the bitterest and longest that the country has ever witnessed.

Document 47: Tax Exemptions for Members of the Armed Forces

Memorandum from the Ministry of Finance to the National Economic Committee, 17 March 1966.

The National Liberation Council submitted for consideration by the National Economic Committee a paper prepared by the Commander of the Ghana Army, Major-General Kotoka, on the terms of service and conditions of pay of members of the Armed Forces.

2. In accordance with a promise which the Major-General gave to his men on the eve of the Revolution, he has recommended that the following reliefs be granted to the officers and men of the Armed Forces:

(i) Total exemption from Income Tax.
(ii) Total exemption from quartering charges.
(iii) Total exemption from payment of electricity, water and conservancy charges.

3. In addition, the Commander has requested that a decree be issued to restore:

   (i) the pension rights of the officers and men of the Armed Forces which were removed as a result of the coming into effect of the Armed Forces Act of 1962, and
   (ii) certain grants made to officers and men under certain conditions, e.g. transfer grants.

4. Although the total cost of granting these reliefs has not been indicated, it is estimated that the loss of revenue involved may amount to about ₵2.4 million in a full year. A loss of revenue to the tune of another ₵2.4 million may be incurred if, as is equitable, the reliefs are extended to cover the officers and men of the Police Force. A loss of ₵4.8 million is undoubtedly not too high a price to pay for the true freedom that has been brought to the Nation by the Armed Forces and the Police.

5. However, in considering the possibility of granting the reliefs requested, the following two points should be taken into account:

   (i) It is in the supreme interest of the Nation that the national budget should be balanced mainly through a reduction of expenditure to the barest minimum. The consequences of following an alternative policy are obvious.
   (ii) Exempting individuals from the payment of taxes and other charges might create dangerous precedents and make it more and and more difficult to administer the Tax Laws.

6. In the light of the above, the following recommendations are made for consideration by the Committee for dealing with the situation:

   (1) The restoration of pension rights and other grants requested by the Commander may be granted immediately.
   Assessment of the total cost involved up to the end of June 1966 and for a full financial year should be obtained from the Armed Forces. (It is not clear whether this applies to the Police Force, if it does a similar line should be adopted.)
   (2) The reliefs in respect of income tax, etc., should be granted since they were in the nature of firm promises by the Commander to his officers and men. However, this should form part of the exercise to be conducted by the Board which it is intended to appoint to review the conditions of service for officers and men of the Armed Forces. Instead of offering these in the form of reliefs the Board should recommend salary and wage rates which on a net basis will have the same effect as if the reliefs had been granted.
   (3) A Committee should be appointed simultaneously to review the terms and conditions of the pay of the Police Force.
   (4) The Committee to be appointed to review the salaries and

conditions of service of the Armed Forces and Police should be warned of the dangers to the economy of increasing Government expenditure through increases in wage and salary rates, if only as a means of inducing them to be moderate in their recommendations.

Ministry of Finance,
17 March 1966.

Part VI: 'A Load of Indebtedness'

Introductory Note

A major issue of economic policy, to which all other economic considerations were subordinated, was that of Ghana's external debts and the renegotiation of these debts. It is with this that the papers in this section are concerned.[1] Document 48 shows the structure of Ghana's external debt service as of December 1965. According to the figures presented here, some 75% of the total debt service was due between 1966 and 1970, but in fact amortization rates for the different categories of debt differed significantly, ranging from 93% for Western private credits to 65% for the Eastern credits, 44% for official credits from Britain and West Germany, and 29% and 24% respectively for long-term loans from the World Bank and US Government (USAID and Export-Import Bank). The terms of many of these loans were 'rigged' against the Ghana Government, and their administration was characterized by abuses of one type or another, a tendency magnified by poor control and overall management by the Nkrumah Government (Document 49). The evidence here shows why suppliers' credits have become one on the most important contemporary mechanisms of exploitation of Third World countries. These difficulties apart, there were serious inherent difficulties in the utilization of some of these credits as a means of development financing (Document 50). In particular the majority of Western private credits were in non-directly productive areas such as transport and infrastructure, with only 15% in manufacturing. Although the credits were usually extended for 5 years or less, fewer than 9% could be expected to generate income within 6 years, while 34% required between 6 and 12 years and the remainder (46%) over 12 years. At least 34% of the Eastern loans were in manufacture, and 61% of the projects financed could be expected to generate income within their maturity period of 12 years.

In spite of the anxiety of the Military Government to come to the negotiating table, the formal terms of rescheduling were much harsher than those sought by the NLC (Documents 51, 52). The main issue of contention was the moratorium interest rate. The Agreed Minutes of December 1966 and October 1968 set out the main outlines of agreement, with the details to be thrashed out subsequently in bilateral negotiations. Bilateral negotiations were completed for the 1966 agreement, but in 1968 negotiations with a number of Western countries broke down over the issue of the interest rate. The cost of 'relief' under the two agreements was an increase in Ghana's overall indebtedness of N₡89.7 million, accounted for disproportionately by the Western creditors (Document 53). In spite of the hostility of the NLC to the socialist countries, the terms of settlement offered were significantly softer than those of the capitalist countries.

The civilian Government of Dr Busia which succeeded the military in October 1969 took a rhetorically harder line on the foreign debts and made a successful demand for the reopening of negotiations. The possibility of repudiation or default was seriously discussed, possibly for the first time. Document 54 sets out the working report of a meeting of the Minister for Finance and Economic Affairs and senior Government officials at Aburi on 25/26 June 1970 (ostensibly to consider strategy for the Consultative Group meeting taking place the following month) at which this possibility was considered. Although a number of possible justifications were advanced – non-viability of projects, tainted contracts, overpricing, and inability to pay – government officials were anxious to avoid any radical action that would alienate the Western creditors. Thus the conclusion was that if there was to be default, it would be 'better to default with consent' in order to avoid 'very sharp repercussions' from the creditor countries.

Documents 55–58 set out the verbatim proceedings of the London debt conference of 7 to 11 July 1970. The contradictory interests of debtor and creditor the impassioned pleas of Ghana's Finance Minister (J.H. Mensah) for a long-term settlement and aid that would 'release Ghana from the load of indebtedness', and the insistence of creditors on high interest rates and short-term formulae that would facilitate their control over Ghana's policies – are clearly brought out in these excerpts. For the first time the 1970 Agreed Minute (Document 59) imposed specific policy guidelines on Ghana. These policy guidelines were to be emphasized at the Consultative Group meeting of 15–16 July, where sometimes trenchant criticisms of Ghana's economic and financial policies were made.[2] Also clear from these excerpts is the role of political considerations in the debt renegotiation process. These considerations are further elucidated in the fascinating report of the Finance Minister (J.H. Mensah) to the Prime Minister on the Debt Conference (Document 60), where diplomatic manoeuvres before and during the conference are also discussed. (Unfortunately it has not been possible to reproduce all sections of the report dealing with these aspects.)

In January 1972 Busia's Government, wrestling with the policy prescriptions of the International Monetary Fund and the World Bank, was overthrown by the Ghana military.[3] However, his fall was followed by the emergence of a more radical regime that was willing to repudiate certain debts and unilaterally reschedule others – on the basis of evidence which had all the time been available to the NLC and Busia Governments. In spite of this militant action, the new Government was granted (in 1974) precisely the type of long-term settlement denied to Busia's openly pro-imperialist Government, incorporating terms which were at the time among the most generous in the world.

Document 48: Ghana's Debt Service Burden

Estimated Contractual Service Payments on External Medium- and Long-Term Public Debt Outstanding, Including Undisbursed, as of 31 December 1965.

Table 48.1 Debt Repayable in Foreign Currency
(In thousands of U.S. dollar equivalents)

Year	Debt Outst. (Begin of Period) Including Undisbursed	Payments During Period		
		Amortization	Interest	Total
Grand Total				
1966	490,742	51,213[a*]	12,148[b]	63,361
1967	439,511	67,820	15,539	83,359
1968	371,711	70,390	15,557	85,947
1969	301,321	59,294	12,578	71,872
1970	242,027	52,370	10,487	62,857
1971	189,657	42,002	8,347	50,349
1972	147,655	25,094	6,621	31,715
1973	122,561	18,544	5,570	24,114
1974	104,017	14,235	4,768	19,003
1975	89,782	9,807	4,159	13,966
1976	79,975	8,330	3,757	12,087
1977	71,645	7,362	3,403	10,765
1978	64,283	6,611	3,097	9,708
1979	57,672	5,793	2,805	8,598
1980	51,879	5,975	2,530	8,505

*Notes appear at the end of the Table.   *continued*

continued

Year	Debt Outst. (Begin of Period) Including Undisbursed	Payments During Period		
		Amortization	Interest	Total

Privately-placed Debt – Suppliers' Credits

Year	Debt Outst.	Amortization	Interest	Total
1966	307,390	45,300	10,220	55,520
1967	262,090	56,935	11,018	67,253
1963	205,155	55,901	9,043	64,944
1969	149,354	45,877	6,492	52,369
1970	103,377	39,790	4,737	44,527
1971	63,587	29,969	2,993	32,962
1972	33,618	13,877	1,633	15,510
1973	19,741	9,167	958	10,125
1974	10,574	6,846	482	7,328
1975	3,723	2,484	163	2,647
1976	1,244	1,010	53	1,068
1977	234	234	7	241

IBRD Loans

Year	Debt Outst.	Amortization	Interest	Total
1966	47,000	–	–	–
1967	47,000	–	1,351	1,351
1968	47,000	1,357	2,683	4,040
1969	45,645	1,436	2,604	4,040
1970	44,209	1,519	2,520	4,039
1971	42,690	1,609	2,432	4,041
1972	41,081	1,702	2,338	4,040
1973	39,379	1,801	2,239	4,040
1974	37,573	1,907	2,133	4,041
1975	35,671	2,018	2,023	4,040
1976	33,653	2,136	1,905	4,040
1977	31,517	2,260	1,780	4,039
1978	29,257	2,392	1,648	4,040
1979	26,865	2,531	1,508	4,040
1980	24,334	2,678	1,362	4,040

continued

Year	Debt Outst. (Begin of Period) Including Undisbursed	Payments During Period		
		Amortization	Interest	Total

Loans from US Government[c] – Total

1966	36,900	50	1,035	1,085
1967	36,850	313	1,117	1,430
1968	36,537	576	1,184	1,760
1969	35,961	911	1,236	2,147
1970	35,050	1,265	1,269	2,534
1971	33,785	1,291	1,296	2,587
1972	32,494	1,318	1,302	2,620
1973	31,176	1,346	1,244	2,590
1974	29,830	1,375	1,184	2,559
1975	28,455	1,405	1,124	2,529
1976	27,050	1,436	1,063	2,499
1977	25,614	1,468	1,001	2,469
1978	24,146	1,501	937	2,438
1979	22,645	1,536	373	2,409
1980	21,109	1,571	807	2,378

Loans from Western [European] Governments[d] – Total

1966	19,000	–	–	–
1967	19,000	368	508	876
1968	18,632	1,072	1,123	2,195
1969	17,560	1,072	1,059	2,131
1970	16,488	1,072	995	2,067
1971	15,416	1,072	932	2,004
1972	14,344	1,072	868	1,940
1973	13,272	1,072	805	1,877
1974	12,200	1,072	741	1,813
1975	11,128	1,072	678	1,750
1976	10,056	1,072	615	1,687
1977	8,984	1,072	551	1,623
1978	7,917	1,067	488	1,555
1979	6,850	1,067	424	1,491
1980	5,783	1,067	361	1,428

continued

continued

Year	Debt Outst. (Begin of Period) Including Undisbursed	Payments During Period		
		Amortization	Interest	Total

Loans from 'Eastern' Countries[e] – Total

1966	80,452	5,863	893	6,756
1967	74,590	10,204	1,545	11,749
1968	64,386	11,484	1,524	13,008
1969	52,902	9,398	1,187	11,185
1970	42,904	8,724	966	9,690
1971	34,180	8,061	694	8,755
1972	26,119	7,125	480	7,605
1973	18,994	5,158	324	5,482
1974	13,836	3,035	228	3,263
1975	10,801	2,828	171	2,999
1976	7,973	2,676	116	2,792
1977	5,297	2,328	64	2,392
1978	2,969	1,651	24	1,675
1979	1,318	659	–	659
1980	659	659	–	659

Loans from USSR[f]

1966	39,559	1,815	332	2,147
1967	37,744	4,920	983	5,903
1968	32,824	4,864	822	5,686
1969	27,960	4,696	689	5,385
1970	23,264	3,853	577	4,440
1971	19,411	3,685	477	4,162
1972	15,726	3,491	383	3,874
1973	12,235	3,466	296	3,762
1974	8,769	2,076	218	2,294
1975	6,693	2,017	168	2,185
1976	4,676	2,017	116	2,133
1977	2,659	1,669	64	1,733
1978	992	992	24	1,016

a. Of which $13,664,000 were in arrears as of 31 December 1965.
b. Of which $3,537,000 were in arrears as of 31 May 1966.
c. USAID and Export–Import Bank
d. Britain and Federal Republic of Germany
e. The major Eastern creditors are the Soviet Union, the GDR, Poland, Czechoslovakia, Hungary and China
f. USSR portion of total 'Eastern' loans

Source: World Bank, Statistical Services Division, 9 March 1967.

Document 49: Abuses in Pre-finance Contracts
From Report of the Auditor-General on the Accounts of Ghana for the Period Ended 31 December 1964, Accra: 1967, pp. 5-6.

37. *Pre-finance Contracts.* Lack of effective coordination in the administration of contracts under suppliers' credit and the absence of adequate records of these contracts have complicated the compilation of statistics of the extent of Government's commitments under suppliers' credit facilities. Consequently, it has not been possible to obtain requisite information on the status of the contracts, and the information given in past reports has necessarily been fragmentary.

38. A Committee appointed by the Government to re-examine the financial provisions and other aspects of pre-finance contracts negotiated by the Government confirmed the view held by this Department that whilst the terms of most of these contracts provide adequate safeguards for the contractors as regards Government's financial commitments and general responsibilities in respect of labour relations and provision of facilities, they do not protect to the same extent the rights of the Government. For example, the Committee noted that all the contracts provide for compensation for the contractors in the event of failure of action on the part of the Government but no corresponding obligation is placed on the contractors for similar acts on their part. In most of the contracts bills of quantities and prices assumed for each category of work are omitted. It is not therefore possible to assess the reasonableness of the cost of the projects in the light of current international prices for identical items. Further it is difficult to decide to what extent reliance can be placed on local sources of supply for certain materials needed to complete the project.

39. Other important findings of the Committee are as follows:

(i) Most of the contracts do not spell out the three distinct but interrelated elements in the financing of the projects, i.e. the total cost of labour, direct materials and overhead expenses, which are to be financed in part by the Government's own down payments and the amount of the credit extended by the suppliers. Generally only the provisions for the repayment of the credit are spelled out. In some few instances the Government's contribution and the credit extended are merged as a consolidated sum to represent the credit granted.

(ii) The interest payable by Government on the credit is calculated differently in many contracts. The rate of interest varies a good deal and has no specific relationship to the type of project or the period of the credit.

(iii) Most of the contracts, in addition to interest, include financial charges for services connected with the guarantee of the loan. These charges are unduly high in relation to the rates of premium on credit insurance quoted by export organizations of the countries from which the credit is obtained.

(iv) Some of the contracts provide for the execution of promissory notes for the entire amount of credit at the time of signing of the contract and for lodgement with Trustees abroad. The promissory notes are to be released by the Trustees from time to time when acceptance certificates of the Government engineers are produced for the equivalent values of each batch of promissory notes. Thus, whatever be the status in the implementation of the contracts, the contractors' interests are safeguarded by the prior execution of promissory notes by the Government for lodgement abroad.

(v) The most vulnerable aspect of the financial provisions is the currency of repayment. In most cases the entire credit is made repayable in foreign currency irrespective of the fact that a sizeable amount of local currency expenditure is incurred in the country. In some cases a large share of the downpayment is also made in foreign currency.

(vi) The most serious defect of the contracts relates to the absence of any recording of the figures of credit committed and utilized by Government either in the Budget Estimates or in the Revised Estimates or the Final Accounts of the Government. The estimates of expenditure which are presented in a summary form in the final accounts are thus incomplete. For example, the estimates of development expenditure of a Ministry or of a Department do not include the amount to be spent by them during the year out of the credit committed to and contracted for by it with foreign suppliers. This omission not only nullifies Parliament's control over expenditure but also weakens the Ministry of Finance's administrative control over the ceiling which is imposed on expenditure incurred by departments. As a result of this anomaly, there is no effective trace of the number of such contracts.

40. The Committee made far-reaching suggestions for improvement in the administration and control of existing and future contracts. So far as this Department is aware, the recommendations of the Committee were virtually ignored by the former Government, with the result that the incidence of the financial burden arising from these contracts has been so high that Government has encountered considerable payments difficulties, especially as regards repayment in foreign currency.

41. The available figures indicate that up to 30 September 1965, 218 external suppliers' credit agreements involving a total amount of £G267,812,176 had been concluded with 21 countries, of which credit taken during the period under review amounted to £G43,925,020. Of the overall commitments as at 30 September 1965, the credit component

amounted to £G204,732,377, whilst downpayments made by Government in fulfilment of its obligations totalled £G63,079,799.

42. The figures quoted in the preceding paragraph do not take account of internal pre-finance contracts to the value of £G1,662,899 for which Promissory Notes on the basis of acceptance certificates have progressively been issued by the Government since the beginning of the period under review.

Document 50: Contractor-Finance Projects*
Table 50.1

N₵ million

Sectors	Less than 6 years (1)	6–12 years (2)	More than 12 years (3)	Others (4)	Total (5)
A. IMF Member Countries					
1. Agriculture	30.1	32.7	–	–	62.8
2. Mining	–	–	–	–	–
3. Manufacturing	–	58.4	–	–	58.4
4. Construction	0.5	0.3	64.6	–	65.4
5. Transport and Communications	3.1	40.1	46.9	4.7	94.8
6. Electricity, gas, water	–	–	66.2	–	66.2
7. Unallocated*	–	–	–	43.0	43.0
Total	33.7	131.5	177.7	47.7	390.6
As a percentage of Total	8.6	33.7	45.5	12.2	100.0

*Includes credits for imports of raw materials and consumer goods as well as projects that do not generate any directly measurable economic returns.

The following contracts are excluded:
 (a) Purchase of frigate
 (b) Drevici group projects
 (c) Atomic reactor, agricultural equipment; pharmaceutical factory, automobile factory; for which contracts prices are not known.

continued

continued

Sectors	Expected to Generate Income in				Total
	Less than 6 years	6–12 years	More than 12 years	Others	
	(1)	(2)	(3)	(4)	(5)

B. Non-IMF Countries

1. Agriculture	4.5	11.2	–	–	15.7
2. Mining	–	–	2.4	–	2.4
3. Manufacturing	–	31.3	–	–	31.3
4. Construction	–	0.2	2.9	–	3.1
5. Transport and Communications	0.2	8.0	4.9	–	13.1
6. Electricity, gas, water	–	0.5	1.7	–	2.2
7. Unallocated*	–	–	–	23.5	23.5
Total	4.7	51.2	11.9	23.5	91.3
As a percentage of Total	5.1	56.1	13.1	25.7	100.0

C. All Countries (A + B)

Total	38.4	182.7	189.6	71.2	481.9
As a percentage of Total	8.0	37.9	39.3	14.8	100.0

Source: Ghana's External Debt Problem: Its Nature and Solution, Accra, April 1970. (Document presented by Ghana Government to External Creditors).

Document 51: Rearrangement of Ghana's Medium-term Debt

Agreed Minute on the Repayment of the Medium-term Debt of the Government of Ghana and others Resident in Ghana. London, December 1966.

1. Representatives of the Governments of Australia, Belgium, Canada, the Federal Republic of Germany, Israel, Italy, Japan, The Netherlands, Norway, Switzerland, the United States of America, and the United Kingdom ('the creditor countries') met in London under the Chairmanship of the United Kingdom from 6 December to 9 December 1966, with

representatives of the Government of Ghana ('the Ghana representatives') to consider Ghana's request for external debt re-arrangement. Representatives of the International Monetary Fund and the International Bank for Reconstruction and Development were also present.

2. The Ghana representatives recalled that at a meeting convened at the Ghana Government's request by the United Kingdom Government in London on the 1 and 2 June 1966,* they had described the grave economic situation the Ghana Government had inherited from the previous Government and the determined and practical steps the new Government, in consultation with the IMF, were taking to rehabilitate Ghana's economy. They had also stated that the Government were determined to meet in due course the country's external financial obligations incurred under the previous Government but that debt rearrangement was needed because the Government were currently faced with foreign exchange difficulties.

Accordingly, the Ghana Government had sought a temporary suspension of the service of transfers under suppliers' credits until an appropriate debt rescheduling or refinancing could be arranged.

They had also drawn attention to the grave imbalance in the years immediately ahead between the estimated receipts from visible and invisible exports, aid and other sources and the considerable payments required for necessary imports and debt servicing.

The representatives of the creditor countries had undertaken to report the Ghana Government's request to their Governments.

The Ghana Government had expressed the hope that at a subsequent meeting it would be possible to negotiate a rearrangement or refinancing of these credits in a manner consistent with the equitable treatment of the creditors and the rehabilitation of the economy in order to facilitate the long-term development of Ghana.

3. Attention was drawn to the terms on which transfers of payments in respect of credits or loans provided by the Governments of, or persons or corporations resident in, the creditor countries to the Ghana Government, or to persons or corporations resident in Ghana, with an original maturity exceeding one year but not exceeding twelve years, and arising under or relating to contracts for the supply of goods or services or both from outside Ghana, concluded before 24 February 1966, should be made.

4. The Ghana representatives stated that the Government would undertake new external borrowing only for purposes of high economic priority and with due regard to the fulfilment of existing debt service obligations. At present new external borrowing with a maturity of one to twelve years was limited under the provisions of a one-year standby arrangement with the International Monetary Fund which became effective in May. The Government considered it essential to bring about

*See Document 13. – *Editor*

gradually a net reduction in the total outstanding amount of such debt and would continue its efforts to achieve this end. Upon the expiry of the present standby arrangement in May 1967, the Government contemplated requesting another standby arrangement with the Fund. They would be prepared to include in this provisions relating to Ghana's foreign borrowing policy.

With effect from the end of December 1966, the Government would provide foreign exchange cover on an up-to-date basis for all authorized current payments other than profits and items of a capital nature. The position in respect of profits would be kept under review and such remittances would be liberalized as the foreign exchange situation improved. The scheme introduced in August 1966 for clearing arrears of current payments was working smoothly and the Government would continue to meet their obligations fully under this scheme. The Government would continue to review the outstanding current arrears on a quarterly basis and would clear these arrears as rapidly as the foreign exchange situation permitted.

The Government would review periodically their policies in the financial, trade and payments fields with the International Monetary Fund, within the framework of Article 14 consultations. This would provide the Governments of the creditor countries with up-to-date information on performance under their economic programme designed to achieve growth with stability. During the consolidation period information would be sent to the International Monetary Fund, on a half-yearly basis, on all new external debt commitments and debt service payments, other than short-term trade and banking credits, undertaken or authorized by the Government. The Government would authorize the Fund to make this information available to the Governments of the creditor countries, with such interpretation as might be necessary.

5. In respect of the credits or loans referred to in paragraph 3 and granted or insured by the Governments or their competent institutions of the creditor countries, the Ghana representatives stated that their Government proposed to make transfers in respect of all debts of principal and interest overdue thereunder on 1 June 1966, and of all such debts due or falling due between 1 June 1966 and 31 December 1968, both dates inclusive ('the consolidation period') in the following manner:

[The formula* adopted here provides, for principal and interest maturing

    A.   On or before the 30 June 1967:
           repayment of 20% between 1 July 1967 and 1 December 1968 and of the remaining 80% between 1 December 1968 and 30 June 1979;

---

*This is a summary of the rescheduling provisions detailed in Art. 5, and not part of the original document.—*Editor*

B. in the financial year ending 30 June 1968:
repayment of 20% in the financial year ending 30 June 1968 and the remainder (80%) between 30 June 1968 and 30 June 1979;
C. between 1 July 1968 and 31 December 1968:
repayment of 20% between 1 July 1968 and 31 December 1968 and of the remainder (80%) between 30 June 1972 and 30 June 1979

Repayments were to be effected in progressively rising instalments, the due date (with a few exceptions) being the end of the financial year, defined as the year commencing 1 July and ending on 30 June of the following year.

Where no date is specified in the formula set out above, transfers in accordance with the said formula will be made in four equal instalments of the total amount due to be transferred in any financial year on the first day of July, October, January and April, except that the first transfer in respect of payment of any debt falling due on or after 1 July 1967 will be made on the original contractual due date for such payment if so required by a creditor country.

The Ghana representatives also stated that it was the intention of the Ghana Government to make available to the International Monetary Fund as soon as possible after the first day of July, October, January and April in each year during the consolidation and delayed transfer periods, information to enable the International Monetary Fund to inform the Governments of the creditor countries of the amount of all transfers made since 1 June 1966 to each creditor country in settlement of debts incurred under the credits or loans referred to in paragraph 3.

6. The Ghana representatives stated that their Government would undertake that if at any time terms which are more favourable than those set out in paragraph 5 are accorded in relation to credits or loans of the type referred to in paragraph 3, whether or not provided by the creditor countries or residents in those countries, terms no less favourable will forthwith be accorded to the creditor countries and/or creditors resident in those countries. The Government of Ghana would supply, through the International Monetary Fund, information on the terms which they accorded to other creditors.

7. The Ghana representatives stated that their Government:

(a) would, if required by a creditor country and to the extent that this was shown to be necessary by the nature of its credit insurance system, direct that during the consolidation period debtors, or their guarantors, resident in Ghana would pay a sum in cedis equal to the full contractual amount of all instalments due to creditors resident in that country into special accounts with the Bank of Ghana where it would remain until transferred or paid in accordance with this Agreed Minute or with the bilateral agreements, or other arrangements referred to in paragraph 9. The Government of Ghana would take steps to notify without delay to the appropriate authority of the creditor country concerned particulars of these payments.

(b) would undertake that the payments made as provided in sub-paragraph (a) would be transferred in the currency in which the debt had been contracted or in the currency of the creditor country in question at the exchange rate ruling on the date of the cedi payment of the instalment in question.

8. The Ghana representatives stated that their Government would arrange that interest would be paid by the Ghana Government on all delayed transfers. The rate of interest to be paid would be determined in the bilateral agreement or other arrangement referred to in paragraph 9, having regard to the cost of borrowing in the creditor country concerned. Each creditor country will use its best endeavours to keep the average rate it charges as low as possible. Such interest would be transferred in the currency concerned half-yearly on the 30 June and 31 December, or as provided in the bilateral agreement or arrangement, except that interest on arrears accruing before 30 June 1967 would be transferred in the following instalments:

(a) one-sixth on 1 July 1967
(b) one-sixth on 1 January 1968
(c) one-sixth on 1 April 1968
(d) one-sixth on 1 July 1968
(e) one-third on 1 December 1968.

The representatives of the creditor countries stated that the debt consolidation could meet only a part of the balance of payments problem as illustrated by the material which the Ghana representatives had put before the meeting. They also maintained that the debt rearrangement must be distinguished from aid and that it could not be provided at concessionary rates.

9. The Ghana representatives said that their Government would be prepared to take all necessary action to give effect to these proposals. In particular they were willing, on the basis of this Agreement Minute, to enter into bilateral negotiations with the Governments of the creditor countries, or the competent institutions or agencies, without delay with a view to reaching full agreements or, at the option of the creditor country concerned, other arrangements, as soon as possible. Such agreements or arrangements would include all necessary consequential provisions, including provisions for their technical application.

The representatives of the creditor countries stated that they would recommend to their Governments that they should enter into bilateral negotiations with the Ghana Government on the basis of this Agreed Minute. Particulars of such agreements or arrangements would be sent by the Ghana Government to the International Monetary Fund who would transmit them to the Governments of all the creditor countries.

10. It was stated by the representatives of the creditor countries and by the Ghana representatives that nothing in this Agreed Minute, or in the bilateral agreements or other arrangements envisaged in paragraph 9, would affect rights and obligations of creditors, debtors and guarantors under or in relation to the contracts referred to in paragraph 3.

11. The Ghana representatives requested that the creditor countries should meet in 1968 to consider further relief to Ghana ... if, in the view of the Ghana Government, such a meeting was necessary. In a spirit of understanding the representatives of the creditor countries took note of this wish. The Chairman stated that the United Kingdom Government would convene a further meeting at the request of the Ghana Government or of any creditor country.

12. The Ghana representatives and the representatives of the creditor countries agreed that the foregoing is a correct record.

Document 52: Ghana's Medium-term Debt: Agreed Minute, 1968

Agreed Minute on the Repayment of the Medium-term Debt of the Government of Ghana and others resident in Ghana, Marlborough House, London, 22 October 1968.

Preamble
1. Representatives of the Governments of Australia, Belgium, the Federal Republic of Germany, Italy, Japan, The Netherlands, Norway, the United States of America and the United Kingdom ('the creditor countries') met in London under the Chairmanship of the United Kingdom from 16 October to 22 October 1968, with representatives of the Government of Ghana ('the Ghana representatives') to consider Ghana's request for a final rearrangement of medium-term external debt. A delegation from France attended as observers and presented their views on the matters under discussion. A representative of Switzerland attended as an observer. Representatives of the International Monetary Fund and the International Bank for Reconstruction and Development were also present.

Review of Performance and Request for further Debt Rearrangement
2.(1) Representatives of the creditor countries, in the light of the information made available to them before and during the meeting, took note that the Ghana Government had faithfully adhered to the provisions for the payment of debt recorded in the Agreed Minute of December 1966,

which were incorporated in subsequent Bilateral Agreements with creditor countries, and had been meeting debt service payments in accordance with the provisions set out in that Minute and Agreements regularly.

2.(2) Representatives of the creditor countries also expressed appreciation of the achievements of the Ghana Government during the first consolidation period.

2.(3) The Ghana representatives expressed their Government's firm intention to continue their efforts to strengthen and develop Ghana's economy. They reaffirmed their Government's determination to meet in due course the legitimate external financial obligations of the country. They maintained that the speed of repayment would, however, be conditioned by the country's capacity to pay. They drew attention in an *aide-mémoire** to the substantial imbalance in the next few years between the estimated receipts from visible and invisible exports, aid and other sources and the considerable payments required for debt servicing and essential imports. To assist their Government's efforts to strengthen the economy and to facilitate the resumption of an adequate economic growth rate, they requested a further rearrangement of debt. They stressed that without such assistance it would be unrealistic to expect that the Ghanaian economy could generate the economic resources needed to meet fully the country's current payments and its contractual obligations.

Debt to be Rearranged

3. The debt to be the subject of rearrangement would be contractual debt maturities falling due in the new consolidation period (as defined in paragraph 5 below) in respect of credits or loans provided by the Governments of, or persons or corporations resident in, the creditor countries to the Ghana Government, or to persons or corporations resident in Ghana, with an original maturity exceeding one year but not exceeding 12 years and arising under or relating to contracts for the supply of goods or services or both from outside Ghana concluded before 24 February 1966.

Undertakings by Ghana

4. The Ghana representatives stated that:

(1) their Government would have due regard to the fulfilment of existing debt service obligations in their policy with respect to new external borrowing;

(2) their Government would endeavour to provide foreign exchange cover for all current obligations as and when they fell due and for the prompt clearance of accumulated arrears;

(3) their Government would continue to review periodically their policies in the financial, trade and payments fields with the

---

*Ghana, *Ghana's Economy and Aid Requirements in 1968.—Editor.*

International Monetary Fund, within the framework of Article 14 consultations. This would provide the Governments of the creditor countries with up-to-date information on performance under their economic programme designed to achieve growth with stability. During the new consolidation period, information would be sent to the International Monetary Fund, on a half-yearly basis, on all new external debt commitments and debt service payments, other than short-term trade and banking credits, undertaken or authorized by their Government. Their Government would authorize the Fund to make this information available to the Governments of the creditor countries, with such interpretation as might be necessary.

Re-scheduling Arrangements

5.(1) In respect of the credits or loans referred to in paragraph 3 and granted or insured by the Governments or the competent institutions of the creditor countries, other than those referred to in paragraph 8, the Ghana representatives stated that their Government proposed to make transfers in respect of all debts of principal and interest falling due between 1 January 1969 and 30 June 1972, both dates inclusive ('the consolidation period') in the following manner:

In respect of each such debt there would be transferred to the appropriate creditor country:

(i) an amount equal to 20 per cent of that debt on the contractual due date except that, in relation to each such debt falling due between 1 January 1969 and 31 December 1969, both dates inclusive, an amount equal to 15 per cent of that debt would be transferred on the contractual due date and amounts each equal to $2\frac{1}{2}$ per cent of that debt would be transferred on 1 January 1971 and 1 January 1972;

(ii) an amount equal to 3 per cent of that debt in two equal instalments on 1 July 1974 and 1 October 1974;

(iii) in equal quarterly instalments on 1 January, 1 April, 1 July and 1 October in each calendar year –

    (a) an amount equal to 7 per cent of that debt in the calendar year 1975;

    (b) amounts equal to 10 per cent of that debt in each of the calendar years 1976, 1977, 1978 and 1979;

    (c) amounts equal to 15 per cent of that debt in each of the calendar years 1980 and 1981.

5.(2) The Ghana representatives also stated that it was the intention of the Ghana Government to make available to the International Monetary Fund, as soon as possible after the first day of July and January in each year until repayment had been completed in accordance with sub-section

(1) of this paragraph, information to enable the Fund to inform the Governments of the creditor countries of the amount of all transfers made on or after 1 January 1969 to each creditor country in settlement of debts incurred under the credits or loans referred to in paragraph 3.

Statement by Representative of Japan
7. The representative of Japan stated that his Government had, with the agreement of the Governments of the other creditor countries, negotiated a bilateral agreement with Ghana in accordance with the Agreed Minute of December 1966, which, while in other respects according with the terms set out in that Agreed Minute, had conformed to the principle that contractual interest would be paid in full on the original due dates. The representative of Japan stated that his Government intended to negotiate a bilateral agreement with Ghana in accordance with this Agreed Minute conforming to the same principle. Such an agreement might result in transfers to creditors resident in Japan exceeding 20 per cent of the total of principal and interest to be transferred during the consolidation period in accordance with paragraph 5 of this Agreed Minute, but the representative of Japan stated that his Government would ensure that the bilateral agreement would, in respect of the whole period of debt re-scheduling arrangements covered by this Agreed Minute, offer terms no more favourable to creditors resident in Japan than those set out in paragraph 5 thereof. Representatives of other creditor countries took note of the statement by the representative of Japan.

Creditor Countries with Very Small Claims
8. The Ghana representatives stated that, for technical and administrative reasons, their Government intended to make transfers on the contractual due dates in respect of maturities under credits or loans referred to in paragraph 3 where the unrescheduled amounts due after 31 December 1968 to persons or corporations resident in a creditor country totalled less than US $35,000.

Interest on Deferred Transfers
10. The representatives of the creditor countries urged that the interest rate on deferred transfers should follow the formula in the Agreed Minute of December 1966, i.e. the rate of interest would be determined by bilateral negotiations having regard to the cost of borrowing in the creditor countries concerned, each creditor country using its best endeavours to keep the average rate charged as low as possible. However, in an endeavour to secure agreement with the representatives of Ghana, and in the context of the other terms of this Agreed Minute, they proposed that each creditor country would charge interest rates on deferred transfers such that the average payable to creditors resident in that country would be in the range $5^1/_2$ per cent to 6 per cent per annum inclusive. This proposal, however,

would not preclude any creditor agreeing to a rate of interest lower than this range.

The Ghana representatives took note of this proposal, and stated that their Government would arrange that interest would be paid by the Ghana Government on all deferred transfers. Such interest would be transferred in the currency concerned half-yearly on 1 July and 1 January, or as provided in the Bilateral Agreement or arrangement. They maintained, however, that interest payments at the rates proposed would, in the context of the general settlement, impose an undue burden on the balance of payments of Ghana unless alleviated by supplementary measures.

The representatives of Ghana and of the creditor countries therefore undertook to recommend to their respective Governments that the rate of interest on deferred transfers should be determined at bilateral negotiations.

Final Settlement
13. Representatives of creditor countries noted and endorsed the expectation of the Ghana Government that this debt rearrangement would represent a final settlement with all creditors.

Conclusion
14. The Ghana representatives and the representatives of the creditor countries agreed that the foregoing was a correct record.

Document 53: Impact of Re-scheduling on Ghana's Debt Service Burden
Table 53.1
(₵ millions)

	Original Principal and Interest (1)	Moratorium Interest (2)	Total (3)	(2) as % of (1) (4)
A. IMF Member Countries				
1966 Agreement	137.3	56.9	194.2	41.4
1968 Agreement	75.3	26.8	102.1	55.6
Total	212.6	83.7	296.3	39.4
B. Non-IMF Member Countries				
1966 Agreement	36.2	5.8	42.0	16.0
1968 Agreement	1.2	0.2	1.4	16.7
Total	37.4	6.0	43.4	16.0
C. IMF and Non-IMF Countries				
1966 Agreement	173.5	62.7	136.2	36.1
1968 Agreement	76.5	27.0	103.5	35.5
Total	250.0	89.7	239.7	35.6

Source: Ghana, *Ghana's External Debt Problem: Its Nature and Solution* (April 1970), p. 66.

Document 54: The Case for Possible Debt Repudiation or Default
'Notes on Seminar on Consultative Group Meeting, 25/6/70' (Report on meeting of Government officials at Aburi on 25 and 26 June 1970).

The case for default: An attempt was made to assess whether there was any case for default on the part of Ghana. The discussion was led by Mr Asante [Solicitor-General]. In the discussion the case for possible repudiation was also examined as well as counter arguments that may be raised by the creditor countries. Both legal and economic reasons were considered. It was pointed out that whereas the 1966 agreed minute left the door open for other debt negotiations, in the 1968 minute no other meetings were proposed. Since the 1968 re-scheduling a number of bilateral agreements have been entered into and Ghana has paid some of these debts, although the new Government has intimated that it did not agree with the 1968 proposals. The situation was that both by intent and by act of Government, Ghana was technically in default already since some of the debts had not been paid as scheduled. Concerning the legal position, despiting [*sic*] the fact that the 1968 agreement had not called for a further review and despiting [*sic*] the fact that in law, agreements must be kept, debtor countries could still call for a review exercise. This was because international agreements allow that where situations change which were not envisaged in the original agreement a review can be undertaken. If the review exercise failed, default could be on the basis of inability to pay. It would appear that on economic grounds a case could have been made for defaulting early in 1966 when the economic situation was really bad (based on reaction to feelers in the World Bank). It was a moot point whether the fact that projects involved in the contracts were not viable could support Ghana's case *caveat emptor*.

The question was then posed as to what could happen if Ghana defaulted, assuming that the review exercise failed. It was pointed out that as a member country of the World Bank the Creditor country could call on the World Bank to impose sanctions to deny aid. The power of the World Bank to impose sanctions derived ultimately from the Bank's articles but generally from the World Bank Board's decisions through the voting of members of the Board. Non-creditworthiness could disqualify a country from being eligible for aid. Creditworthiness of a country is determined by the state of the economy, i.e., its balance of payments position, its ability to pay debts, which would include the question whether obligations are honoured by the country or not. However, the World Bank's action to impose sanctions would not be automatic if there was a reasonable case for the country in default to have defaulted. In this connection the case of Tanzania was cited as an example. It was thought that there was a case for at least repudiating some of the debts on the basis of tainted contracts. The case here would be that the contracts were 'vitiated by corruption'. Determination of vitiated contracts could be done on the basis of the common law of the country provided for it or if the terms of the contract itself included a clause against corruption. It was pointed out that laws of most of our creditors including Britain (the major creditor) provided for repudiation. Second, most of the contracts signed by Ghana included a clause on corruption. It was suggested that it might be a good idea to make an example as a matter of principle, and it was observed in particular that the case involving Parkinson Howard in the construction of the motorway had enough basis to sustain repudiation. Further, it would be good to pick for repudiation those contracts with exaggerated prices which were guaranteed by the creditor countries.

Default could take a number of forms:

1. A public announcement;
2. Technical default without announcement;
3. An announcement at the conference with or without the agreement of the creditor countries.

It was to be decided which alternative would be used. Generally it was felt that in order to avoid very sharp repercussions from the creditor countries it might be better to default with consent if there was a reasonable chance for this consent. This would mean accepting other obligations as under the contracts, but invoking inability to pay. As precedence the cases of some Latin American countries were cited. . . . Since consent was unlikely it would be better not to leave any loopholes by seeking the consent of the creditor countries before defaulting. The better act would be to state considerable cause for default and announce this at [sic] the talks were not fruitful. In this connection also, it was considered that in principle it might be better not to default completely but table a unilateral proposal that Ghana should announce at the end of the talks and implement it on her own. Such a proposal needed to be worked out as an alternative to the original Ghana proposals.

Possible Arguments Against Ghana Defaulting
The other side of the coin was what possible arguments the creditor countries may raise quite justifiably against default on the part of Ghana against refinancing. The arguments would include the state of the economy, Ghana's ability to pay, the re-scheduling agreement, the social and political conditions in the country and the objectives of the government. In general it was felt that the feeling of the creditor countries was that Ghana's economy was quite healthy and that her ability to pay was good. A listing of points would include:

1. Healthy economy.
2. That although the balance of payments was in deficit this was a short-term problem...
3. That refinancing precedents do not really apply to Ghana (i.e. the Indonesian case cannot be cited).
4. That documentation so far prepared was not good enough to support our case.
5. That the programmes now announced do not include specific policies to support intentions.

Attention was then turned to possible reaction from the creditors on Ghana's default. It was thought that the creditors' reaction to default will depend on whether they think we can really pay or not. In sum, they probably think we can pay. Whereas we can make a case for repudiating some debts we cannot default. The argument of non-viable projects can at best sustain only re-scheduling.

Document 55: Proceedings of the Ghana Debt Conference, Marlborough House, London 7–11 July 1970.

Record of the Opening Session, 7 July 1970

1. Speech by the Parliamentary Under-Secretary of State Foreign and Commonwealth Office *(Chairman)*

I am glad to welcome you all to this meeting on behalf of Her Majesty's Government.

It is a special pleasure to be able to welcome the distinguished Minister of Finance of Ghana, Mr Mensah, to these deliberations. He and most of his colleagues in the Ghana delegation are certainly no strangers to London and he knows, I am sure, that we are always delighted to see him here. I am especially glad that the Minister has been able to spare the time from his very many heavy commitments in Accra, so soon before budget time, in order to lead his country's team at these talks.

This is, of course, a measure of the importance to Ghana of the matters we are to discuss. Indeed, their importance extends beyond Ghana: it has implications and repercussions worldwide and reflects a range of problems affecting very many developing countries in their commercial and financial relations with the rest of the world.

So although whatever we decide here will make its first and main impact on Ghana and Ghana's creditors, we must not underrate the significance of what we do, in a wider context.

As you know, our purpose is to enable Ghana and those of her main creditors who have previously met here in 1966 and 1968 to discuss the recent request by the Government of Ghana for re-examination of the Ghana debt problem.

We shall have an opportunity in these next few days to discuss the case circulated by the Government of Ghana at the end of April which set out the arguments and statistics supporting the Ghana Government's request for further debt relief.

I feel sure that I speak for everyone here today when I say that we all share a common approach to these problems: we are sympathetic towards Ghana's aspirations; we are anxious to make a fair and objective appraisal of the problems involved; we are determined to arrive at a solution which will correspond to the realities of the situation and so far as possible will meet the interests of all those represented here.

Despite the complexities of the problem and the difficulties of reconciling our varying interests, I am confident that, with goodwill and perseverence on the part of every delegation here, we can together arrive at an outcome for the conference which will be a victory for no one but a success for us all. . . .

I suggest that we should all agree to treat our proceedings at this meeting as strictly confidential and that nothing should be said by any of us to the press about what takes place apart from any press statement which we might agree upon before we conclude our business. . . .

3. Speech by the Leader of the Ghanaian Delegation (J. H. Mensah)

... You are all aware that this meeting stems from the request, which was made at the time of the presentation of the 1969/70 Budget of Ghana by the National Liberation Council Government, that creditor countries should consider a multilateral conference to agree on further debt relief to Ghana. The background and the reasons for this request were presented in the following terms by the then Government, of which I also happened to be the member responsible for Finance:

> The measures that Government has taken in the last three years to release financial resources for debt repayments, and to reduce the inflationary pressures which arise from Government deficits, are well known. They have entailed denying ourselves many imported but essential goods. They have necessitated reductions in Government expenditure, involving the retrenchment of labour. And they have meant the holding back of the development of the country practically throughout the entire period of office of the National Liberation Council. The devaluation of the cedi in 1967 was the most drastic measure taken to hold down the demand for imports and to encourage exports.
>
> As a result of all these measures and events, Ghana's balance of payments position is stronger than it has been for many years. But it is quite clear that given the most likely trends in our balance of payments we are highly unlikely in the near future to find room, in the amounts now envisaged for meeting the debt service obligations as they now stand.
>
> There are no reasonable economic forecasts on the basis of which it could be expected that this country could find the resources for debt service on a substantial scale without resort in the near future to internal measures severe beyond what is conceivable or humanly reasonable.
>
> At the same time, the people of this country demand that the course of national progress should be resumed. As a Government, we must respond to this demand – and this goes for both the present Government and any succeeding civilian Government.

I assure you that this request was not made without the most careful consideration. We were aware that our own Government was on record as expecting that, to use the words of the Agreed Minute of October 1968, 'This debt rearrangement (i.e. the 1968 formula), would represent a final settlement with all creditors.' We were also aware that the Governments of creditor countries had 'noted and endorsed this expectation of the Ghana Government.'

Some of you may know that at the time of the overthrow of the Nkrumah regime in 1966 there were many voices, including some very responsible voices, which were raised in favour of a general repudiation of the massive load of debt with which that regime had saddled the country. There was justifiable public anger at this inheritance much of which was represented on the ground by assets of little economic value or worse, by private fortunes of politicians and contractors, illegally acquired at the expense of the public. The Government of Ghana after four years is still engaged in unravelling the tangled mess of incompetence and corruption that was built up in the last four short years of the most incredibly irresponsible Government of the Nkrumah regime. With patience we hope eventually to be able to deal, as the laws of Ghana require, with all improprieties and malfeasances that surrounded the incurring of so much of these debts.

Despite this unsavoury legacy of the Nkrumah regime, the National Liberation Council did not heed the call for repudiation. Instead, it undertook to honour all the legitimate debts of the previous regime on the understanding that feasible arrangements would be made for the payment of these debts.

The agreements that were reached between the National Liberation Council and the creditor countries afforded a sizeable and immediate relief, both to the Government budget and to the balance of payments of the country, from the massive liabilities to debt service which would otherwise have fallen on Ghana. I should once again place on record the appreciation of the people of Ghana for the promptness and the statesmanlike concern among the governments of creditor countries in dealing with this problem.

The principles on which these rearrangements were arrived at seemed then to be fairly settled principles and feasible in the light of economic facts. As I have said, our own Government accepted the 1968 settlement as a final one. In retrospect, I think we can all agree that there are two aspects of these settlements that were inadequate. First, there was the principle of a short consolidation period of two or two and half years, followed soon thereafter by a repayment period, the total length of the whole arrangement being held within the limits of the established norms for medium-term credit. Second, there was the principle of the levying of a moratorium interest charge in return for the facility of the postponed repayment obligations.

Debt relief was intended to contribute towards the amelioration of pressing budgetary and balance of payments deficits. In the document which the Government of Ghana has submitted to this conference,* I think we have shown convincingly that these were not imbalances that could be expected to disappear within the fairly short period that is covered by the medium-term commercial credit. Partly, the problem is inherent in the structural imbalance between production and demand which characterizes the economy of Ghana. This has the result of making our economy

---

*Ghana Government, *Ghana's External Debt Problem: Its Nature and Solution* (April 1970) – *Editor.*

dependent upon imports to such a degree that it is relatively unmeaningful to apply to the debt problem of Ghana the traditional measures of debt service ratios and other mechanical formulae. Structural economic change is precisely one of the objectives of economic policy in Ghana during the coming decade, to which I will refer again presently.

As regards moratorium interest, it is only necessary to point to the fact that its imposition has led to an increase of nearly 40% in the original amount of debt which was the subject of re-scheduling agreements in 1966 and 1968.* I hope that in the consultations that have gone on among the creditor countries in recent months, a clear consensus has emerged as to how to treat this question. In our view, it is an impossible contradiction that we should, by our mutual arrangements, increase by more than NC80 million the sums that Ghana is liable to pay back to your countries, on account of the Nkrumah debts, while at the same time the governments of all the countries represented here are making strenuous efforts to assist with the rehabilitation of our economy.

The Government of Ghana accordingly submits the following proposals:

(i) that the time horizon within which a new debt rearrangement is made should bear a closer relationship to the time span within which, by a consensus of views founded on technical considerations, the necessary surpluses for the repayment of the debt could be generated; this relates to both the budgetary and the balance of payments resources that are required for debt service;

(ii) that arrangements be made so as to remove the load of moratorium interest charges that have been imposed under the previous settlements, and that a formula be chosen for the future which does not involve such a large increase in the sums that Ghana would have to pay year by year in return for the debt relief facility during the period that the reconstruction of the economy is still going on.

Between December 1968 and June 1969, Ghana continued steadily with the process of concluding bilateral agreements with creditor countries to implement the terms of the multilateral settlement. As I have said when we were faced with the problems of finding the resources to support the 1969/70 budget of the NLC Government and with the projections of resources and requirements of the economy as a whole in the immediate future we were persuaded that the liabilities resulting from the application of the 1968 agreement could not be supported by the economy or by the budget. From that time onwards, and especially after the Government of Ghana had submitted a formal request for a fresh look to be taken at the debt problem, there obviously arose a logical

---

*See Document 54. – *Editor.*

contradiction between continuing a series of negotiations which were supposed to enshrine these agreed terms in solemn contracts on the one hand and our knowledge and expectations regarding the economy on the other hand. The matter of the interest rate to be paid for the facility of debt service deferment has proved particularly difficult to negotiate. . . .

It is the view of the Government of Ghana that the new arrangements that are made to deal with these debt problems, if they are to be viable, should be made on substantially different principles from those that were applied before. Firstly they must start to form a certain consensus regarding the economic trends towards which it is desired to make a contribution by means of debt relief.

In the document submitted to this conference, we have outlined the economic consequences of two simple socio-political assumptions. The first is illustrated by what is called the 'low growth model'. In this our economists have explored the consequences of pursuing a policy under which Ghana was expected to maintain a rate of economic growth which just kept pace with the rate of population growth. In the second model they have explored the consequences of following a policy which attempts a rather faster rate of growth with a view to providing the resources for some structural economic change, including the diversification of exports, for a modest increase in the standard of living of the people, and for an eventual position of relatively self-reliant economic growth.

I hope the conference can agree that the second model is the only one that is even minimally feasible as the economic policy of a freely elected government.

What emerges is that on either hypothesis the resource gap that has to be covered by fresh efforts on the part of the Government of Ghana itself, of the donor countries which are supporting the Ghana economy during its period of rehabilitation, and of the creditor countries will be large. . . .

Between 1966 and the end of 1969 N₵116 million of external resources have been transferred to Ghana by the principal aid-giving countries and by the World Bank group in the form of balance of payments support and project aid. As against this, repayments of debt service liabilities on these supplier and contractor debts of the former regime have up till now totalled US$56.5 million to member countries of the IMF, of which about US$20 million were in respect of moratorium interest charges. During the same period, about US$10 million of principal repayments and moratorium charges have been paid to non-member countries of the IMF from whom hardly any fresh capital assistance has been obtained. In other words, substantially more than one-half of all aid received by Ghana since 1966 has been offset by foreign exchange transfers for the repayment of these medium-term debts.

It has to be borne in mind moreover that the pattern of sources of new aid is substantially different from the pattern of the destination of debt service payments. This situation has inevitably impaired the ability of the Government of Ghana to continue to attract aid from those countries who are not major creditors but who wish to contribute substantially to the economic development of our country.

... Since 1966 Ghana has already had to pay some US$22 million in moratorium interest charges to her creditors in consideration of debt rearrangements which in the event have proved to be still inadequate. It is the belief of the Government of Ghana that the new climate of enlightened international opinion on this matter should make it possible for the present conference to agree to the removal of this particular element from the new debt rearrangement.

We therefore request that if it is considered necessary to levy any interest charges on the refinancing loans which we have proposed in order to obviate this element of a massive moratorium burden, then these loans should be granted at an interest rate of not more than 2 per cent.

Based on our reading of the best economic forecasts which are available to us ... we have proposed that Ghana be granted a grace period of 10 years during which no debt repayments would be made. . . .

It is only some such solution that would afford a long enough period of time for the rehabilitation and the structural transformation of the economy. . . .

The Government of Ghana does not expect that the commercial export financing and credit guarantee institutions of many of the countries which hold portions of these medium-term debts could extend their rules of operation in order to accommodate the terms that we are proposing. The grace period, the interest rates, and the capital repayment period that we have suggested are all suitable for Government financing, but in our experience they are not suited to commercial credit transactions. Besides, the principle of moratorium interest at relatively high levels could not, it seems to us, be surmounted within the context of another debt rearrangement that tried to preserve intact the essential characteristics of the original commercial arrangements.

We have consequently proposed that the governments of creditor countries make to Ghana refinancing loans equivalent to the amounts that would be required to repay at their present due dates, the original contract liabilities and in their turn allow the Government of Ghana to repay these refinancing loans on contemporary aid terms.

In the Government of Ghana's document to this conference a proposal has been made that all the medium-term debts be refinanced, as of July 1969, on the uniform terms of a 40 year amortization period, a 10 year grace period, and no more than a 2 per cent interest charge. . . .

In its foreign exchange management the Government of Ghana has since 1966 aimed at systematically reducing the large volume of arrears on account of commodity trade and invisible transactions which it inherited at the time of the *coup* in 1966 . . . The shortage of foreign exchange has, however, left one legacy which is yet to be removed. I refer to the system of mandatory 180-day credits in respect of which it is estimated that Ghana now holds N₡100 and N₡110 million worth of external credits. It is also estimated that in consideration of the extension of this type of credit the cost of imported goods to Ghana is at least 15% higher than it would otherwise be. If this is so, then it must have cost the country close to N₵75 million to service this type of trade credit between 1966 and 1969. The Government is anxious to do away with this expensive method of financing imports and a start has already been made with putting some import items on a sight basis or on other freely negotiated payment basis as between the Ghanaian importer and the foreign supplier.

Owing to the tight foreign exchange reserve position, progress in this area has had to be necessarily slow and as of last year less than 9% of total imports had been put on a sight basis. It has, therefore, been proposed in our document that as a part of the solution of the debt problem a multilateral arrangement might be sponsored whereby, through the normal banking system in the countries where these credits originate, a refinancing operation on medium-term basis would be undertaken. Such an arrangement would save a substantial amount of foreign exchange which could be devoted to national development and to the raising of the standards of living. . . .

The tasks of economic policy to which so many of your countries have contributed so generously since 1966 are, I think, seen by all of us in the same terms. We have to consolidate the economic progress that has begun to emerge in Ghana after many years of stagnation. In this process we have to strengthen the social momentum towards self-sustained growth that is emerging. We have to ameliorate the immediate hardships under which the people of Ghana have lived for so many years. Above all, we have to consolidate the unique political evolution which has taken place in our country; we have to prove that national development under free political institutions is possible, is more desirable, and is more firmly based. . . .

The people of Ghana are watching to see whether, after three and half years of military rule and a smooth transition to a freely elected government they can also expect to see the pace of national development equal and surpass what they witnessed in the last year of the previous dictatorship. I think that all the governments represented here have an interest, like my own Government, in seeing the political transition in Ghana consolidated, confirmed and crowned with material success.

It is in this perspective that I call upon the representatives of the governments here assembled to release Ghana from the load of indebtedness which we have contracted under the 1968 arrangement and subsequent bilateral agreements, and to put in their place arrangements for debt repayment which will enable us to accomplish the social and political tasks to which we have jointly set our hands. The price tag is some N₵33 million a year during the ensuing decade. Do we have the political will and imagination to face up to it?

Document 56: Proceedings of Ghana Debt Conference
Record of the Second Session, 7 July 1970

1. Speech by Chairman of Conference, on behalf of the Creditors
Mr Minister, I should explain that I am speaking now on behalf of all the representatives of the creditor countries participating in this Conference...

The creditors have examined the figures in the Ghanaian document and they are clear that a serious problem which confronts the Ghanaian economy is the balance of payments. They agree with the Government of Ghana that, without a sound balance of payments, long-term growth will not be possible. They have noted the suggestion by the Minister of Finance that we might establish an expert group to discuss the balance of payments projections. The creditors have conducted an examination of the available figures for the next two years among themselves with the assistance of the IMF and the IBRD. . . .

I said just now that the creditor countries agreed with the government of Ghana that without a sound balance of payments, long-term growth will not be possible. Equally, they are clear that a sound balance of payments demands above all else control over the other sectors of the economy if scarce foreign exchange is to be used to the best advantage. Consequently they were especially interested in the Ghana Government's measures directed to these ends. They welcome in particular the Ghana Government's stated intention to control recurrent expenditure, and to increase government revenue; and to ensure that cocoa sales are managed so as to secure the most favourable prices; and the efforts to encourage non-traditional exports.

Turning now to the debt situation the representatives of the creditors countries have asked me first to draw attention to the fact that a number of them have not yet succeeded in completing bilateral agreements with Ghana as called for under the 1968 Agreement Minute. Of the countries represented here this afternoon those in that position are Belgium, Italy, Japan, Norway and the USA. The creditor countries regret very much that this situation still exists two years after the conference and they consider it essential that those agreements should now be concluded without delay in accordance with the terms of the Agreed Minute. I am sure, Mr Minister, that you will want to give this urgent attention as soon as you return to Accra.

Second, they have asked me to express to you their disappointment at having once again to consider Ghana's debt situation. When agreement was reached in 1968 to re-schedule 80 per cent of the medium-term debt incurred before 1966 and falling due between the beginning of 1969 and the middle of 1972 the settlement was, as you yourself said this morning Mr Minister, regarded as being a final one. The creditor countries therefore very much regret that the Government now wish to re-open this and the earlier very advantageous settlements. In their view the debt service burden, anyway over the next couple of years, is not excessive by comparison with that of many of the developing countries.

Creditor countries readily acknowledge that there will be balance of payments gaps this year, and next. The amount of these gaps will largely depend on the amount Ghana receives for cocoa and other exports, the amount and type of aid which aid donors are prepared to provide and the effectiveness of the policies adopted by the Ghana Government not least in securing the right relationship between the import programme, the development plan and available foreign exchange resources. Overall debt service payments on medium-term debt are relatively minor in relation to the picture as a whole, particularly over the next two years. Creditor countries do, however, acknowledge that Ghana has a case for additional resources. In view of the extent to which it hinges on the need for accelerated economic growth, they consider that it is more a case for additional aid than a case for further debt relief on top of that already provided. Indeed in the document circulated in April it was made clear that Ghana was seeking not only debt relief but also aid so as to permit development rather than stagnation. Some of the creditor countries represented here are willing to help in this respect and some have already indicated their willingness to attend the meeting of the Consultative Aid Group to be held here on 15 July under the aegis of the World Bank.

Looking further ahead and on the basis of the figures contained in the document circulated in May* the creditor countries realize Ghana's debt servicing burden may become noticeably heavier after mid-1972 when payments of principal on the medium-term debt become larger. It is not possible, however, now to foresee at all clearly what conditions will be like after mid-1972. For example we cannot forecast the movement of cocoa prices which are at present rather depressed compared with the high levels of a year ago. And we may in two years' time be in a better position than we are now to estimate the likely benefits to Ghana of the oil strike which has been made offshore. All in all the position after mid-1972 is extremely obscure though there are definite signs of promise on the horizon. In view of these uncertainties the creditors countries' representatives have asked me to offer on their behalf to hold a further debt conference of the countries represented here before mid-1972. At such a conference we should be in a better position to review the medium-term debt obligations falling due after mid-1972.

However in recognition of the powerful appeal which you made in your opening statement, they would be prepared to consider making certain concessions for the period between now and mid-1972. To be specific, what they have in mind would be to offer relief on concessionary terms of one-quarter of the amounts due between 1 July 1970 and 30 June 1972 in respect of principal and interest on medium-term debt incurred before February 1966 and covered by the 1966 and 1968 agreed minutes, assuming that these

*The reference is to *Ghana's External Debt: Its Nature and Solution.* – Editor.

have been fully implemented. It is, of course, the assumption of the creditor country representatives that the Ghana Government would quickly and effectively implement the policy intentions clearly set out in the Ghana Government's memorandum to the Consultative Group and in the One Year Plan for 1970/71 – measures designed to constrain the level and to improve the composition of imports; to stimulate and diversify exports; to control the level of current government expenditure; to raise additional tax revenue and encourage domestic savings; and to support these measures by appropriate monetary policies. I believe it would be helpful to the creditor country representatives if you, Mr Minister, could later on in the Conference go into rather more detail about the arrangements which your Government intends to take in these fields and also if you would give us an assurance that bilateral arrangements will be concluded without delay in accordance with the terms of the 1968 agreed minute.

The creditor countries have also noted the Ghanaian proposal that a multilateral arrangement might be sponsored for re-financing the 180-day credits through the normal banking system. They doubt, however, whether it is practicable or indeed possible to contemplate the formation of a government-sponsored consortium to raise sums for this purpose.

That is the end of what I have been asked by the creditor countries' representatives to say to you.

Document 57: Proceedings of the Ghana Debt Conference
Response of Ghana's Minister of Finance to Creditor Countries Proposal, 8 July 1970.

Yesterday morning I outlined the position of the Government of Ghana on the debt question. This position consists essentially of saying:

1. That a long-term solution should be sought within the context of economic development and structural adjustment.
2. That the resource gap that would emerge from attempting to achieve this objective would be very large.
3. That debt relief should be utilized along with domestic government policies and inflows of external aid to fill this resource gap.
4. That consequently the existing debt rearrangement which was based on short period of adjustment was inadequate and unacceptable to the Government of Ghana.

2. I have no mandate to discuss the debt problem on the basis of a personal appeal to representatives of creditor countries. My instructions are to seek a settlement that fits in with the balance of payments position of Ghana as it is at present, and as it can be reasonably forecast.

3. I am disappointed that while agreeing with the proposition that 'without sound balance of payments long-term growth will not be possible', the creditor countries have failed to examine seriously long-term balance of payment factors.

4. It is admitted that long-term projections are on such a greater or lesser degree of uncertainty, but one has to act on the basis of certain expectations. Specifically it is difficult to understand how the creditor countries could accept long-term export projections as a basis for the very far-reaching decisions which they have taken in support of the reconstruction of Indonesia but now plead technical difficulties in arriving at a long-term decision in support of reconstruction of Ghana, even though both countries are primary exporting countries and therefore subject to degrees of export instability...

7. I am disappointed that in the statement of the creditor countries no attempt has been made to offer a solution that pretends to fit in with any agreed programme for the long-term rehabilitation and structural readjustment of the Ghana economy.

8. Previous debt rearrangements have been on the same hand-to-mouth basis that is now proposed. If anybody could pretend that the balance of payments constraint on Ghana's economic development would be relaxed in a short period, then the two-year solution offered by the creditor countries would have some significance.

9. In my statement to the conference yesterday, I had proposed that while adopting a long-term solution to the Ghana debt problem, provision might be made for periodic review in case extraordinary factors intervened. I think that the Governments of the creditor countries should be able to face the prospects of a long-term arrangement giving the possibility of intermediate re-examination of the fact.

10. Any forecasts of the gap between the resources and the requirements in the economy during a long-term period are large. If this were not so, the offer of the creditor countries to make an arrangement covering two years postponing only 25% of the debt service liability would have some meaning. The Government of Ghana invites creditor countries to propose a long-term viable agreement. Part of our criticisms of previous settlements was that they were based on hand-to-mouth agreements which necessitated periodic reviews at short intervals. The two-year relief offered threatens to get Ghana and the creditor countries into the same position again. This should be avoided . . .

15. It was the request of the Government of Ghana that the creditor countries agree with us that in the light of all the above considerations, the 1968 agreement on the debt rearrangement was no longer tenable.

16. It was suggested in the statement that the resource gap would partly be met through transfers of additional resources in aid. The Government of Ghana maintains its position that both types of transfer are required to cope with the respective resource gap. The Government of Ghana considers it . . . particularly regrettable that the creditor countries could

only indicate their willingness to attend a meeting of the consultative group as an explanation of the offer of the debt relief made. I indicated in my statement yesterday there was great doubt regarding the possibility of additional aid flowing into Ghana at the present time to fill the gap beyond what is now in the pipeline. If individual creditor countries have the mandate to indicate specific levels of additional aid in terms of actual transfers which they expect to be able to afford to Ghana in the next two years, the conference should hear such declarations. In the absence of such commitment, the Government of Ghana does not see much substance in the statement that various countries are willing to attend the consultative group meeting next week.

17. I propose for the above reasons the following:

(a) That our respective groups of experts get together to sort out the long-term projections as well as the forecasts for 1970–71 and 1971–72 and advise the conference as to a reasonable basis for its further decision.

(b) That the creditor countries consider once again the long-term problem that the Government of Ghana has requested should be re-examined and in this regard provide some indicators as to the respective contributions of aid, debt relief, internal measures and export intensification towards a solution.

(c) I would emphasize once more the willingness of the Government of Ghana to participate in periodic reviews of the facts and undertaking of the respective parties within the framework of the long-term solution. . . .

(e) That Government of Ghana is also convinced that the problem of commercial credit which was submitted to the conference has not been given the consideration which it deserves.

Document 58: Proceedings of Ghana Debt Conference
Creditors' Statement, Second Session 8 July 1970

1. The Chairman's Reply to the Ghanaian Delegation on their Case for Further Debt Relief

The Chairman opened the proceedings by reminding the Conference that it had been agreed that the representatives of the creditor nations should meet together to discuss the points raised by the Representative of Ghana and also that a Working Party should be formed to examine the Balance of Payments statistics. The Working Party was still in session and he understood that a considerable time would of necessity elapse before their report was available.

In the meantime, the representatives of the creditors had had their meeting and had authorized him to give replies to some of the points raised by the Representative of Ghana. These were as follows:

(a) The Representative of Ghana had asked the Conference to consider relief being given over a much longer period than 2 years. The creditors had discussed this and now confirmed that they could deal only with the period under discussion, that is, 1 July 1970 to 30 June 1972. The representatives of the creditors had no authority to consider a longer period than that. Their Government did, however, accept that a longer term problem existed and indeed, they had made this clear yesterday. The Representative of Ghana wished for agreement on a longer term settlement with periodical reviews, but the creditors adhered to the view that the only solution to which they were free to agree was a two year settlement now with provision for a further conference after the expiry of the two-year period. The Representative of Ghana might think this inconsistent with the creditors' expression of disappointment that it had been found necessary to meet so soon after the 1968 agreement, which had been considered final. Now the creditors wished to say that anything beyond 1972 would not be ruled out by an agreement completed in 1970.

(b) The next point to be considered was the position of the creditors with regard to the bilateral agreements still outstanding from the 1968 Conference. The representatives of the creditor nations had stressed that these were to be taken into account in reaching any agreement concluded at this Conference. Any transfers falling due during the period July 1970 to June 1972 which were covered by the 1968 agreement would come in for further relief during that period.

(c) The Chairman was then able to clarify the phrase 'concessionary terms' used in the creditors' reply to the Ghanaian case. The Chairman had authority to speak specifically on this point. The proportion suggested for relief would be one-quarter and the proposal was that the alternative terms for relief would be such as to provide a grant element amounting to 61%. This would be in accordance with the policy of the Development Assistance Committee of the OECD. There were different ways in which this could be achieved. The following text was then distributed to the Conference for consideration:

'There shall be offered relief of one-quarter of the amounts due between 1 July 1970 and 30 June 1972 in respect of principal and interest on medium-term debt incurred before February 1966 and covered by full implementation of the 1966 and 1968 Agreed Minutes.

Creditor countries shall have the choice of providing this relief by one or more of the following means:

(i) refinancing loans having a grant element of 61 per cent, or
(ii) partial and temporary deferment of interest and/or principal due between 1 July 1970 and 30 June 1972 for a period of 10 years without interest, i.e. which would be equal to a grant element of 61 per cent, or
(iii) additional programme aid having a grant element of 61 per cent, where disbursements of such aid can be agreed to promptly and completed by 30 June 1972 and over that period provide at least the equivalent of the agreed amount of debt relief for each of these two years, over and above the level of aid disbursed during the period July 1969 to June 1970.'

(d) The Chairman said that another point raised by the Representative of Ghana was the relationship between debt relief measures and development aid. The Representative had asked for an indication of the magnitude of the aid which countries represented at this Conference might make available to Ghana. They accepted that a relationship existed between these but the instructions the Chairman had from the representatives of the creditor nations was that they had no instructions from their Governments as to what they might be prepared to give in the development aid field. The Chairman therefore had no alternative but to say that this Conference was not in a position to discuss aid, which must therefore await the work of the Consultative Group. However, creditors would make available the work done by the Working Party to those departments of their Governments concerned with development aid so that this might be used in formulating future proposals.

(e) Lastly, the Minister had referred to the problem of short-term credits. The representatives of the creditor nations sympathized with the desire of the Ghanaian Government to see a reduction of 180 day credit terms to sight methods of payment. However, the creditors did not think it would be appropriate for them to intervene in methods of ordinary business transactions. Their view is that their work should be directed to the medium-term field. The Chairman, therefore, regretted that he was unable to add to what he had said yesterday on this subject.

Document 59: Ghana's Medium-term Debt: Agreed minute, 1970

Agreed Minute on the Rearrangement of Medium-term Debt Repayments due from Ghana between July 1970 and June 1972, London, 11 July 1970

...4. Relief to be made available[4]

(1) Relief would be made available in respect of the amounts falling due as defined in sub-paragraph (2) below in respect of credits and loans as defined in the Agreed Minutes of 9 December 1966 and 22 October 1968.

(2) The relief should be of 50 per cent of the amount due between 1 July 1970 and 30 June 1972 in respect of principal and interest on medium-term debt as defined in the Agreed Minutes cited in sub-paragraph (1), and covered by full implementation of those Minutes. Creditor Countries should have the choice of providing this relief by one or more of the following means:

  (a) refinancing loans having a grant element of 61 per cent*, or
  (b) Partial and temporary deferment of instalments of interest and/or principal due between 1 July 1970 and 30 June 1972 for a period of ten years without interest, i.e. which would be equal to a grant element of 61 per cent,* or
  (c) additional programme aid having an average grant element of 61 per cent*, where disbursements of such aid can be agreed to promptly and completed by 30 June 1972 and over that period provide at least the equivalent of the agreed amount of debt relief for each of these two years, over and above the level of aid disbursed during the period July 1969 to June 1970.

5. Undertakings by Ghana

(1) The Ghana representatives stated that:
  (a) their Government would promptly conclude bilateral agreements under the 1966 and 1968 Agreed Minutes with those countries with whom such agreements had not yet been concluded;
  (b) the policies of their Government would embrace restraint on Government current expenditure; the improvement of agricultural production; the promotion of exports; the improvement of tax policies; and the introduction of more effective foreign exchange policies, as well as a review of the tariff structure and the limitation of imports to goods having a high degree of economic and social essentiality.
  (c) their Government would continue to review periodically their policies in the economic, financial, trade and payments fields with

---

*Using a 10 per cent discount rate; the Creditor Countries' Representatives stated that this was in accordance with Development Assistance Committee practices.

the International Monetary Fund and with the International Bank for Reconstruction and Development;

(d) their Government would seek to negotiate with Creditor Countries present but not participating at the present Conference and with other Creditors rearrangements no less favourable to Ghana in respect of payments due in the period from July 1970 to June 1972. . . .

6. Conclusion of Outstanding Bilateral Agreements

Where a bilateral agreement in accordance with the terms set out in the 1968 Agreed Minute had not at the date of the signing of this Agreed Minute been concluded, and where amounts were for this reason outstanding and payable on or before 30 June 1970, such amounts would become payable upon the conclusion of such an Agreement according to the terms of the 1968 Agreed Minute. Notwithstanding that such payments might then be made during the period of debt relief as defined in paragraph 4(2) they should not be subject to the terms of this Agreed Minute. . . .

10. Further Review

The conference concluded that a further meeting of the same nature should be convened before mid-1972 to review Ghana's debt situation in the longer term. On the basis of that review and in the light of prevailing conditions and of forecasts of likely trends the Creditor Countries would consider what additional debt relief measures might be required. The Ghanaian Representative urged that that Conference should seek a long-term solution to Ghana's debt problem. The Creditor Countries' representatives took note of this statement. In the interim, the periodic IMF consultations under Article XIV and IBRD reviews as well as the meetings of the IBRD Consultative Group for Ghana and bilateral consultations would provide all countries concerned with current information on Ghana's economic progress. The Conference proposed that their Governments should invite the IBRD in consultation with the IMF to assist those participating in the proposed further conference to prepare the documentation for it. . . .

Document 60: Finance Minister's Report on Ghana Debt Conference

J. H. Mensah, 'Report of the Ghana Delegation to the Ghana Debt Conference, London 7-11 July 1970' (n.d.).

[This report, submitted by J. H. Mensah, Minister of Finance and Economic Planning and leader of the Ghana delegation to the Prime Minister, Dr Busia, reviews the debt conference and assesses Ghana's gains. The report also contains an account of Ghana's relations with each of the Western creditors and the diplomacy that preceded the debt renegotiations. This account confirms the extent to which Ghana had fallen under the influence of the United States, and, to a lesser extent of West Germany. Unfortunately this part of the report (the first 12 pages) was not intact and cannot be reproduced in its entirety. Only a few excerpts can be quoted here. These reveal that intelligence information gathered by the Ministry of External Affairs before the conference indicated that Ghana was unlikely to obtain any further debt concessions at the conference, leading to suggestions by advisers of the Busia Government that Ghana should turn the meeting into a political exercise to 'attain objectives other than those of financial relief'. These objectives, and the possible obstacles, are discussed by Mensah in a revealing passage:

> The political evolution in Ghana is obviously worth something to the West. Precisely how much in terms both of actual sums of money offered and of major principles conceded is the question that has to be probed. Apart from the congressional squeeze on aid funds, we are operating against a general background of isolationism in the United States engendered by the Vietnam war. Some voices in the American Administration are asking [sic] that Ghana should not be allowed to move from her previous position of extreme involvement with the East to one of extreme involvement with the West. This is not because a pro-West Ghana is undesirable, but because a close involvement of America with another poor country to whom the Eastern bloc is potentially hostile creates another point of ideological rivalry when the whole tendency is towards de-escalating the cold war. On the other hand, in the final analysis America must take steps to help a democratic and pro-West Ghana to survive. The problem is to estimate the price tag on this American interest. (pp. 2-3)

Mensah goes on to explain why the Western creditors were unwilling to grant the concessions sought by Ghana in London:

> It became clear in the course of the negotiations that the creditor countries were haunted by the fear of being cajoled into yet another Indonesian-type debt settlement involving a long moratorium and long amortization period and relatively low interest rates. Our demand for an immediate long-term settlement with provision for periodic review was stiffly resisted on the unconvincing ground that

no reliable forecasts could be made now in respect of our country's economic fortunes beyond the next two years! Nor would they be moved by the logic of the fact that most of the Creditor countries had subscribed to a long-term settlement for Indonesia, which as a primary producing country, was subject to the same economic vicissitudes as Ghana from the point of view of balance-of-payments projections.

According to Mensah the reason for this reluctance was that an 'Indonesian' settlement for Ghana would thereby 'increase the probability of across-the-board settlements of this nature with other developing countries' (p. 8). Mensah notes the vicious circle entailed in Ghana's relationship with the creditor/donor countries; 'substantially more than half' of all aid given since 1966 was offset by foreign exchange transfers for medium-debt repayment. The problem boiled down to the relationship between Ghana and the Europeans on the one hand and the Americans on the other: 'broadly, the Americans are putting money into Ghana while the Europeans are taking money out'. (p. 11)]

Now read on:

III(c) The nature and extent of the proposals and 'concessionary terms' offered by the Creditor Countries

39. It has been mentioned above that the Creditor Countries initially offered to extend relief of *twenty-five per cent* of the amounts falling due between 1 July 1970 and 30 June 1972 in respect of principal and interest on medium-term debts as defined in the Agreed Minutes of 1966 and 1968. This would have implied the foregoing by them of N₵5.25 million during the 1970/71 financial year and an equivalent amount the following financial year. Considering the size of our resource gap, we pressed for a review of the amount of proposed relief. After some hard bargaining, including the detailed joint evaluation of our balance of payments estimates previously referred to, the Creditor Countries agreed to vary the relief offer from *twenty-five per cent* to *thirty-three and one-third* per cent.

40. In the final stages they offered relief of *fifty per cent* if we would agree to the package *including the preservation of moratorium interest charges from the previous settlements.* This implies that for the next two financial years, a total amount of *N₵21 million* has been released by the Western creditor countries from debt servicing obligations and can be used for economic development. If our Government is able to negotiate with other Creditors not represented at the Conference rearrangements no less favourable to Ghana in respect of payments due in the period from July 1970 to June 1972, our total debt relief for the two-year period would amount to *N₵26 million.* . . .

III(d) The Question of Moratorium Interest as considered for postponement of repayment obligations

46. Our delegation launched a violent onslaught against the practice of levying moratorium interest in consideration of postponement of repayment obligations. We made it quite clear that the new Government of Ghana did not find it possible to live with a system which 'piles charge upon charge and debt upon debt' under a moratorium arrangement. Such an arrangement might perhaps be necessary in normal commercial transactions but in dealings between Governments the idea was out of step with advanced international thinking. We accordingly requested that a formula be found to exclude moratorium interest in the settlement proposed by the Creditor Countries, in other words that the moratorium interest falling due within the next two years on the basis of the 1966/68 settlements should be waived altogether.

47. When the Creditor Countries proved adamant, we made the radical proposal that the operation of the 1966/68 Agreements should be suspended in so far as payment of moratorium interest was concerned, pending a thorough re-examination of the whole question of moratorium interest at the next Conference!

48. The result of our efforts in the matter of moratorium interest is summed up in the following passage from the draft Agreed Minute:

> In consideration of the amount and nature of the relief to be provided they (i.e. the Creditor Countries) took note of the importance attached by the Ghana Government to the question of moratorium interest. . . . The Creditor Countries wanted to state that the effect of this relief (i.e. the relief of 50% of amounts due in the next two years) was on average broadly equivalent overall to relief of approximately two-thirds of the moratorium interest and approximately one-quarter of the principal payable. (Paragraph 3 (3) of draft Agreed Minute, attached as Appendix III).

49. For the creditor countries it was important that the moratorium interest charges arising out of the 1966 and 1968 settlements should be counted in, without any *qualifications*, together with the original contractual principal and interest obligations as at the time of the *coup* in determining the total liability of which a proportion would be deferred. The above formulation, in which they themselves made a distinction between the relief that was being offered on the original liabilities and the relief that was being offered on the moratorium interest charges, therefore represented a major change in their position.

50. In response to further pressure they proposed an alternative formulation in these words:

> The creditor countries wanted to state that the effect of this relief regardless of the combination of relief measures used under

paragraph 4(2) was on average, because of the similar 61% grant element, broadly equivalent overall to the *reduction of moratorium interest costs* by more than a half.

Technically, this represented a further advance in the sense that it referred to a 'reduction' in the moratorium charges. However, the language is more obscure, and representatives of creditor countries would not accept the principle of a 'waiver' of moratorium interest charges. I therefore stuck with the original formula. But in any future negotiation we can start from the position that a distinction between the two sorts of liabilities has already been conceded.

51. The economic effects of the above concession as against an outright waiver of moratorium interest are, of course, not the same. Yet the concession is significant in that it represents an explicit deference to our Government's concern over the levying of moratorium interest charges. It is my impression that if this matter is vigorously pursued at the next Conference it should be possible to secure a complete waiver of the accumulated load of moratorium interest in any settlement that might be reached at that Conference.

52. In the meantime it should be noted that this objectionable feature has been omitted from the present 1970 settlement. That already means a great deal in cash terms. But it means even more in principle: no future debt rearrangement for Ghana will involve the levying of moratorium interest charges. I chose this as the sticking point on which one could, if necessary have broken off negotiations. Our moral position would have been very strong in the event of a collapse over this issue. But the gains recorded as indicated above made it inadvisable to go over the brink with it.

53. The formula which I chose was to gain acceptance for the position that since this was a matter of such importance to our Government I could not reach a final settlement without further discussions in Accra. This gives us an opportunity to keep open the question of moratorium interest charges when conveying the Government of Ghana's reaction to the offer of the creditor countries.

III(e) Conclusion of Outstanding Bilateral Agreements

54. The relief offer made by the Creditor Countries was predicated on the condition that our Government would 'promptly conclude bilateral agreements under the 1966 and 1968 Agreed Minutes with those countries with whom such agreements had not yet been concluded'.

55. In our opening statement to the Conference we had explained that the delay in concluding these arrangements was due partly to the 'logical contradiction between continuing a series of negotiations which were supposed to enshrine (the terms of the 1968 Agreed Minutes) in solemn contracts on the one hand and our knowledge and expectations regarding

the economy on the other hand...' and partly to the matter of the interest rate to be paid for the facility of debt service deferment. We had confirmed that, nevertheless, the Government of Ghana recognized the principle, which had been embodied in previous debt settlements, that all Creditor Countries should be treated alike. Accordingly, we had proposed that the sums outstanding under the unsigned agreements should, on the conclusion of the Agreements, be offset against balance of payments transfers which the Conference foresaw to be paid by Ghana at the time that repayments of debt service charges would*... we had made it clear that our Government was unable to accept the rates of interest concluded so far.

56. The reaction of the Creditor Countries was that the amounts outstanding under the unsigned agreements, totalling about N₵2 million, would become **immediately** payable upon the conclusion of such agreement according to the terms of the 1968 Agreed Minute. Regarding the rate of interest, they reacted that while it was not for the Conference to lay down rates of interest, it was not to be supposed that the countries concerned would be prepared to reach agreements 'not generally in line with bilateral agreements already concluded'.

57. Of course the demand for **immediate** payment of the amounts due, on the conclusion of the agreements concerned, was unacceptable to us. We pressed for a recognition of our Government's right to negotiate terms superior to those already negotiated. This recognition was reflected in the final formula adopted which omitted any obligation on Ghana to make 'immediate' payment of these arrears.

58. The position with regard to the unconcluded agreements under the 1968 settlement is therefore, as follows: Our Government is obliged, as part of the 'package deal' formulated at the Conference, to conclude the outstanding bilateral agreements. The rate of moratorium interest and the mode of payment of the outstanding sums are, however, still subject to bilateral negotiation.

59. It is accordingly recommended that the Government takes prompt measures to resume negotiations leading to the conclusion of the outstanding bilateral agreements. It is further recommended that in the negotiations our Government's position on the whole principle of moratorium interest should be forcefully restated and that notwithstanding the Creditor Countries' statement that the Creditor Countries concerned would expect substantially the same treatment as that given to others with whom bilateral agreements have already been concluded, our Government should bargain for the lowest possible interest rates and the best possible arrangement for repayment of the arrears...

---

*Original document indecipherable at this point—*Editor.*

IV. Other Undertakings by Ghana

64. Apart from the undertaking to conclude promptly bilateral agreements under the 1966 and 1968 Agreed Minutes with those countries with whom such agreements had not yet been concluded, our Delegation stated, as part of the 'package deal'

   (a) that the policies of our Government would embrace restraint on Government current expenditure; the improvement of agricultural production; the promotion of exports; the improvement of tax policies as well as review of the tax structure.
   (b) that our Government would continue to review periodically its policies in the economic, financial, trade and payments fields with the IMF and IBRD;
   (c) that our Government would seek to negotiate with Creditor Countries not represented at the Conference, (that is to say our Eastern European creditors and Yugoslavia and UAR) re-arrangements no less favourable to Ghana in respect of payments due in the period from July 1970 to June 1972;
   (d) that our Government would apply in favour of the Creditor Countries the 'most favoured nation principle' in any future negotiations with others involving the provisions of the relief offer, and
   (e) that our Government would supply through the IMF or direct to Creditor Countries information on the terms which our Government accorded to other Creditors.

65. These 'undertakings' are, in comparison with the concessions made by the Creditor Countries, relatively light. In fact, they amount to no more than a restatement of our Government's own intentions and a recording of certain consultative procedure [*sic*] which are routinely in force. It has always been the intention of the Government to conclude the outstanding bilateral agreements. What has stood in the way of progress is the issue of moratorium interest. The Government is still free to negotiate the best possible interest rates and the best possible repayment terms.

66. As regards the policy measures to be pursued by our Government, they are no more than what were defined in our Debt Document.* Periodic review of policies with IMF and IBRD has already become a regular feature in our dealings with these international bodies and has been of great assistance to us in policy execution. Regarding the negotiation of rearrangements with other Creditor Countries not represented at the Conference it is in our Government's interest to seek similar relief from these Creditors. Moreover, since it is our Government's intention to seek even better terms from these other Creditors, the undertaking to observe

---

*Ghana's External Debt: Its Nature and Solution.—Editor.

the 'most favoured nation principle' in relation to the Creditor Countries represented at the Conference is of no practical consequence to our Government.

67. In sum, the 'undertakings' given by us in the draft Agreed Minute are such as our Government can readily and conveniently honour. It is accordingly, recommended that our Government endorses them . . .

Informal Contracts

73. Apart from the formal negotiations, our Delegation made several informal contacts, both before and during the Conference, with a number of the delegations of the Creditor Countries, particularly the United States and the German representatives. The confidential information gained from these informal contacts proved very useful in the formulation of our strategy during the formal negotiations. We were thus enabled to extract to the limit of their capacity all the concessions which the Creditor Countries were prepared to give in the circumstances. The French representative also conveyed to us in confidence some of her Government's instructions regarding the position to be taken by her in the Creditor's caucus.

74. These confidences are naturally to be taken with a pinch of salt. But it is a measure of the very friendly relations exisiting between Ghana on the one hand and Germany, USA and France on the other, that our Delegation got so much cooperation from the representatives of these countries . . .

VII. Memorandum to the Draft Agreed Minute

75. These are the pointers to the political and diplomatic campaign which we must carry out if Ghana is to obtain a final settlement next year . . .

VIII. Delegation's Conclusions and Recommendations

77. Considering the initial difficulties which our Government encountered in its endeavour to gain acceptance of our request for a meeting to rearrange our medium-term debts, and having regard to the general pessimism with which the world in general viewed the outcome of the Conference, it is the view of our Delegation that the results of the Conference are quite favourable to Ghana. Ghana has achieved an immediate relief of fifty per cent of the amounts due in the next two years, which means the release of a total sum of N₵21 million to be channelled into economic development. In addition a further sum of N₵5 million would be released if similar rearrangements are concluded with other Creditor Countries.

78. This interim relief is itself a recognition of the fact that the 1966 and 1968 Agreements were inadequate; it indeed undermines the very

foundations of those agreements.

79. Although the Conference was unable to formulate a long-term settlement, yet the agreement to convene a further meeting in eighteen months' time to consider what further measures might be taken underscores the temporary nature of the present arrangement and leaves the door open for a settlement based on long-term considerations.

80. In the light of the foregoing considerations our Delegation submits the following recommendations:

(i) that the Government should accept the draft Agreed Minute as an Agreed Minute and authorize me to inform the Chairman of the Conference accordingly;

(ii) that political and diplomatic activities be initiated both in Accra and in the capitals of the Creditor Countries between now and the next Conference, with a view to securing a commitment of the Creditor Countries to a long-term settlement on the liberal terms and conditions proposed by us at the next Conference;

(iii) that our Government, in concert with the Governments of the Creditor Countries who participated in the Conference, should invite the IBRD in consultation with the IMF to assist in the preparation of documentation for the next Conference;

(iv) that prompt measures be taken to conclude bilateral agreements under the 1966 and 1968 Agreed Minutes with those countries with whom such agreements have not yet been concluded, bearing in mind the general desire of the Government to obtain the lowest possible rate of moratorium interest and the best possible repayment terms;

(v) that necessary steps be taken to negotiate with the other Creditor Countries not represented at the Conference (i.e. our Eastern European Creditor Countries and Yugoslavia and the UAR) rearrangements no less favourable to Ghana in respect of payments due in the period from July 1970 to June 1972;

(vi) that the Government should promptly enter into bilateral negotiations on the basis of the draft Agreed Minute with the Governments of the Creditor Countries or the competent institutions or agencies with a view to reaching formal agreements as soon as possible for the implementation of the present offer of relief by the Creditor Countries.

Document 61: Lt. Col. Acheampong's Statement on Ghana's External Debts
5 February, 1972.

Fellow Citizens,

When we took over power on 13 January 1972 we informed the nation that one of our major objectives was to bring to an end the economic mismanagement of our country by the Busia Government. In furtherance of this objective, we have undertaken several measures to reintroduce sanity into our economic management. With the cooperation of everyone of you, we are resolved to sustain these efforts . . .

Let me now turn to the external debt problem. On assuming responsibility for the administration of this country, the National Redemption Council intimated that a statement would be made on Ghana's external debt problem as soon as the Council had reviewed the entire external debt situation of the country. Within the past few weeks, this review has engaged the urgent attention of the Council, and we are now in a position to announce the Government's policy on this matter in the following terms.

As of 12 January 1972, the total principal amount of external debts arising out of medium-term suppliers' credits was $294 million. The interest that would accrue on these debts as they have been re-scheduled at present amounts to another $72 million. The long-term debts also totalled $231 million. In addition to these, there is a short-term debt totalling some US$286.26 million made up of arrears on import payments of US$66.96 million, 180-day credits of US$138.82 million and arrears on service payments of US$80.48 million.

The total public external debt of Ghana may be classified into three main categories, namely, long-term debt arising from long-term loans other than suppliers' credits, debt arising from suppliers' credits and short-term debt as I have just defined.

It will be readily appreciated from the foregoing that the external debt problem of Ghana has assumed major dimensions, and that the difficulties it poses for the well-being of our economy are, indeed, formidable.

It is well known that the medium-term debts arising from suppliers' credits concluded before 24 February 1966, have been the subject of various debt settlement conferences between previous governments of Ghana and Governments of creditor countries. What needs to be emphasized at this stage is that a substantial number of these contracts were clearly inimical to the interests of Ghana. The reports of several commissions of enquiry and other investigations clearly establish that some of these contracts are tainted and vitiated by corruption and other forms of illegality. In some cases, there has been a fundamental breach of contract on the part of the contractors. A substantial number of the projects financed by the suppliers' credits were not preceded by any feasibility studies establishing their viability. The prices quoted in respect of these projects were inflated, and the repayment terms did not admit of the projects generating sufficient resources to amortize the debts. It is not surprising, then, that most of these projects have proved hopelessly unproductive. Only 8.6 per cent of the projects, in value terms, could have paid for themselves in the repayment periods granted under these credits. These conclusions are sustained by the findings of impartial international institutions such as the World Bank. While the Nkrumah regime cannot escape responsibility for entering into these dubious transactions, a substantial part of the blame equally attaches to the governments of creditor countries, as well as the contractors, for promoting and guaranteeing these contracts.

Although the two previous Governments persistently reserved their right to examine these contracts, they proceeded to negotiate with creditor countries for debt relief on the basis that all the debt obligations were valid. It is a notorious fact that all efforts on the part of previous Governments to obtain long-term debt relief from creditor countries in 1966, 1968 and 1970 ended in abject failure. The creditor countries have insisted on their 'pound of flesh'. They have persistently refused to view the solution of our debt problem in terms of a developmental perspective. The short-term relief resulting from the several debt conferences was conceded at the cost of a staggering moratorium interest of approximately $62.0 million which has further complicated the debt problem. The National Redemption Council has no reason to believe that the resumption of negotiations on previous patterns would prove fruitful this time.

In the light of this record of insensitivity on the part of creditors to Ghana's long-term requirements, what alternatives are open to us? The two previous Governments forcefully pointed out to the Governments of the creditor countries what must be obvious to any impartial observer of our economic situation, namely, that our foreign exchange resources simply could not at once sustain the debt service obligations and meet our minimal development targets. Ghana has been classified by the World Bank as not fit for conventional loans and our capacity to service these debt obligations is conspicuously limited. Nonetheless the creditor countries which participated in the various debt conferences have proved singularly unsympathetic and unresponsive to our well-documented case.

After carefully examining the balance-of-payments prospects for the foreseeable future, the National Redemption Council is satisfied that the external debt obligation of Ghana that remains after the 1966, 1968 and 1970 debt settlements would drastically limit the ability of any government of Ghana to provide the basic necessities of life for the people or to carry out any modest programme of economic development and growth. The settlement required of Ghana is based upon the premise that Ghana would persist in a policy of harsh stabilization measures with attendant reduction in living standards and the retrenchment of human as well as material resources. There would be insurmountable difficulties for any government in generating surpluses on the budget. It would be impossible for the economy to generate the real resources that could be transferred to Ghana's creditors. It would also be naïve to expect the external payments position to permit Ghana to find the required foreign exchange to make these transfers.

It is totally unacceptable to the National Redemption Council that the standard of living of the average Ghanaian now or in the foreseeable future should be substantially lower than it was ten years ago owing to the inability of the Government to generate economic growth, increase employment opportunities or to allow the importation of a sufficient volume of essential commodities.

The National Redemption Council cannot fail to take cognizance of the frustrations which have been unleashed by the dismal failure of the previous Governments to achieve a long-term solution to the external debt problem and the growing disenchantment of the public with conventional methods which have proved futile in the past.

In these circumstances, the National Redemption Council cannot accept any of the debt settlements concluded either multilaterally or bilaterally with creditor countries since 24 February 1966.

Furthermore, any policy to be adopted with respect to Ghana's external debt problem must have the following basic ingredients:

> First, the National Redemption Council will not proceed on the naïve assumption that the debt obligations which have been the subject of previous debt settlements are valid and unimpeachable. Those who maintain that the Government of the National Redemption Council is under any obligation to make any payments to them in settlement of any debt obligations must establish to the National Redemption Council the validity of the contracts under which these debts obligations were incurred, and the viability of the projects in respect of which these contracts were entered into.
>
> Second, the National Redemption Council will neither tolerate nor condone any departure from the high standards of public integrity and probity with respect to the conclusion of any transactions involving previous Governments of Ghana.
>
> Third, the National Redemption Council will not accept any arrangements for the servicing of debt obligations which must necessarily result in economic suicide for this country; we shall not preside over the economic disintegration of Ghana.
>
> Fourth, we do not propose to engage in any sterile multilateral negotiations.

More specifically, the National Redemption Council has taken the following position with regard to the various categories of our external debts. Let me first address myself to the suppliers' credits contracted during the Nkrumah regime. In accordance with well-settled principles of the laws governing suppliers' credit contracts, and in consonance with our declared policy of eradicating all forms of improper conduct or moral turpitude from public life, the National Redemption Council unequivocally repudiates all contracts which are vitiated by corruption, fraud or other illegality. All debts and other obligations arising under such contracts are cancelled with effect from today. The National Redemption Council also owes a duty to the people of Ghana to repudiate all debts and other obligations arising from contracts where there has been a fundamental breach of such contracts on the part of contractors. These grounds were relied upon by the previous Government in cancelling the Drèvici contracts in January 1970. The National Redemption Council is satisfied that on the same grounds the available evidence is sufficient to sustain the cancellation of contracts of the total value of $94.4 million entered into with the following companies – Parkinson Howard Group of Companies, Seawork Limited, Newport Shipbuilding and Engineering Company, and Swan Hunter and Richardson. All indebtedness arising under these contracts is accordingly cancelled with immediate effect. I should stress that this action is only a first step.

The Government of Ghana will repudiate all other contracts on such grounds if appropriate evidence becomes available at a later stage. In this regard the National Redemption Council wishes to make it clear that all suppliers' credits entered into before 24 February 1966 will be subjected to a thorough and rigorous review.

The National Redemption Council considers that the repudiation or cancellation of contracts and debt obligations on the foregoing grounds is perfectly legitimate under any civilized legal system. The Government of Ghana would be prepared to go to arbitration in respect of all disputes arising from our action, and for this purpose we would be willing to submit to the jurisdiction of the International Centre for the Settlement of Investment Disputes, Washington DC, USA.

With regard to other debts arising from suppliers' credits, the National Redemption Council does not propose to adhere to the policy of accepting them unconditionally as valid without any review. Such debts would only be accepted as valid and binding on the National Redemption Council Government if the following preconditions are complied with:

> First, the contractors concerned must establish to the National Redemption Council that such debts arose out of valid contracts;
>
> Second, it must be further established that the contracts are not otherwise vitiated by fraud, corruption or other illegality; and
>
> Third, the National Redemption Council must be satisfied that the said contracts were in respect of technically and economically viable, as well as productive projects.

The National Redemption Council Government would in principle be prepared to accept and pay all debts arising from suppliers' credits which are duly established as valid and binding in accordance with the criteria which we have just stipulated. However, having regard to our critical economic condition and balance-of-payments position, the National

Redemption Council wishes to declare in emphatic terms that the Government of Ghana cannot honour such debt obligations on any terms other than those currently applicable to credits granted by the International Development Association. In effect such debts would be paid over a 50-year period, including 10 years of grace. Ten per cent of the debts would be settled during the second 10 years, and the remaining 90 per cent over the following 30 years. Since we have rejected the debt settlements entered into by previous Governments, the capital amounts to be considered under this formula would be exclusive of all accumulated moratorium interest.

With respect to debts arising from suppliers' credits contracted after 24 February 1966, the National Redemption Council Government will accept them as valid and binding without further examination. However, on economic and balance-of-payments grounds, the Government has no alternative but to pay such debts on the terms applicable to credits granted by the International Development Association.

The National Redemption Council wishes to make it clear that the cumulative effect of these policy announcements on our indebtedness arising from the suppliers' credits contracted during the Nkrumah regime is as follows:

> First, one-third of the principal amount of the debt arising from these suppliers' credits is repudiated outright.
>
> Second, the accrued moratorium interest of US$72 million on this principal amount is emphatically rejected.
>
> Third, no debt obligations arising from the remaining contracts will be accepted by the National Redemption Council Government unless the contractors concerned have satisfied the conditions we have laid down, and
>
> Fourth, there will be no payment of any debt arising from any suppliers' credit for the next 10 years.

In the case of short-term debts, defined as the total of arrears on import credits, 180-day credits and liabilities of service payments, the National Redemption Council will, in principle, accept liability to pay these debts. These obligations arise in respect of goods which have in fact been consumed in Ghana and there would be no basis for denying liability. Nevertheless our economic situation makes it impossible to settle these debts on the original terms. In the circumstances, the National Redemption Council has instructed the Bank of Ghana to make a steady, if even small, reduction in our short-term indebtedness as the nation's resources will permit.

As to long-term debts which arise principally out of long-term loans and credits granted by the World Bank, International Development Association, the Government of the United States of America and the Governments of other donor countries, the National Redemption Council considers that the relevant loan and credit agreements are not open to the objections raised to suppliers' credits, and it is accordingly the intention of the National Redemption Council to honour them in accordance with the terms already agreed....

30. Fellow Ghanaians, I speak to you this evening in a sombre mood. It is a mood generated by the challenge of the times. The measures which I have announced this evening throw a challenge to all of us. We are indeed in a critical situation. We cannot expect to be bailed out by some miraculous intervention or the generosity of other countries. What we are declaring to the whole world now is that we have the will-power and the human and material resources to be self-reliant. With determination and hard work, we will demonstrate to our satisfaction and prove to the world that a small and harassed country can stand up to the formidable array of forces which has always sapped our national confidence, inhibited our independence and undermined our self-sufficiency. We cannot as a nation continue to be buffeted by forces which we are powerless to control. We cannot continue to live a life of illusion and self-deception. Once we have fully grasped the implications of the stark realities facing us, we will have to embark on a vigorous programme of increased productivity in all sectors of the economy. We will have to distinguish essentials from non-essentials. We will have to rearrange our order of priorities. Above all we will have to adopt a revolutionary attitude to our whole manner of living. In short, we will have to prove that we are truly independent and self-reliant in all respects. I trust that you will not let Ghana down, and that together, we can wage a successful economic war on poverty, economic mis-management and other evils which have hitherto beset our development.

Thank you and God bless you.

Document 62: Repayment of Ghana's Medium-term Debt: Agreed Minute 1974

Agreed Minute on the Repayment of the Medium-term Debt of the Government of Ghana and Others Resident in Ghana, Rome, March 1974.

Preamble

(i) Representatives of the Governments of Belgium, France, the Federal Republic of Germany, Italy, Japan, The Netherlands, Norway, the United Kingdom and the USA ('the creditor countries') met representatives of the Government of Ghana in Accra from 11 to 18 December 1973 and in Rome from 11 to 13 March 1974 to seek a solution to Ghana's external debt problems.

Representatives of the Governments of Denmark and Switzerland attended as observers. Representatives of the IBRD and IMF were also present.

Section I—Debt to be Re-scheduled
The re-scheduling arrangements set out in Section II below shall apply to:
- (a) all principal and contractual interest payments due after 31 January 1972 in accordance with the Agreed Minutes of the 1966, 1968 and 1970 Debt Conferences and originating from medium-term contracts to which those Agreed Minutes relate; and
- (b) all principal and contractual interest payments due after 30 June 1972 under medium-term contracts to which those Agreed Minutes relate which fell due under those contracts after 30 June 1972 and which have not been previously re-scheduled; and
- (c) interest at the rate of $2\frac{1}{2}\%$ per annum on all the payments referred to under head (a) above in respect of the period beginning on 1 February 1972 and ending on 30 June 1972.

(ii) The payments referred to under heads (a) and (b) of paragraph (i) of this Section are in respect of credits and loans to the Government of Ghana or to persons or corporations resident or carrying on business in Ghana
- (a) arising under or relating to contracts concluded before 24 February 1966 for the supply of goods or services, or both, from outside Ghana; and
- (b) provided or insured by the Governments or competent institutions of the creditor countries; and
- (c) with an original maturity exceeding one year but not exceeding 12 years.

(iii) Where, however, the total of the payments referred to in paragraph (i) due to the Government of, and persons or corporations resident in, or carrying on business in, any one creditor country amounts to less than US$1.5 million such payments will for administrative and technical reasons be excepted from the provisions in Section II. Such payments will be transferred forthwith unless otherwise agreed between the Governments of Ghana and the creditor country concerned.

(iv) Moratorium interest accruing in accordance with the Agreed Minutes of the 1966, 1968 and 1970 Debt Conferences will cease to be payable after 31 January 1972, except as may be agreed in cases to which paragraph (iii) of this Section applies.

Section II—Re-scheduling Arrangements
(i) The representatives of the Government of Ghana stated that their Government would, except as provided in Section I (iii), transfer to the creditor country concerned the amounts of the payments and interest referred to in Section I (i) in 36 equal and consecutive half yearly instalments commencing on 1 January 1983.

(ii) The representatives of the Government of Ghana further stated that their Government would transfer to the creditor country concerned interest at the rate of $2\frac{1}{2}\%$ per annum from 1 July 1972 on the amounts referred to in paragraph (i) of this Section, to the extent that they have not been transferred to the creditor country concerned, as follows:

(a) the interest accruing between 1 July 1972 and 30 June 1974, both dates inclusive, would be transferred in 5 equal and consecutive half-yearly instalments commencing on 31 December 1974;

(b) the interest accruing after 30 June 1974 would be transferred in consecutive half-yearly instalments commencing on 31 December 1974 . . .

Section V—Miscellaneous Provisions

(i) The representatives of the Government of Ghana stated that their Government would transfer forthwith all payments due up to and including 31 January 1972 and all moratorium interest accruing up to that date in accordance with the Agreed Minutes of the 1966, 1968 and 1970 Debt Conferences and originating from medium-term contracts to which those Agreed Minutes relate, whether or not a bilateral agreement had been concluded.

(ii) The representatives of the creditor countries stated that they would make available to the Government of Ghana by 31 March 1974 lists of the medium-term contracts made before 24 February 1966 to which this Agreed Minute relates and as soon as possible, to the extent that they are able to do so, documentary evidence of those contracts or of any negotiable instruments given in connection with those contracts.

Section VI—Implementation

(i) The representatives of the Government of Ghana stated that they would recommend to their Government that it should take all necessary action to give effect to this Agreed Minute, in particular they were willing to recommend to their Government that it should enter into bilateral negotiations with the Governments of the creditor countries, or the competent institutions or agencies, with a view to implementing this Agreed Minute by means of formal agreements or, at the option of the creditor country concerned, by means of other arrangements. Such agreements or arrangements would include all necessary consequential provisions, including provisions for their technical application.

(ii) The representatives of the creditor countries stated that they too would recommend to their Governments that they should enter into bilateral negotiations with the Government of Ghana on the basis of this Agreed Minute.

(iii) These negotiations would begin as soon as possible after 31 August 1974 provided:

(a) that by 30 June 1974 the Government of Ghana has indicated which of the contracts made before 24 February 1966 and the negotiable instruments given in connection therewith they do not accept as valid it being understood that the Government of Ghana will be deemed to have accepted the validity of all contracts and of all negotiable instruments given in connection therewith which have not been challenged by 30 June 1974 provided that such acceptance of validity will not preclude the Government of Ghana from questioning the performance of such contracts and the amount of any claims relating thereto; and

(b) that by 31 August 1974 the creditor countries have not notified the Government of Ghana that the total of the debt outstanding on the contracts challenged by the Government of Ghana is such as to call in question the re-scheduling arrangements specified in Section II of this Agreed Minute.

Section VII—Disputes

The representatives of the creditor countries and the representatives of the Government of Ghana stated that:

(i) Any dispute as to the validity of any contract to which this Agreed Minute, relates (including any contract already challenged or arising out of or in relation to any such contract (including the performance thereof), or in relation to any negotiable instrument given in connection with any such contract, will be resolved:

  (a) by any appropriate procedures laid down in that contract for the resolution of such disputes: or
  (b) by such other means as the parties to the dispute may agree.

  Provided that, if the dispute is not resolved in accordance with the foregoing provisions of this paragraph, nothing shall preclude the parties to such a dispute from seeking such remedies as are available to them in any competent court of law.

(ii) Any sums determined, as a result of the resolution of a dispute in accordance with paragraph (i) of this section, to be due to any of the creditor countries, or to any persons or corporation resident in or carrying on business in any of the creditor countries, will be paid to them after the dispute has been so resolved and on terms no less favourable than those specified in Section II.

Section VIII

The representatives of the Government of Ghana and of the creditor countries hereby agree that the foregoing is a correct record.

Notes

Notes to Introduction

1. Roger Genoud was one of the few to see this clearly. See his *Nationalism and Economic Development in Ghana*, New York: Praeger 1970. This introduction is not a comprehensive analysis of the Nkrumah and military regimes. For fuller treatment of some of the themes discussed here, see my forthcoming manuscript, *Ghana: Development, Class, Underdevelopment*, esp. ch. 2, 'Planning for Underdevelopment: "Socialism"'.

2. E.G., joint ventures with the state and state interventionism. For a defence of state interventionism, cf. OECD, *Development Assistance, 1970 Review*, Paris 1970, p.20, where it is argued that 'if development [in Third World countries] is to proceed successfully and economic inputs are to be used efficiently, a central role must be well played by political leaders and government bureaucracies in each of these sectors and in guiding research of their problems. The relative absence of other centres of leadership and innovation in most developing countries puts inevitably in the hands of government a much larger share of policy-making and implementation than we in the more industrialized countries are currently accustomed to'. Regret is expressed that 'full acceptance of the dependence of successful development on political performance has been slow in making its way among the experts'. This reasoning may be compared with some of the positions presented in the following documents.

3. Ghana, *Seven-year Development Plan for National Reconstruction and Development 1963/64 to 1969/70*. For more extended analysis of this pattern of industrialization, see my forthcoming manuscript.

4. Compare the main text of the *Seven-year Development Plan* and the CPP *Programme for Work and Happiness*.

5. B. D. C. Folson, 'The Marxist Period in the Development of Socialist Ideology in Ghana, 1962–66', *Universitas*, Vol. 6, No. 1, May 1977.

6. Marvin P. Miracle and Ann Seidman, *State Farms in Ghana*, Madison: University of Wisconsin, Land Tenure Centre, March 1968; J. Gordon, 'State Farms in Ghana', in A. H. Bunting (ed), *International Seminar on Agriculture*, New York: Praeger 1970.

7. This was one of the issues of contention between the Nkrumah government and the bureaucracy.

8. 'Structural Crisis, Class Formation and the State in Ghana', unpublished

paper prepared for conference on Challenges of the Social Sciences in the Eighties, CEESTEM, Mexico City, October 1981.

9. Without devaluation, the burden of stabilization would fall primarily on agricultural exporters (cocoa), while with devaluation the urban working classes would be expected to shoulder the main burden. This explains the difference between the Nkrumah stabilization of 1965 (see Document 1) and that of the NLC.

10. Closing address to the Bretton Woods Conference by Henry Morgenthau, US Secretary of the Treasury and President of the Conference. United States Treasury Department, *Articles of Agreement: The International Monetary Fund and the International Bank for Reconstruction and Development*. The United Nations Monetary and Financial Conference, Bretton Woods July 1–22, 1944, p. V.

11. 'The principal interest of the United States in the [International Monetary] Fund results from its interest in stable monetary conditions throughout the world without which neither international trade can prosper nor foreign investments be safe. As a large trading nation whose foreign trade is likely to grow in the years to come, and as the greatest creditor nation of the world, the United States requires a well-operating world economy . . . The United States is not likely to require assistance from the Fund; but it does require a stable world and thus has a great interest in all agencies and institutions which promote and maintain this stability.' Michael A. Heilperin, *International Monetary Reconstruction: The Bretton Woods Agreements*, New York: American Enterprise Associaton 1945, pp. 52–3.

12. 'The United States will, of course, play a leading role in the management of the [International Monetary] Fund. Not only will it hold 28 per cent of the total voting power in the Fund, it will also have in its territory the seat of the Fund's principal office and the right to designate the depository where *half* of the Fund's assets, including gold, will be held, at least initially. Thus in terms of both influence and safeguards, the United States will occupy a leading position, corresponding to its equally leading contribution to the Fund's resources.' Ibid., p. 53.

13. Secretary of the Treasury Morgenthau, op. cit., p. V.

14. M. Heilperin, op. cit., p. 86.

15. This may seem paradoxical in view of the origins of the IMF. But as Tew explains: 'The Fund's charter was drafted by experts who vividly remembered the competitive exchange rates of the 1930s and who saw in the Fund a bulwark against a recurrence thereof in the post-war world. But since competitive devaluation is a malady peculiar to times of widespread depression, there has in fact been little or no sign of it in the prosperous (and indeed inflationary) period since the Fund's commencement of business in March 1947. The Fund therefore has rarely, if ever, been called upon to restrain its members from unjustifiable devaluations. On the contrary, the need has rather been for a modicum of discreet prodding to help members overcome their reluctance to devalue in circumstances where their internal cost structure had become so out of line with international prices that realignment was clearly impracticable at the existing exchange rate . . . Not infrequently an appropriate degree of devaluation has been an ingredient in the stabilization schemes . . . in which the Fund has participated'. Brian Tew, *The International Monetary Fund: its Present Role and Future Prospects*, Princeton University: Essays in International Finance No. 36, March 1961, p. 13. For an excellent general introduction to the IMF and its mode of operation, cf. Cheryl Payer, *The Debt Trap: the IMF and the Third World*, Penguin 1974.

16. Osvaldo Sunkel, 'Inflation in Chile: An Unorthodox Approach', *International Economic Papers No. 10*. See also the papers by Dudley Seers and David Felix in notes 51 and 85.

17. Sector Distribution of World Bank Group Operations in Latin America and Caribbean Countries (1974) ($/million)

Agriculture	952.49
Education	168.05
Electricity	3071.16
Industry*†	1,144 64
Population	5.00
Telecommunication	190.60
Transport	1837.42
Urban Development	20.00
Water	294.80
Total	$7,684.16

*Includes Fisheries.

1.	Of which:	Brazil	431.16
1.	Of which:	Columbia	272.60
1.	Of which:	Mexico	190.08

Source: World Bank, *The World Bank Group in the Americas* (May 1974).

For Comparative purposes, see data for West Africa in World Bank, *Annual Report 1978*, p. 44.

18. International Finance Corporation, *IFC Annual Report* Introduction. In 1977 the 'mixed sector' was also made eligible for IFC investment.
19. William L. Bennett, 'Developing Private Enterprise Internationally: The story of IFC Operations in 30 countries', *Commerce* (Chicago Association of Commerce and Industry), Vol. 62, No. 2, March 1965.
20. For practical demonstration of the conditions attached to IFC financing of investment banks, see Document 39.
21. See for instance IBRD, *The World Bank Group in the Americas*, Washington: May 1974, p.5.
22. IBRD/IDA, *Annual Report* 1966–67, p. 6.
23. The US through holding by far the largest single subscription in the IMF quotas, controls the largest vote in both the IMF/IBRD (25.92%), with Britain, the next largest subscriber, controlling 10.73%. West Germany and India were the third and fourth largest shareholders. (Reference is to 1968 data.) Recently however the US has been worried at some loss of influence in the Bank owing to changes in quota holdings.
24. *Globe and Mail* (Toronto), 6 February 1980.
25. See IBRD, *The World Bank: Questions and Answers* (Washington: March 1976), pp. 6 and 7.
26. See Documents 1 and 2 in this volume.
27. See Document 15 (my emphasis).
28. Document 21.
29. Ghana, *Economic Survey 1965*, p. 51.

30. *Daily Graphic* (Accra), 3 March 1966.

31. For enunciation of the 'welfare state', see Nkrumah's speech on the tenth anniversary of the CPP in June 1959 and Folson, 'Marxist Period in the Development of Socialist Ideology in Ghana', op. cit. The basic assumptions (though not the terminology) are restated in the *main text* of the Seven Year Development Plan, which may be contrasted with Nkrumah's launching speech. These differences help to explain the defection of the 'right-wing' of the CPP to the side of the rebels in the 1966 coup.

32. But with its insistence on 'non-political' and 'free, democratic unionism', this 'bourgeois democracy' should be seen as a powerful instrument of labour control, as is only too clear in Document 46 and in the 'democratization' of the Ghana TUC by Busia in September 1971.

33. The fullest statement of these objectives is in Kwame Nkrumah, *Consciencism: Philosophy and Ideology of Decolonisation*, London: Heinemann 1967, which tries to reconcile the (contradictory) themes in Nkrumahist 'Socialism'. For a more extended exposition and critique, see my 'Planning for Underdevelopment: "Socialism"'

34. It is necessary to emphasize that the interests of imperialism in the 1966 coup were more complex than appears in this discussion or in these documents, which deal almost exclusively with economic (rather than 'political') issues. Clearly with the leading imperialist powers in the coup, the US and West Germany, political considerations outweighed the economic (the reverse was probably the case with Britain).

35. See Documents 35 and 36.

36. J. H. Mensah, United Nations Advisory Mission to Ghana, 'Report on the Cocoa Processing Industry in Ghana and Related Questions', October 1966, p. 23.

37. Ibid., p. 24.

38. Ghana, *Report by the Auditor-General on the Accounts of Ghana: Public Boards and Corporations 1967–68/1968–69*, Accra-Tema: Ghana Publishing Corporation 1971, p. 24.

39. R. M. Lawson and E. Kwei, *African Enterpreneurship and Economic Growth: The Case of the Fishing Industry in Ghana*, Accra: Ghana University Press 1974, pp. 232–3.

40. Ghana, *Report of the Commission of Enquiry into the State Fishing Corporation*, Accra-Tema: Ghana Publishing Corporation, (n.d.) p. 148. The astonishing saga of the Soviet vessels is recounted here (pp. 61–2) and also in Lawson and Kwei, op. cit. The report cited here is particularly critical of the Economic Committee of the National Liberation Council (the military government), which had been 'most negligent' in its handling of the boats issue.

41. IBRD, *Towards More Effective Self-Reliance: The Role of the Manufacturing Sector in Ghana*, Washington: 1974, p. 4.

42. See Document 45.

43. Ghana, *Report of the Commission on the Structure and Renumeration of the Public Services in Ghana*, Accra-Tema: GPC 1967, pp. 25–30.

44. Ghana, *Report of the Committee on Review of Salaries and Pensions in the Public Services of Ghana*, Accra-Tema: GPC, 1969.

45. This is no joke. See Document 48.

46. Literally, 'the rich get richer while the poor get poorer'. The quotation is from a letter from Bentum, Secretary-General of the TUC, to General Ankrah, Chairman of the NLC (Document 45).

47. J. M. Livingstone, *Britain and the World Economy*, Pelican 1971, p. 46.

48. Nassem Ahmad, 'From "Liberation" to "Redemption": Economic Policy Between the Coups', *Universitas*, Vol. 3, No. 1, October 1973.

49. As a percentage of total state revenues, cocoa receipts rose from 17% in the early 1960s and 7% in the mid-1960s to 30.4% in 1968, 37.4% in 1970, and 42.1% in 1971.

50. See Ahmad's study of the effects on the 1971 devaluation on manufacturing prices, 'From "Liberation" to "Redemption": Economic Policy Between the Coups', op. cit.

51. IBRD, *Economic Stabilization in Ghana*, Washington: 24 May 1968 (Report No. AF-75a), p. 14.

52. This is a standard problem with IMF stabilization. E.g. David Felix's critique of the programme in Chile, 'Structural Imbalances, Social Conflict, and Inflation: An appraisal of Chile's recent anti-inflationary effort', *Economic Development and Cultural Change*, Vol. VIII, No. 2. (Jan. 1960).

53. IBRD, *Economic Stabilization in Ghana*, op. cit., pp. 23-4.

54. Ghana, *The Budget 1965*, pp. 10-13.

55. Report of World Bank mission, November 1965.

56. 'Notes taken at meetings held between the World Bank Mission and the National Planning Commission and Ministers and Principal Secretaries/Secretaries on 22 September and 24 September 1965', Accra (n.d. - confidential), paragraph 31. Part of this document has been reproduced as Document 2.

57. See Document 29.

58. For the US and World Bank positions, see Documents 13 and 30. Also Ruth First, *Barrel of a Gun*, pp. 393-4. The Chamber of Commerce demands are recorded in *4th/5th Annual Report of the Ghana Chamber of Commerce, 1965/67*, pp. 10-15. For the foreign companies, e.g. John Holt to R. S. Amegashie, member of the National Economic Committee, 14 May 1966.

59. This was the case with American supplies under PL.480, proposed IFC loans to the National Investment Bank (Document 39), and less directly, West German KFW loans to the same bank in 1968 and 1970.

60. See Document 31 following.

61. Document 41.

62. Document 17. The unsourced quotations below are from this and the document referred to in note 60.

63. Study for the United Nations by Fernando Fajnzylber, quoted in Richard J. Barnet and Roland E. Muller, *Global Reach: The Power of the Multinational Corporations*, New York: Simon and Schuster, 1974, pp. 152-4.

64. A brief but revealing insight into the relationship between MNCs and banks in Ghana is offered in the *Report of the Committee of Enquiry into the Affairs of R. T. Briscoe (Ghana) Limited*, Accra-Tema: GPC, 1976, pp. 24-25. Briscoe, a subsidiary of the Danish multinational East Asiatic Company Limited, was able to obtain over ₵1 million from one local bank in unsecured overdrafts.

65. OECD, *Development Assistance 1970 Review*, p. 76.

66. Christopher Tugendhat, *The Multinationals*, Pelican 1971, p. 169.

67. For data on overpricing by MNCS see Ronald Muller, 'The Multinational Corporation and the Underdevelopment of the Third World', in Charles K. Wilber (ed), *The Political Economy of Development and Underdevelopment*, New York: Random House 1973. In his study of import overpricing in Colombia, Constantine Vaitsos found average overpricing of 155% in the pharmaceutical industry, 40% in the rubber industry, and 16.6% in electronics. The Colombia import price for two drugs, Valium and Librium, was respectively 82 and 65 times those ruling on the

international market. 'Interaffiliate Charges by Transnational Corporations and Intercountry Income Distribution', Ph.D. Dissertation, Harvard University, June 1972.

68. The African Manganese Company, a subsidiary of US Corporation Union Carbide, was found to have consistently underpriced raw manganese exports to the processing facilities of a sister subsidiary in Norway. In the early 1970s Union Carbide turned over its assets in AMC to the Ghana Government to avoid punitive action.

69. 'Foreign Trade Malpractices': Speech by Lt. Colonel Acheampong, chairman of the National Redemption Council, 22 May 1972.

70. Between 1970 and 1975 Briscoe had illegally 'transferred' some DM 25.3 million to EAC in Denmark, through the simple expedient of routing all its imports (of German cars and machinery) through the parent company, which padded invoices for Ghanaian customers and retained 'profits' thus earned in Denmark. *Report of the Committee of Enquiry into the Affairs of R. T. Briscoe . . .*, op. cit.

71. Ibid., p. 24.

72. R. Barnet and R. E. Muller, *Global Reach: The Power of the Multinational Corporations* op. cit., p. 263.

73. Ibid., p. 214.

74. The importance of control over accounting and auditing in corporate strategy was confirmed once again by the investigation into Briscoe, whose expatriate Financial Controller – 'a craftsman at juggling with figures', in the words of the investigating committee – had schemed with the expatriate auditors (Peat Marwick of Lonrho fame) to cover up the company accounts.

75. Akilakpa Sawyerr, 'Multinational Corporations and Manufacturing in Ghana: A Tale of Two Projects', University of Ghana: Faculty of Law (mimeo), 1979.

76. OECD, *Development Assistance 1970 Review* p. 86.

77. See Document 33.

78. Ministry of Finance and Economic Planning, *Budget Statement for 1970/71*, Accra, 1970, p. 50. In the topsy-turvy logic of the time, at the opening of the Takoradi factory in December 1968, Nana Anaisie, paramount chief of Sekondi and one of the Government appointees on the Board, 'on behalf of the Directors of the company . . . expressed the hope that the Ghana Cement Works will play a useful role in our bid to make Ghana economically independent' – *Ghana Cement* (house journal of GCW), Vol. 1, No. 1, 1969, pp. 16–17.

79. *Ghana Cement*, op. cit.

80. Evidence at hearings of inquiry into award of contract for importation of clinker by Ghana National Procurement Agency, Accra, August 1978.

81. Between 1970 and the end of 1978, the supply contract with Norcem was terminated or allowed to lapse three times and new contracts signed with four separate new suppliers. In each case the new contract was in turn terminated and re-awarded to Norcem.

82. Report by the Auditor-General on the Accounts of Ghana, op. cit., p. 30.

83. Compare the statement on this division in the report cited in note 81 above and the analysis on the same corporation in Document 39.

84. IBRD, *Towards More Effective Self-Reliance* op. cit. Annex I, p. 3.

85. P. Pinstrup-Anderson and Tweetin, 'The value, cost and efficiency of American food aid', *American Journal of Agricultural Economics*, No. 53.

86. This was consistent with the experience of most Latin American countries

that adopted stabilization policies in the 1950s and 1960s, with the possible exception of Brazil. Cf. Dudley Seers, 'A theory of Inflation and Growth in Underdeveloped Economies based on the Experience of Latin America', *Oxford Economic Papers*, June 1962. According to Seers, the 'sharp set-back in output [resulting from stabilization] was only recovered, in *per capita* terms, with difficulty and after some delay' in all the countries except possibly Peru, while unemployment and price inflation persisted.

87. See Document 15.

88. The World Bank reports on the Ghana economy from 1968 are sometimes noteworthy for their sense of defeat, particularly with regard to agricultural policy, the devaluation, and the upward growth in public spending. In addition to the reports noted in Notes 50 and 52, see IBRD/IDA, *The Current Economic Position and Prospects of Ghana Vol. IV: Public Finance*, Washington: October 1970.

Notes to Documents

Part I

1. The World Bank report goes on to comment on the foreign exchange situation, agriculture and industry. For the situation in agriculture see Document 20, and for industry, Document 29.

2. 24 August 1966. In this address President Nkrumah stated that the bilateral agreements would be maintained and extended to other African countries. In the same address he asserted, in apparent reference to the IMF and the Western countries, that 'under no circumstances will (Ghana) allow those who now control and manipulate the world price of cocoa to alter, hamper or curtail our programme of industrial and agricultural development, and the expansion of our educational and other social services'.

3. For Ghana's estimated debt service schedule as of December 1965, see Document 49.

4. Broadcast by Lt. General Ankrah, *Daily Graphic* (Accra), 3 March 1966. The highlights of this broadcast were: the introduction of a Welfare State; the private sector to be retained as the largest sector and the state sector to be restricted to 'key and basic projects'; no nationalization of private enterprises or forced state participation; urgent review and possible sale of state enterprises to the private sector; and introduction of 'controls of a general nature' to ensure that workers were not exploited.

5. See Document 49.

Part II

1. For the role of the DAS in the evolution of Ghanaian economic policy, see Ronald Libby, 'External Co-optation of a Less Developed Country's Policy-Making: The Case of Ghana 1966–72', *World Politics*, Vol. 29, No. 1.

2. This section is a summary of the recommendations made in the main Report. Page numbers at the end of the recommendations refer to the relevant pages in the main Report. 'Interim Report' refers to an earlier report submitted by the Committee in April 1966.

Part III

1. For a detailed analysis of the operation of these Agreements and the

justification for them, see Christopher Stevens, *The Soviet Union and Black Africa*, London: MacMillan 1976.

Part IV

1. Some explanation of the background to the two clinker grinding mills at Takoradi (built by the Polish Government) and at Tema is necessary.

The contract for the Polish project was signed in October 1964 between the Ministry of Industries and Cekop of Poland. It called for the construction of a cement plant with an annual capacity of 400,000 tons at a contract price of £1.3 million, financing to be provided through a Polish credit. It had originally been planned to establish an integrated cement industry at Nauli in the Western Region, utilizing deposits of local limestone in the area; however, owing to technical problems associated with the development of these deposits it was decided as an interim measure to construct a factory at Takoradi utilizing imported clinker. An agreement had also previously been signed with the British firm, Parkinson Howard, in December 1963 to build a plant with a capacity of 200,000 tons at Tema at a contract price of £0.4 million, initially with the intention of supplying cement to the Shipyard and Dry Dock projects.

Thus at the time of the coup Ghana had two cement plants with a total capacity of 600,000 tons, one at Tema already completed and a second (the Polish project) still under construction at Takoradi. The Ghana Government had entered into a management agreement with Associated Portland Cement Manufacturers Limited (APCM) for the operation of the Tema factory and for the supply of clinker for ten years. However, the cost of production at the two factories differed significantly. Production cost was an estimated £5/18/- per ton of cement at Takoradi, and £6/12/- per ton at Tema. One of the main reasons for this was that the cost of clinker supplied by Associated Portland to the Tema factory ranged from £5/12/- to £6/5/- per ton, while Polish clinker supplied to Takoradi ranged from £4/2/- to £4/4/- per ton. Consequently the Takoradi factory was the only one capable of producing cement at or below the landed cost of imported cement.

2. Documents relating to the first round of negotiations were not available to the editor.

3. The Draft Clinker Agreement has been omitted.

4. Also omitted. The new terms from APCM for deliveries of clinker were 77/- per metric ton for a one year contract, 76/- per ton for two years, and 75/- per ton for three years. This was a considerable reduction from the company's previous terms (noted above) ranging between 112/- and 125/- per ton!

5. This draft differs from the Master Agreement signed on 25 May 1967 in respect of the capitalization of the new company (£1 million instead of £0.4 million), down-payment from the Government and Norcement for purchase of the two factories (£0.75 million instead of £0.3 million) and the clinker delivery price (77/- per metric ton instead of 79/-). All other major provisions remained unaltered.

6. This is a reference to a critical study on the enterprises of Noel Drevici, an Armenian businessman, prepared after the coup by three of his employees and forwarded to the NLC with a covering memo by the Political Committee. Shortly after writing this study, the three employees (an Accountant, a Chief Nutritionist, and a Chief Security Officer) lost their jobs. In the memo to the NLC the Political Committee hinted at links between Drevici and certain members of the Economic Committee, and urged the NLC to request the IMF to investigate the Ghana assets of Drevici.

7. For an analysis of the general conflicts between the Political and Economic

Committees, see the author's unpublished doctoral thesis, *Military Rule and the Politics of Demilitarization in Ghana, 1966-69*, University of Toronto, 1973, pp. 258–65.

Part V

1. These comments refer to the original *draft* of the 'Industrial Relations Act (Act 299) (Amendment) (No. 2) Decree, 1967'. The passages in the draft to which the TUC objected proposed to repeal certain sections of the Industrial Relations Act of 1965. The effect would have been to abolish the check-off system, the sponsorship by the TUC of trade union applications for collective bargaining certificates, the power of the Minister for Labour to extend collective agreements under clearly stated conditions, as well as the modification of the collective bargaining process itself through the introduction of 'Labour Boards'.

Part VI

1. For an analysis of Ghana's external debt renegotiations, see 'International Debt-Renegotiation: Ghana's Experiences', *Africa Development*, Vol. 9, No. 2, 1985.

2. Particularly by the United Kingdom. See 'Report on Consultative Group Meeting, London: 15–16 July 1970' (no date or author indicated), pp. 7–9. The policy issues are examined in my paper quoted in footnote 1 above.

3. An excellent analysis of this appears in Ronald Libby, 'External Co-optation of a Less Developed Country's Policy Making'. Also the paper in footnote 1 above.

4. Paragraphs 1 to 3 inclusive of the Agreed Minute summarize the presentations at the Conference, while paragraph 4 following deals with the substantive terms of the agreement.

Institute for African Alternatives

The Institute for African Alternatives was established in 1986 to encourage research and discussion on contemporary problems in Africa. The Institute is located in London (UK) and consists of a suite of offices, a lecture hall, a common room and study rooms.

IFAA is headed by a Council consisting of the following:

Prof. Bade Onimode (Nigeria) Chair
Dr. Tsehai Berhane-Selassie (Ethiopia)
Dr. Fatima Babikar Mahmoud (Sudan)
Dr. Kwame Ninsin (Ghana)
Prof. Haroub Othman (Tanzania)

Prof. Abdoulaye Bathily (Senegal)
Prof. Ben Magubane (South Africa)
Mr. Kempton Makamure (Zimbabwe)
Prof. Nzongola-Ntalaja (Zaire)
Mr. Ben Turok (U.K.)

Activities

Research and Debate: The Institute facilitates research on African problems and encourages debate around current issues.

Conferences, Workshops, Seminars: A major annual conference is held at IFAA with invited speakers from across Africa, as well as a special annual conference on African women. Workshops are also held on a specialist basis and seminars on particular topics. Where possible proceedings are recorded and published.

Lectures and Classes: From time to time a lecture series is arranged. Classes are also run on such topics as History of Africa, Development problems, Neocolonialism, History of African Women, Southern Africa etc. A residential 3 months course on "Policy Making, Development Policy and African Women" is under preparation.

Publishing: An important role is the publication of conference proceedings at IFAA, books by associates of IFAA, occasional lectures and other materials.

An African Women Development Newsletter is underway which will appear quarterly and be distributed in at least six countries in the first instance.

Documentation Centre
A start has been made to create a specialist documentation library and it is hoped to expand this greatly in due course.

Address: IFAA
23 Bevenden Street
London N1 6BH
UK

Telephone: 01-251 1503
Telex: 923753 Ref W6019